THE *Religion*
OF *Maturity*

BY . . . . . JOHN WICK BOWMAN

THE *RELIGION*
OF *MATURITY*

Go on to maturity . . . . HEB. 6:1

ABINGDON-COKESBURY PRESS
New York . . . . . Nashville

THE RELIGION OF MATURITY

COPYRIGHT, MCMXLVIII
BY STONE & PIERCE

K

PRINTED IN THE UNITED STATES OF AMERICA

TO

Louise

ἧς διὰ τὴν ἐν Χριστῷ τελειότητα
τοῦτο τὸ βιβλίον δυνατὸν ἐγένετο

Preface

THIS book is in some measure a sequel to *The Intention of Jesus*. The second chapter of that work, entitled "The Wide Outlook," in which I dealt with Jesus' attitude toward the religious groups in the Judaism of his time, drew more adverse criticism from reviewers than other parts of the book. I was, of course, prepared for this. The issues involved are highly controversial. Then, too, I had of necessity to be somewhat cryptic in stating my views in that chapter because of the limited space at my disposal.

The generous invitation extended by the Board of Trustees and Faculty of Princeton Theological Seminary to deliver the lectures on the L. P. Stone Foundation in the spring of 1946 afforded me an opportunity of restudying the problems involved in that chapter and of presenting my conclusions with regard to them in somewhat greater detail. May I take this occasion, therefore, to render my most hearty thanks, both to those who gave me this opportunity and to the faculty and students of the institution, for the cordial manner in which they heard my first draft of the views herein expressed. The original lectures, however, have been entirely rewritten for the purposes of this volume.

Those who take up this book with the expectation that they will find here something approaching an exhaustive treatment of the

7

sects found in postexilic Judaism will be disappointed. There exist already a large number of such studies, as well as innumerable monographs dealing with various phases of the complicated series of problems involved. It has not been my wish to add to this list. For this reason the student will find no treatment of the Zealots, Essenes, or Therapeutae, nor any attempt at giving a complete view of those sects which are treated.[1] I have indulged myself in the belief that I could presuppose such authoritative guides. Accordingly I have merely selected here and there from the vast accumulation of source materials, both primary and secondary, such items as in my judgment indicate which way the theological winds were blowing among these sects and, to labor the metaphor, their temperature and humidity. The danger in such a method is patent: others may hold that items which I have failed to choose are important or even determinative for securing an adequate understanding of the position of a given religious group. It has seemed to me, however, that there was no other way than that adopted if my purpose was to be achieved. The average reader would become lost in a maze of details to such an extent that my aim and conclusions would be dissipated in the mist had I done otherwise. I can only hope that my choices have not been too far amiss or motivated by too biased a judgment.

The thesis which appears to me to emerge as a result of the inductive approach to the problems of this study, and which therefore I am endeavoring to demonstrate, is: first, that the Old Testament scriptures claim to contain an objective revelation from God given through a line of prophets to his people; second, that postexilic Judaism exhibits on man's part a number of religious responses sincerely intended to implement this divine revelation which is equally acknowledged by all true Jews, the chief of these responses —those of altar, book, and throne—being given some examination

---

[1] It has been interesting to me to discover that, after my making this decision to eliminate treatment of the minor Jewish sects in this book, Millar Burrows in his recent volume *An Outline of Biblical Theology* came to my aid by his support of the thesis that such sects "have no significance for biblical theology." (P. 152.) The reader will note that my book purports to be an essay in just that field.

herein; and third, that the New Testament scriptures assert that the religious response agreeable to God was revealed through Christ and his apostles, who therefore, whatever else they severally may have been, are in any event to be included in the prophetic category.

Throughout this study I have endeavored to keep before me, and to allow my judgments to be influenced by, the scientific observation that points of view, concepts, and so eventually entire fields of study, philosophies, sciences, and religions are to be known and evaluated by the factors wherein they differ, as well as, or even more than, those wherein they agree. To de-fine is to mark out the boundaries of an idea as of any material object, that is, to show where it differs from other points of view. If this canon of the inductive method had been observed by students of comparative religions, there would be far less confusion than actually exists today regarding the merits and demerits of many of these religions. To note, for example, that there are prophetic elements in the teachings of the sects studied in this volume proves nothing that is not already known before the study is undertaken. Everyone is aware that all the religious movements within Judaism stemmed originally from Hebrew prophetism. The same method, accordingly, that succeeds in equating prophetism with apocalypticism serves also to equate both with Pharisaism and the last in turn with Sadduceeism. But if this method is a correct one, why, then—it is proper to inquire—did rabbinism utterly reject apocalypticism, and why were there constant disputes between the Jewish sects throughout their history? The method that serves merely to prove everything to be equal to everything else should be discarded at the start by the serious student in every field, including that of religion. The question of importance regarding any religion is not the origin of the concepts with which it deals but rather what it does with them after they are accepted.[2] It is here that the tone and

---

[2] To quote Professor Burrows again, "Ideas, like men, must be judged on their own merits, not by their pedigrees"; cf. *ibid.*, p. 62, and my own *Intention*, pp. 88-89.

value of the religion with which one is dealing are made manifest.

My indebtedness to biblical scholars is patent on every page of this book. The mere listing of their names and works would require far more space than the limits of this volume permit. I am also deeply conscious of the debt I owe to my students in India and America throughout twenty years of teaching. On the whole they have taught me perhaps more than I have learned from books. Their eager response to the "truth in Christ" and their frequent insights as shown in modest question or heated argument have been of inestimable help to me. That I do not acknowledge them by name is only because I cannot recall from whom I gleaned this or that original thought. But I am sure that many of them will find here contributions which they have made; and if they are pleased with the result attained by uniting their ideas with those of their colleagues, I shall feel rewarded for the effort expended.

In concluding may I express the hope that, if my book should chance to fall into the hands of those of Jewish faith—kinsmen of Jesus "according to the flesh"—they will feel that I have dealt not unkindly with those various expressions of the "faith of Israel" at which I glance and will sense my earnest wish at every point to be fair and sympathetic.

JOHN WICK BOWMAN

Contents

V. THE RELIGION OF MATURITY

PART

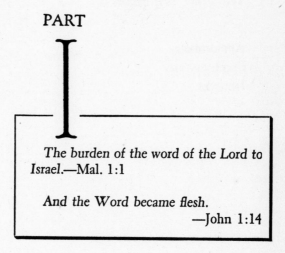

I

The burden of the word of the Lord to Israel.—Mal. 1:1

And the Word became flesh.
—John 1:14

THE PROPHETIC WORD

Synopsis

Chapter 1:—We shall do well to approach the phenomenon of Hebrew prophecy on the prophet's own terms, if we entertain any hope of really understanding it. These terms include the ideas: that the prophet's sole AUTHORITY is "the word of the Lord" which comes to him, that his METHOD of receiving this is one of simple audition, that the INTENTIONED EFFECT of his work is that growth in moral stature of which Israel throughout her history has given such outstanding examples, and that the FINAL GOAL of all his efforts is the creation of the "redemptive community."

Chapter 2:—Though the prophet was neither philosopher nor systematic theologian, still the revelations he received contained the elements of a "body of thought." Taken together, these constituted what we may term an "ethical monotheism," some of whose characteristic concepts were that God is SOVEREIGN over the life of man, that God reveals himself as the RIGHTEOUS ONE, and that this righteous God exerts HIS WILL in making certain demands on man. The prophet had an eschatology in which the three figures of Yahweh, the Messiah, and the Suffering Servant held the center of the stage.

Chapter 3:—Jesus' attachment to the prophetic view appears in his steeping his thought in the prophetic scriptures and in his use of the prophetic literary models. More conclusive still are his sharing their SPIRIT OF FREEDOM, his stress with them on THE UNITY OF THEOLOGY AND ETHICS, and his intentional fulfillment of the prophetic concepts of THE MESSIAH AND THE SUFFERING SERVANT.

CHAPTER

1

The Revelation of the Word

Sir William Ramsay once re-
marked, "Christianity is the religion of an educated mind." Perhaps it would be more nearly correct to say that it is the religion
adapted to mature persons, education being but one of the factors contributing to maturity. This, then, would be part of the
truth about Christianity, though not all of it. For it requires no
proof beyond what is provided by simple observation that the Christian faith has an appeal for persons at every stage of their development, and not for adults alone. In this book we shall confine our
attention to the suggested modification of the Scotsman's thesis—
that Christianity is the religion of maturity.

This judgment is made with three marks of maturity particularly
in mind. These are: *poise*, that assurance, resulting from a sense
of adequacy, which frees from fears and fancies; *originality*, the
power to bear fruit, to propagate one's kind, and so to project one's
likeness beyond the horizon of a single life span; and *disinterested-
ness*, the releasing of potential energy in unselfish service. Such
maturity is the product of growth, and it bears witness to the
presence of creative life whose roots are sunk deep into the soil
of the past. Christianity as the religion of maturity is no exception
to this, and it will be our endeavor here to trace out some of its
roots. We begin with the phenomenon of Hebrew prophecy.

15

There is general agreement, one imagines, that here we are in the presence of moral stature seldom, if ever, equaled elsewhere. It would be easy to multiply the plaudits accorded the prophets by men of insight of nearly every race and age. The words of three must suffice. The prophets of Israel, writes a contemporary Christian scholar living some thirty centuries after the first utterance of the creative voice he is describing, "ushered in the greatest movement in the spiritual history of mankind." [1] Seventeen hundred years earlier Origen of Alexandria, accounted the foremost student of Scripture who ever lived, is replying to the cultured paganism of his day as represented by the Epicurean Celsus. With fervor he writes of the prophets' "leading a life of almost unapproachable excellence, intrepid, noble, unmoved by danger or death," and of their "firm adherence to truth, and their faithfulness in the reproof of the wicked." All this they were and did, says Origen, "for they looked always to God and to His blessings, which, being invisible, and not to be perceived by the senses, are eternal." [2] Turn to the Scriptures themselves. With their accustomed mingling of formal simplicity with boldness of conception they assert, "God spoke of old to our fathers by the prophets; . . . he has spoken to us by a Son." (Heb. 1:1-2 R.S.V.)

These three tributes to the prophets stress respectively the high spiritual quality of their message, their moral earnestness, and the divine source of their inspiration. In so doing they fasten upon three characteristics which find illustration time without number in the lives and writings of these great men. Micaiah ben Imlah, as he stands before Kings Ahab and Jehoshaphat, is quite unconsciously speaking for all his successors when he says, "As the Lord liveth, what the Lord saith unto me, that will I speak." (I Kings 22:14.) Henceforth the Hebrew prophet is to be known as a man who hears what God the Lord speaks to him and who listens to God alone. He is characterized by a sort of divine arrogance, with which

[1] Julius A. Bewer, *The Literature of the Old Testament,* p. 87.
[2] *Contra Celsum* vii. 7.

is fused, however, real humility—the latter being the natural product of the prophet's keen awareness at once of God's ethical holiness and his own sin. He is to prove in consequence an individualist of a pronounced type, but an individualist curiously conscious of his own unworthiness! He will display on his shield, not, after the fashion of Athanasius, *Vaticinator contra mundum*, but instead the simple "Thus saith the Lord," thereby hiding the man behind the Divine Word.

Such considerations as these raise for the earnest student a series of problems relating to the source and nature of the prophet's authority, his method or technique in dealing with this authority, and the effect of his message upon his own and later times.

The Prophet's Authority—"The Word of the Lord"

It is customary to speak of the prophetic movement in Israel as originating toward the close of the eleventh century B.C.[3] and of the first attempts at historiography from the prophetic standpoint as embodied in the work of the Jehovistic writer who flourished after the middle of the tenth century or later.[4] No doubt the second of these dates will prove reasonably acceptable to the general reader, and in any case the development of my thesis does not require a more accurate judgment on the point. But to think of the prophetic movement as beginning with the great figures who came upon the Hebrew scene from the eleventh century B.C. forward is to limit that movement temporally after a manner out of accord with the mind of the prophets themselves. Such limitation, moreover, can scarcely be justified from the standpoint of an adequate definition of the term "prophet."

To begin with the definition, Professor William F. Albright has shown that

the correct etymological meaning of the word [*nabhî'*, prophet] is . . . "one who is called (by God), one who has a vocation (from God)," as

[3] See W. F. Albright, *From the Stone Age to Christianity*, p. 232.
[4] For dates cf. S. R. Driver, *An Introduction to the Literature of the Old Testament*, pp. 123 ff.; Albright, *op. cit.*, p. 190; Bewer, *op. cit.*, pp. 60-73.

appears from the fact that this is almost always the sense which the verb
nabû, "to call," has in Accadian, from the middle of the third millenium
to the middle of the first.

Accordingly Professor Albright defines the figure in question thus:

The prophet was a man who felt himself called by God for a special
mission, in which his will was subordinated to the will of God, which was
communicated to him by direct inspiration.[5]

The elements of this definition, it will be noted, are the divine
"call," a sense of "mission," the sublimation of the prophet's will,
and the consciousness of inspiration or, as I should prefer, of the
revelation of God's will in the situation.

The relevance of the several parts of this definition can be verified
by observing the characteristics of those styled "prophets" in the
prophetic writings. For the prophetic call one may note the familiar
experiences of Moses (Exod. 3), Samuel (I Sam. 3:1-21), Isaiah
(Isa. 6), and Ezekiel (Ezek. 2:1-7); for the sense of mission, the
same and like passages; for the assurance of the divine revelation,
the example of Micaiah just referred to and the description of the
coming prophet "like unto" Moses in Deut. 18:18, together with
the often repeated "oracle of the Lord" (cf. Zech. 12:1), "the word
of the Lord" (Ezek. 7:1), or "Thus saith the Lord" (Amos 1:3);
for the prophet's subordination of will, a passage like this from the
Prophet of the Exile: "The Lord Jehovah hath opened mine ear,
and I was not rebellious, neither turned away backward. . . . Therefore have I set my face like a flint, and I know that I shall not be
put to shame." (Isa. 50:5-7; cf. Ezek. 2:8.) It would be easy to
multiply references here, but the facts are too well known to require further elaboration.

It is not open to dispute, I take it, that a marked feature of
the Hebrew prophetic movement was the liberality of the prophets'
own employment of this definition. Indeed, they never endeavored

[5] *Op. cit.,* pp. 231-32.

to limit its application in any way not imposed by the nature of the definition itself. To have done so would have been for them a sign of betrayal of the highest principle for which they claimed to stand—the freedom of the human spirit to speak and act without let or hindrance as guided by the Spirit of the Lord of Hosts. It would have been blasphemy to their mind either to stifle the Spirit of the Lord through whomsoever he might choose to utter his Word or to endeavor to relegate to themselves the title of having spoken in his name. The impertinent question, "Which way went the Spirit of the Lord from me to speak unto thee?" (I Kings 22: 24), intended as it obviously was to quench the Spirit in a budding prophet, became for them, therefore, the mark of the "false" prophet.

Accordingly prophetism knew neither cultural nor class distinctions. Among its elect ones it numbered priests like Jeremiah and Ezekiel; a judge and Levite, Samuel; a statesman of the caliber of Isaiah; a herdsman, Amos; a king, Saul; and many others, the status or profession of some of whom—like Hosea and Micah—we do not even know. Equally on its own reckoning prophetism knew no temporal boundaries. For the Word which was its inspiration, being the Word of God, transcended the dimension of time. The patriarch Abraham, therefore, was named a prophet by the prophetic writer who flourished about the middle of the eighth century B.C., or earlier (Gen. 20:7 [E]), and the same writer counted Miriam a prophetess (Exod. 15:20). About the same time or even earlier a prophetic historian spoke of Deborah as both prophetess and judge (Judg. 4:4 [J or E?]).[6] Similarly, Moses, who long antedated the prophetic movement as it manifested itself from the eleventh century onward, became for the prophetic scriptures and has remained for the Jew in succeeding ages the great exemplar of all prophets.[7]

---

[6] Cf. also Huldah in II Kings 22:14 (R$^{D1 \text{ or } 2?}$) and II Chr. 34:22, and note the saying in II Kings 17:13.

[7] Deut. 18:18 (D¹); Jer. 15:1; Mark 9:4-8; Heb. 3:2; M. Aboth 5:18. Cf. in M. Sanh. 11:5 the comments on Deut. 18:18-20.

19

At the other extreme of time, also, the prophet looked forward to a day when the reputed wish of Moses—"Would that all the Lord's people were prophets, that the Lord would put his Spirit upon them!" (Num. 11:29)—would be fulfilled. Joel voiced this sentiment in the eschatological passage at 2:28-32, which the later church held to have been fulfilled at Pentecost (Acts 2:17-21). The church of the New Testament, therefore, was merely carrying forward the prophetic tradition and spirit in professing its mission to be the prophetic one of proclaiming a "gospel of the kingdom" and its ministry a ministry of prophets.[8]

In the New Testament the two Greek words "apostle" (ἀπόστολος) and "prophet" (προφήτης) are associated as belonging to the same category, and it is no doubt intended that individuals so denominated have essentially one mission to perform.[9] Of these terms, the second had been used in the Septuagint to translate the Hebrew nabhī';[10] and it was natural, therefore, to adopt it with reference to the New Testament figure who professed to be the recipient of that divine charisma or afflatus of the Spirit which issued in a word of revelation (cf. I Cor. 14:29-31). "Apostle," on the other hand, had appeared but once in the Old Testament Septuagint, where it translated the verb shālach (send); its normal equivalent therefore would be shālīᵃch, messenger.[11] The origin of its New Testament usage is in doubt. Harnack attributes this to a Jewish source, whereas Kirsopp Lake prefers Antioch (Syrian) as the center of its origination.[12] In the present state of the evidence a decision is impossible. But whatever the locus of its first usage, the term gives undoubted expression to the tradition that Jesus had "sent" his

---

[8] Acts 15:32; I Cor. 11:4; 12:10, 28, 29; Did. 11:3 ff.; 13:1 ff.

[9] Cf. Eph. 2:20; 3:5; 4:11; I Cor. 12:28-29; Did. 11:3, and Martin Dibelius on Ephesians in Handbuch zum Neuen Testament.

[10] E.g., Ps. 74:9; Isa. 37:2; Jer. 1:5, et al.

[11] I Kings 14:6.

[12] Cf. The Beginnings of Christianity, V, 48, 50; Adolf Harnack, The Mission and Expansion of Christianity, I, 327 ff.; B. F. Streeter, The Primitive Church, pp. 146 ff.

disciples forth as missionaries of the gospel of the kingdom. Hence the original band of the twelve were shᵉlichīm or "apostles."

As emissaries of the Incarnate Word this favored band, together with Paul and a few others who could claim to be apostles because of having been specially commissioned by the Lord, stood upon a higher plane of privilege and responsibility than the prophets who had only the Spirit.[13] Hence in the end the term "apostle" was restricted to them, and "prophet" remained to denote the charismatic or Spirit-filled ministry which was perpetuated in the church and which professed to be in direct line with the older prophets, sharing with them the knowledge of the word of revelation and the sense of the divine commission.[14]

It is easy to overlook the significance of this aspect of timelessness in the prophet's definition of himself and in the application of that definition within the prophetic scriptures. Professor Norman Porteous, while giving expression to a very important truth, nonetheless in my judgment fails at this point in writing:

These men [the prophets] were Hebrews of the Hebrews, inheritors and not creators of a religious tradition, possessed of a religious experience which is in part to be explained by the fact that other men had walked with God before them and had passed on to them profound thoughts about Him and His ways with men.[15]

Who are these "other men" who had known God before the prophets' day? Such a statement appears to limit the prophetic category in a way that the prophets—who thought of it, so to speak, as retroactive, viewed in the light of the brilliant galaxy who appeared after the eleventh century B.C.—would not have tolerated. In their view any man anywhere who had "walked with God," who had really known him and had received from him in fellowship a commission, was a prophet. And to their mind the impor-

---

[13] This seems to be the implication of such a passage as I Cor. 9.
[14] Probably the latest use of "apostle" in the unrestricted sense is to be found in Did. 11:3 ff.; cf. Streeter, op. cit.
[15] H. Wheeler Robinson, ed., Record and Revelation, p. 217.

tant thing to remember was that, whatever his culture and whenever he may have lived, such a man shared with all other prophets a knowledge of God which his contemporaries did not share with him. At this point, therefore, the prophet claimed an experience which was timeless, which transcended every culture, and which sat in judgment on every culture. If we are to attempt to understand the prophets and to evaluate them with a degree of fairness, we must begin with this, their own inclusive definition of the term "prophet," in mind.

The like criticism is relevant concerning much that has been written on "the religion of Israel," in which it is assumed that there was a body of religious faith and experience common to all Israelities that existed to a degree, at any rate, irrespective of the prophets and their contribution to it. That Israel had, as all other peoples have had, a religion, no one would care to deny. Israel had indeed a variety of religions throughout her history. I am interested here only in the equation of "the religion of Israel" with that high teaching about God which it is the wish of the writers of Scripture to promote and which those who employ the phrase appear to want us to believe was a sort of "religious common factor" within Israel as such.

Those who hold this view generally assume that Hebrew prophecy represented a more or less "popular" gift for religious experience, that the prophetic awareness of God was shared by the people rather widely, and that no great disparity was to be found between the intellectual, moral, and spiritual levels of people and prophets.[16] It cannot be said with too great vehemence that in the history of Israel's development no justification can be found for such a view. Indeed it would be far nearer the truth to say that the Hebrew prophet lived in a world set apart from his people. Our Lord represented the true state of affairs when he said, "Woe unto you! for ye build the tombs of the prophets, and your fathers killed them"

[16] See Bowman, "The Bible as Revelation," *Theology Today*, Jan., 1945, pp. 455-69.

(Luke 11:47). Israel's long history furnishes a sad list of examples in proof of this judgment.

The opposing thesis, with which we are dealing, appears to be based "on an exaggerated theory of the social origin of knowledge." [17] I would be the last to deny "the partly conscious and partly unconscious influence of the community" on the prophets, as well as on other religious leaders and outstanding men in various spheres. Modern psychology has gone far toward demonstrating the fundamental truth to be found in the Hebrew idea of the "community": our lives or "selves" are indeed group lives and group selves, and no man lives a Robinson Crusoe existence within any society anywhere.[18] Nonetheless, as Professor John Newton Thomas has observed:

If there is no such thing as an isolated individual, there is also no such thing as a community without individuals. . . . It is significant, for instance, that the eighth century prophets did not arise outside of Israel: it is equally true and significant that they did not remain on the religious level of Israel.[19]

The tone of Israel's religious experience was raised progressively by the prophetic word, true; but as this development proceeded, the prophets were ever climbing higher and higher. In the end, therefore, as C. H. Dodd has written, "the prophets appear rather as the towering summits of a mountainous landscape, which from its foothills to its mountaintops shows the same geological structure." [20] Were it otherwise, the work of the prophets would have been an even more signal failure than it actually was. But it needs to be remembered first and last that on the prophets' own claim at all events—and as Israel's history goes far toward demonstrating— it was out of their unique sense of "mission" and the guidance

[17] See John Newton Thomas, "The Authority of the Bible," *Theology Today*, July, 1946, pp. 159-71.
[18] See P. S. Minear, "The Biblical Sense of Community," *The Journal of Religious Thought*, I, 2 (1944), 77-96.
[19] Thomas, *op. cit.*, p. 168.
[20] Quoted by Thomas from *The Authority of the Bible*, p. 138; see further my book *The Intention of Jesus*, pp. 68-77, 227-28.

given them by the word of the Lord, which they claimed to possess, that this religious development proceeded apace.

One further point is to be noted as implicit in the definition we have been discussing. The prophet needed no ordination or other sanction for his ministry beyond the divine "call," even as the content of his "message" was its own sole validation. Here was a man who took the concept of revelation so seriously that he asked no human approbation of his ministry. He walked forth into the market place or the temple; he stood before kings and commoners alike; he took a long journey into distant lands or cities; he called the masses to a mountaintop—all this to give his ringing message. And in every case he made the simple claim, which obviously he intended should be taken in all seriousness, that he was speaking as God's mouthpiece. He delivered himself of instruction, but instruction of a unique kind—the Torah of God himself—and he demanded that men listen to it in the name of God alone. Amos spoke for all his fellows when he declared his own motivation: "The Lord Jehovah hath spoken; who can but prophesy?" (3:8b).[21]

The Prophet's Method—Listening to God's Voice

The prophet's method of apprehending the divine revelation accorded with his claim that God had spoken to him. This method was one of *audition* or listening. And there is here a uniqueness which must not be lightly passed over. For this technique of the prophet is as truly *sui generis* as the Greek philosopher's use of reason to deduce from the universe its secrets, or the Hindu rishi's insight into the meaning of natural phenomena, or the modern Solon's scientific method of induction. It was based on the prophet's simple response of attention to the voice of God, which was always the aggressive element in the prophet's mystical experience. To employ Deissmann's expressive phrase, the prophet on his own

[21] A prophet on occasion was, of course, anointed by his fellows (I Kings 19:16), and miracles as "signs" were performed by some (I Kings 17:14-16). Neither the one nor the other, however, may be said to have been "characteristic" of the prophetic office or necessary to support the prophet's claim to have heard the word of revelation.

24

account was a "reacting mystic," [22] that is, one who never endeavored to induce the revelation of which he was the recipient but rather merely listened to the divine voice.

A glance at the religious situation in the Hebrew prophet's day will serve at once to indicate the difficult nature of the religious problem he had to face and to throw into relief the form of his own solution. The religious and even psychopathic phenomena prevalent at that time are familiar to all students of religion. Enchantment and sorcery, divination and augury, witchcraft, wizardry and necromancy, and the ecstatic trance—such terms as these on the border line between magic and religion suggest in part the trend of the popular religious interest inside the territories occupied by Israel and Judah and in contiguous lands from, at least, the third millennium B.C. forward.[23] Esoteric knowledge of future events, or of the will of the gods, or of the destiny of individuals, peoples, and nations, was ascertained by means of teraphim (household gods), Urim and Thummim (divining attachments to the high priest's breastplate), casting of lots, and examination of the livers and other organs of certain animals.[24] Dreams, trances, and visions also played a large part in the foretelling of future events.[25]

There can be no doubt that from very early times under the prophetic influence the endeavor was made to distinguish between these phenomena with a view to commending some and condemning others. The various prophetic strata in the Hexateuch, the Latter Prophets, the Deuteronomists, and the Chronicler are one in their entire condemnation of sorcery, necromancy, and the like as wholly pagan and unworthy methods of ascertaining the will of God.[26] The "false prophet" was a product, at least in some in-

[22] *The Religion of Jesus and the Faith of Paul*, p. 196.
[23] See Albright, *op. cit.*, pp. 232 ff.
[24] Judg. 17:4-6; 18:14; II Kings 23:24; Ezek. 21:21.
[25] For dreams see Gen. 20:3-6; I Kings 3:5; for visions, Num. 24:4, 16; II Chron. 9:29. Trances are not mentioned in the Old Testament, but the act of "falling down" in Num. 24:4, 16 probably should be so interpreted (cf. the gloss here in the A.V.).
[26] Exod. 22:18; Lev. 19:26, 31; Deut. 18:10; II Kings 17:17; II Chron. 33:6.

stances, of contact with such phenomena, particularly as these appeared in the pagan religions. Skinner has even suggested that the false prophet was a survivor "of the old patriotism, from which Elijah divorced religion." [27] Micah condemned such prophets and their pagan practices on moral grounds (3:5-8), while Jeremiah (14:14; 24:9-10) and Ezekiel (13:6-23; 22:28) accused them of being men of a "lying vision" and a "lying divination."

Psychological considerations, however, suggest that the very heat displayed by the prophets in their denunciations of these spurious manifestations is itself proof of their sense of the similarity between the two movements, the true and the false. The magic of the devil's emissaries and the miracle of the Lord's prophets have always been disquietingly similar in outward appearance. And in fact the prophetic writings acknowledge an identity of background—if not of origin—for some of these phenomena. The ancient seer (rō'eh, chōzeh), originally a kind of "diviner" of a type which had its origin in "Mesopotamia and spread in all directions as early as the middle of the second millennium B.C.," [28] was the immediate forerunner of the prophet.[29] This relationship is significant in view of the unfortunate association of the seer with ecstatic manifestations of a type common to religions of both primitive and advanced varieties. The Maulawiyah and Rufa'iyah dervishes of Islam, the Delphic Pythia, the Sibyl of Cannae, the Bacchantes and Dionysiacs among the Greeks—these and many other examples of the phenomena in question are familiar to all. The suggestion lies to hand, then, that the Hebrew seers and prophets were swept into this flood of ecstasy and are to be explained on parallel lines. Add to this the fact that there was undoubtedly some psychic abnormality among the prophets, as in the case of Ezekiel.[30]

Though in the nature of things no final answer can be given to

[27] I am indebted to Wheeler Robinson, *Redemption and Revelation*, p. 151, for the reference; see Skinner, *Prophecy and Religion*, p. 187.

[28] Albright, *op. cit.*, p. 231.

[29] I Sam. 9:9; cf. T. H. Robinson, *Prophecy and the Prophets*, pp. 30, 35.

[30] See Edwin C. Broome, Jr., "Ezekiel's Abnormal Personality," *Journal of Biblical Literature and Exegesis*, Sept., 1946, pp. 277-92.

the series of problems raised by these facts, there are several considerations which point toward a working hypothesis relative to them. (1) In the first place, *the vehicle of the revelation* claimed by the prophet tends to be of the higher sort or sorts among those usually reckoned as possibilities. Thus, though the Deuteronomist associates, if he does not identify, the prophet with the "dreamer of dreams" (13:1-3), it is a notable fact that no prophet by name is ever said to have experienced a revelation in this fashion.[31] There is rather an unmistakable effort at differentiation between those who experienced the dream revelation and those who had the vision; and the generally moral and spiritual level of those in the latter class, which includes a number of the prophets, is strikingly higher.[32] It would seem, therefore, that the prophetic scriptures are feeling toward a distinction which, as Wheeler Robinson observes, Jeremiah makes when he "ranks the vision higher than the dream, and the audition perhaps higher than the vision." (23:9-11, 28.)[33]

2) If *abnormality of a psychic type* existed among the true prophets, it was evidently kept under control by other factors in the prophets' personalities. That "the spirits of the prophets are subject" to them (I Cor. 14:32) was an axiom recognized in Israel during the periods of major prophetic activity. Professor Albright has pointed out that

the ecstacism of the prophets of the Tyrian Baal . . . belongs to the Dionysiac type, while that of the early prophets of Yahweh described in I Sam. 10 and 19 has nothing orgiastic about it. . . . Perhaps the Yahwistic movement arose partly as a reaction against pagan ecstaticism,

[31] The nearest to an exception to this statement is the case of Daniel, who is called "the prophet" by "Matthew" (24:15) in an insertion made by him into Marcan material (Mark 13:14).

[32] Dreams are said to have brought revelations to Abimelech, Jacob, Laban, Joseph, Pharaoh, Gideon, Solomon, Daniel, Nebuchadnezzar, Joseph (husband of the Virgin), and the Magi. Visions from God were seen by Abraham, Balaam, Samuel, Nathan, Isaiah, Iddo, Ezekiel, Obadiah, Nahum, and Habakkuk from among the seers and prophets, and additionally by Daniel, Zacharias (father of the Baptist), Ananias of Damascus, Peter, and Paul. See my book *Introducing the Bible*, pp. 31-32.

[33] Op. cit., p. 151.

27

which must have threatened the religion of Israel as few other movements of history.[34]

As for Ezekiel's abnormality, Albright reiterates what everyone knows, that this is a "tendency which he shares with many other spiritual leaders of mankind. A certain 'abnormality' is required to divert a man's thoughts and his emotional experiences from the common treadmill of human thinking and feeling." [35] In like fashion Mr. Broome, while observing that "Ezekiel exhibits behavioristic abnormalities consistent with paranoid schizophrenia," at the same time concludes that "his religious significance is by no means impaired by our diagnosis of a paranoic condition, as William James convincingly argued in the case of other great spiritual leaders." [36]

3) A third consideration concerns *the nature of the audition* in Wheeler Robinson's comment on Jeremiah. As I have already remarked, this became the normative method of the prophet's apprehension of the divine voice or word. This is indicated by the common formulas "Thus saith the Lord," "The Word of the Lord came unto . . . ," and the like. It need scarcely be remarked that no one acquainted with the high moral teachings of the prophets, which were the acknowledged content of the word they heard, will be prepared to equate the voice heard by them with the "voices" of the insane. To state the nature of a proper alternative explanation, however, is by no means easy. Dr. Robinson suggests that these prophetic auditions were "really normal experience of the reflective or intuitive kind, interpreted unconsciously through the current psychology, and assigned to Yahweh" in accordance with the tendency to attribute to divine influence states of consciousness which had first been objectified.[37]

It will of course be acknowledged that the "subjective" element is present in all such auditions. For how could a divine revelation

---

[34] *Op. cit.,* p. 233.
[35] *Ibid.,* pp. 248-49.

[36] *Op. cit.,* pp. 291-92.
[37] *Op. cit.,* p. 143.

28

be apprehended except through the normal channels of man's intellectual processes? Further, the interpretations of this subjective element will differ with the varying psychologies which men hold from age to age. But it is surely begging the question to affirm that these auditions were the product of either reflection or intuition. The prophets, like other men, no doubt reflected on the contents of their minds and like them experienced their intuitions. Reflection, however, presupposes the presence of a previous content upon which the mind may react, and the problem before us is that of discovering the source of that content which the prophet claimed to be the word of God to him. Similarly, as regards the prophetic intuitions, the problem is: Granting that there were such, how are they to be explained? Were these men "religious geniuses," or were they, as they claimed, really in contact with the living God?

Perhaps the answer to both questions at once is to be found in the exceptionally high character of the subjects of the prophetic auditions. A study of the writings of these men shows that the tribute paid them by Origen [38] was in the highest degree deserved by them. This is not to say that they were in consequence "deserving" of the revelation which came to them, nor do I wish to be understood as affirming that it came to them because of such (wrongly) conjectured desert on their part. The prophets themselves would have been the first to deny this. As Professor Paul S. Minear writes:

There is no suggestion in the case of Amos and the other prophets that the revealer must have an unusually clear mind, unusual preparation in the way of moral growth or devout meditation. Contemporaries did not speak of the prophets as being outstanding either in their piety or in their human wisdom.[39]

Nonetheless, a study of the prophetic writings of the Old Testament scriptures reveals the fact that these men were subjected to

[38] See above, p. 16. [39] *Eyes of Faith*, pp. 153-54.

the rigor of a moral and psychological conditioning calculated to make or break the strongest natures. They were surrounded by the unethical and irreligious allurements of the paganism of both East and West over a period of several hundred years, and the story of how they resisted these enticing charms is one of the thrilling sagas written into the experience of man. To affirm, then, that these men of God were conditioned and therefore adequate for the reception of a word from God is quite other than to say that they were granted it because of a worth residing in them in consequence of that same conditioning. The affirmation of the latter half of this sentence would represent the ultimate reach of the human *hubris*, a sort of out-Pelagianizing paganism of a type which has no kinship with the spirit of the Hebrew prophets. But equally the denial of the former half represents an unrealistic approach to the facts of history and psychology which appears to be characteristic of much so-called neo-orthodox thought and teaching.

Granting, then, the fact of this conditioning of which we speak, how are we to explain it? Surely it is unreasonable to deny that it may have been God who made contact with the prophets and who engendered in them a sense of moral loneliness which he would one day seek to satisfy. It is equally unscientific to deny that it may have been he who progressively sought to dissipate that sense of loneliness by filling the aching void with the reality of his own fellowship. Objectivity of the prophetic voice is by no means incompatible with the psychological and moral conditioning to which we have been referring. On the contrary there would seem to be every reason to believe that the two are the natural complements of each other. College subjects are not taught in kindergarten; intellectual conditioning here advances apace with advance in knowledge. Jesus' principle—"To him who has will more be given" (Mark 4:25 R.S.V.)—applies in the world of our everyday life. Analogously, one would expect the same to be true—as our Lord affirmed that it was—in the moral and spiritual realms, and that if there is a God who as the Great Teacher has something to say to men, he would condition them for receiving it.

It is significant in the light of these a priori considerations to discover that the voices from heaven reported to have been heard within the pages of Scripture were heard only by those equipped to hear them. Balaam, Moses, Elijah, the three on the Mount of Transfiguration, Paul on the Damascus Road—all these could hear what the commonalty of men had not the means of apprehending. Others "said that it had thundered" (John 12:29), or heard only the sound of a voice (Acts 9:7), or else were utterly unconscious of any voice whatever, as in the Marcan account of the "voice" at the baptism of Jesus.[40] It is equally significant that, whereas the democratic nature of Hebrew prophecy to which we have before alluded [41] allowed for any man's becoming a prophet, actually only those subjected to the rigorous conditioning to which we have referred ever heard the "voice" which alone could constitute a man a prophet. Abraham in Ur and Haran, Moses in Egypt and Midian, Samuel in the household of Eli, Hosea in a broken home, Amos in his pastures surrounded by the contemporary paganism of the nations, Jeremiah in Anathoth and among his own people—all of these were first prepared in the school of realism to see life "in the raw," to experience the meaning of human frailty and sin, and so to discover for themselves the need of the salvation God would hold out for his people through their instrumentality. The voice which they heard then broke in upon their lives as *an emotional kind of knowledge* akin to that provided in the consciences of men and partaking of the sort of spontaneity usually associated with the latter.[42] It was characterized like conscience by the presence of a series of moral imperatives which created a sense of obligation and presented the prophet and his people with a challenge to act for God, to fulfill

[40] I am following here the argument and in part the words in my *Intention of Jesus*, p. 36.

[41] See above, p. 19.

[42] Emil Brunner's definition of conscience as "an emotional kind of knowledge, like the inarticulate groaning of a prisoner in his dungeon" was in my mind as I wrote these lines; see *The Divine Imperative*, p. 156.

all righteousness, and to deal worthily with their fellow men. Little wonder, then, that the prophets interpreted this voice, as men usually do their consciences, as the voice of God. In the end we cannot demonstrate the objectivity of either of these voices any more than we can prove the objective reality of any spiritual datum. And it is much to the prophet's credit that he sets forth his message without any attempt to do so.

4) *Relevance of the prophet's message.* A fourth consideration suggestive of the validity of the prophet's claim to speak for God arises out of the observed relevance of his message for the needs of his day. Much has been written regarding the *vaticinium pro eventu* and *post eventum*. It would have been more illuminating had students of the prophets spent more time noting that their deliverances were always *vaticinia in situ* and never *in vacuo*. They were never the armchair dicta of a philosopher divorced from life. Rather they spoke to the occasion and presented a practical way for its confronting on the part of God's people. This is instructive, and the infinite variety of the prophets' messages corresponding with the needs of the hour as they arose throughout a span of centuries, coupled as this consideration must always be with the other— namely, that these voices sounding forth from their writings across the intervening years have seemed to bring a message sorely needed by man wherever it is heard—appears to reflect a deep and very practical interest in the welfare of men. It seems, moreover, to suggest the presence of a deep moral concern somewhere at the heart of things—a concern so profound that successive men throughout centuries are shaken out of their complacency and made to view life from the standpoint of great universal truths and norms which appear to be governing their lives. This concern, they are made to realize, incarnates itself in saving acts, and it is to instruct them regarding the significance of these acts that the word comes to them *in the situation and when the need is great.*[43] This series of acts and

---

[43] See Bowman, "The Bible as Revelation," *op. cit.,* relative to revelation as constituted of an *act* plus a *word.*

32

words was stored up by the prophet in his treasury of memory.[44] He had learned, as John Mackay has written, that "the Road to Tomorrow leads through Yesterday"; and by every milestone he had set up a "memorial" which read, "Lo, God was in this place and I knew it not." [45] But the prophet became convinced of it, and it is by the light of his believing interpretation of the events of history that we are asked to judge the validity of the revelation of the word he claimed to hear.

The Effect of the Revelation—Growth in Moral Stature

We turn now from the prophet's technique of audition to what is even more fundamental for an estimate of the genuineness of his message which he claimed to be from God, namely, the ethical product of this message in terms of life and character. One of the prophet-inspired psalms contains these sentiments:

> Trust in the Lord, and do good;
> Dwell in the land, and feed on his faithfulness.
> Delight thyself also in the Lord;
> And he will give thee the desires of thy heart.
> Rest in the Lord, and wait patiently for him.
>
> . . . .
> Cease from anger. . . .
> Fret not thyself, it tendeth only to evil-doing.
> But the meek shall inherit the land,
> And shall delight themselves in the abundance of
>   peace. (Ps. 37:3-4, 7-8, 11.)

The Hebrew term to describe the type of character herein exemplified ('ānāw) is translated "meek" but might perhaps more appropriately be rendered "serene." This was the man who under every circumstance had learned to "wait patiently" for God, confident that however dark the clouds might be, however strong the

[44] This thought is taken from a paper on "Memory as a Prophetic Concept" read by James Muilenberg at a meeting of the Pacific Coast branch of the Society of Biblical Literature and Exegesis.
[45] Heritage and Destiny, p. 1.

forces that opposed, God would be able to work his will and that his will would contrive his people's good.

Such serenity of spirit became the Hebrew ideal character, largely through the influence of the prophets, and it has continued to be such throughout the history of Judaism. The Psalms are redolent with its praise.[46] And contemporary with Amos the prophetic author of Num. 12 (E) held up the concrete example of Moses as the exemplar of this serene type of person. He gave, moreover, a clear example of the way that meekness served to please God. When Aaron and Miriam complained against Moses on this occasion, the Lord himself "came down in a pillar of cloud" in defense of his "very meek" servant. The moral of the tale was stated in the not-uncertain terms: "Wherefore then were ye not afraid to speak against my servant, against Moses?" The larger implication of this narrative is clear: meekness, serenity of spirit—the product of genuine belief in and trust on God—was the characteristic mark of God's true man.

Amos—the prophet whose terrific indictment of the rich of his day for selling "the needy for a pair of shoes," for "trampling upon the poor" and "turning aside the needy in the gate" from their lawful rights, is still extant (5:13-15)—was the first to see in poverty the opportunity for developing this serenity of mind and heart. It was possibly under his influence that the "poor man" ('ānī) by a legitimate use of the pun came to mean "poor in spirit" through the term's formal similarity to 'ānāw, the "meek man." This "poor man" was taught to cry unto the Lord as his only sure resource, and the settled character of meekness or serenity thus acquired was given the highest place in ethical living. Isaiah, Zephaniah, the great Prophet of the Exile, and above all the Psalms followed Amos in delineating this character and in extolling its praises.[47]

Israel's history and the notable success of those who have

[46] Pss. 22:26; 25:9; 37:11; 45:4; 76:9; 147:6; 149:4.
[47] Ps. 34:6; Isa. 11:4; 61:1-3; Zeph. 3:12.

emulated this serenity of spirit are the best possible testimony to the effectiveness of the prophetic word at this point. The prophet's view of history, wherein divine act and divine word were but two moments of one divine fact, found at once its counterpart and vindication in the living character which the creative word produced. For the divine act manifested itself in the character of serenity to be found in every Israelite who shared the prophetic spirit. It would be needlessly prolix to recount the many examples of this throughout Israel's history. The author of the Epistle to the Hebrews has collected and displayed a galaxy of these in his notable eleventh chapter. Also more modern writers have called attention to the courage effected by the prophetic message as this expressed itself in "moral and political reformation." [48] Such fruitage in life and character, be it noted, does not arise from cheap emotionalism. The courage to stand before kings or to maintain a quiet faith under adversity requires a deeper source. And the fact must not be allowed to escape us that the prophet attributed this source to his knowledge, acquired "mouth to mouth, even manifestly" (Num. 12:8), from the Moral Governor of the world himself. This claim on the part of the prophet, coupled with the undoubted effect of his message in the matter of character building, constitutes a major factor which we have no right to ignore as we endeavor to form a judgment relative to the source of his teaching.

Franz Werfel in his drama entitled *The Eternal Road* has given us a moving picture of the Jewish people throughout the centuries. And the theme he has chosen to present is the serenity of spirit of this great people as in each generation the adversity which stalks along its road overtakes one and another group in its company. Even at the end of the drama as they go away into exile, the ancient and modern versions being displayed together, they sing, "When the Lord brought the exiles back to Zion, we were as those that

[48] Albright, *op. cit.*, p. 233.

dream. Then were our mouths filled with laughter and our tongues with singing." [49]

The Word's Societal Product—The Redemptive Community

Revelation, it should be remembered, is for the sake of redemption.[50] This was a fact which the prophets were never allowed to forget, for the "hound of heaven" kept constantly urging them forward to the chase. Thus spoke Jeremiah: "And if I say, I will not make mention of him, nor speak any more in his name, then there is in my heart as it were a burning fire shut up in my bones, and I am weary with forbearing, and I cannot contain" (20:9). This is that moral concern at the heart of things, which we have already considered, cropping up again. If the prophet attempted to bottle up the word of revelation within himself, instead of that serenity of spirit which was its anticipated result it became the cause of disquietude and inner conflict—the sure sign of repression and possible precursor of psychosis.

For the prophetic word was for the people—eventually for all peoples everywhere. As one of the oldest strands of prophecy foresaw, Zion would one day become "the spiritual metropolis of the world, and the nations" would journey "thither to learn Jehovah's ways, and to hear His Word." [51] This theme is developed in identical words by Micah (4:2-3) and Isaiah (2:2-4) and probably emanates, therefore, from a source older than either of these.

But before this "Movement to Zion," as Father Hebert calls it,[52] could eventuate, three things were to happen: the prophetic word would *call into being* a "redemptive community," *discipline* that community in the midst of adversity till it had achieved an unshakable faith in God, and *inspire* it to become the flaming evan-

---

[49] I am indebted to Walter Marshal Horton for the discovery of this great and moving drama. See his *Our Eternal Contemporary*, pp. 3 ff.

[50] The bringing of these two concepts together in its title is one of the genuine insights provided by Wheeler Robinson's book on this theme.

[51] R. L. Ottley, *The Hebrew Prophets*, p. 41.

[52] *The Throne of David*, p. 80.

gelist of a gospel destined to save the entire world. There need be no doubt that the prophets were severally conscious of sharing at once in all three of these tasks. For it was not in accord with the genius of the prophetic word to think of any of the three as ever finally fulfilled. The people of God was always in the process of being called into existence, even as its moral disciplining was a perennial task and its evangelistic opportunity a never-ending responsibility.

Historically a beginning was made with the calling forth of a nuclear people of God and its fashioning into a "redemptive society." This was done, according to the prophetic historian, when "the Lord said unto Abram, Get thee out of thy country . . . , and I will make of thee a great nation , . . , and in thee shall all the families of the earth be blessed" (Gen. 12:1-3 [J]). Thus was the people of God first brought into being by the creative word mediated through the prophet. Its re-creation was a never-ending task, however, and recurred in Egypt, at Horeb, in Moab, as well as at countless times and in numerous situations in succeeding ages (Deut. 4:33-38; 5:2; 29:1). The pangs of this rebirth were felt by Hosea as he reclaimed his adulterous wife (1:9; 2:23). Jeremiah's "new covenant" is quite obviously another chapter in this story of the birth and rebirth of God's people (31:31-35), as are also the doctrine of the "remnant," and Paul's teaching regarding the one "new man," wherein the prophetic universalism finds final and full expression with the entrance of the Greeks into the "redemptive society."

Again, the prophetic word discharged the task of disciplining the now-constituted people of God. The Hebrew prophets who flourished from the eleventh century B.C. onward have been termed the "watchmen of the Theocracy." [53] They were not only evangelists; they had also the task which Paul called οἰκοδομή (often translated "edifying"), the building up of God's people in life and character until they should attain maturity. They were the reposi-

---

[53] The phrase is Kittel's. Cf. Ottley, op. cit., p. 9.

tories of what Father Hebert has termed "the faith that inspired Israel to win its moral victories and to cleave to its God with invincible faithfulness through defeat and captivity." [54] They called men to repent and turn to the Lord, and they preached a lofty ethic in which the note of social righteousness was prominent. Their strident symphonies included an entire moral and spiritual repertoire: Amos' thundering judgments on man's sin, Joel's pleading for repentance, Hosea's wooing note of unrequited and forgiving love, Second Isaiah's vicarious suffering, Jeremiah's regenerating covenant, Ezekiel's cleansed and sanctified people. It was a moral catharsis such as no other people in all history has experienced.

And it failed, though not wholly or finally. But in its first phase the "redemptive community" failed at the point of self-abandon. This is perhaps not strange, for no people has ever yet repented and turned to God with complete resignation. "It sounds paradoxical to claim," writes Father Hebert, "that Israel's missionary vocation springs out of its exclusiveness. But so it is." [55] The Lord is a "jealous God"; hence his worship must be hedged round and guarded by a people devoted to the task. In different ways both prophet and priest in Israel would have agreed to this proposition. But the prophetic word went beyond the exclusiveness to envisage a universalism which should require self-abandon of the "chosen people" if it was to fulfill its word-appointed task. For this exclusive, jealous God of Israel is for all people, and all people are unto him.[56]

It was here that Israel failed. Her fault as the redemptive community was that she refused to redeem. Numerous were the endeavors of the prophets to have her achieve her saving function in the world. But they always failed. Out of this failure was evolved the doctrine of the "remnant"—that faithful group within God's people who should take over the redeeming function of the whole and thus form the nucleus of a new people prepared to realize its evangelizing responsibility.[57] So far as the Scriptures are concerned,

[54] *Op. cit.*, p. 24.
[55] *Ibid.*, p. 74.
[56] Isa. 45:22; Mic. 4:2; Zech. 2:11.
[57] Isa. 10:20-22; 49:5-7.

the struggle between Paul and the Judaizers was the last phase of this sorry misinterpretation of the prophetic word and of the tragedy which such lack of moral insight was bound to bring upon God's people. It is a simple statement of historic fact, therefore, to say that thereafter the challenge to achieve the status of the prophetic redemptive community passed from Judaism to the Christian Church.[58]

[58] Professor Burrows in this connection observes: "Since Israel actually failed to meet the divine requirements, her history is one of only fleeting glory followed by disaster, which was recognized as just punishment." *Op. cit.*, p. 146.

CHAPTER

2

Thus Saith the Lord

P ROFESSOR EMILE CAILLI-
et has written of the passage in the *Pensées* in which Pascal "states
that man, when alone, carries on an inner conversation," and he
adds the illuminating remark that the kind of conversation which
results is an index to each man's character.[1] There can be no doubt
that the prophets were no exception to this general rule and that
like other men they too conversed within themselves regarding the
discursive materials presented to them in the word which they
heard. But, as we have seen,[2] they never reduced what they discovered there to anything approaching a *system of thought*. They
were not, therefore, philosophers or "wise men" as some in the
Hebraic tradition, as well as in the Greek, aspired to be. They were
not even theologians in the modern sense of that term. They did
not deduce proposition two from postulate one, nor did they reason
from hypothesis x to conclusion y. They merely listened to the
word which they heard and, after submitting it to the rigor of their
inner conversation, gave it forth again as a series of divine imperatives united solely by the somewhat tenuous, because ever-changing,
bond provided by the nature of the personality through which it
had passed.

[1] *Pascal—Genius in the Light of Scripture*, p. 24.
[2] Above, pp. 29, 32.

Our approach to the prophets, however, cannot fail to be analytic for the reason that the word which they heard is no longer for us the living thing it was for them. It lies rather in their writings as so much golden ore to be discovered and mined and analyzed. Then only can we hope to apply it to the complex situation of our day as while alive it applied itself in theirs.[3] When this method is adopted for the writings of the prophets, several ruling ideas about God and man and their mutual relations appear to stand out as normative for an understanding of the word which came to these men. That they were aware of the existence of these "norms" in their teachings there can be no doubt, as they were intelligent men. I present them here, therefore, without hesitation as leading concepts of the prophetic word.

The Sovereignty of God

It has become customary to speak of the prophets as having a "philosophy" of life and of the universe or history. In the light of what has been said hitherto regarding the prophetic auditions it would be more accurate to say that they had a *science of God and of his relation to his universe.* For what they had to say on these subjects was the product of observation—of seeing the acts and hearing the word of God. He was Sovereign Lord of the world and of men because his word came to the prophets as a divine imperative that would brook no disobedience. When men disobeyed his word, the prophets observed the punishment which he meted out upon them as nations and as individuals; and when they obeyed, these observers were privileged to see something of his gracious dealing with them.[4]

The probable translation at Exod. 3:14, "I will be that I will be"

[3] This is not to deny, of course, what we have already affirmed—that the "prophet" is wrongly conceived to be temporally restricted to a particular age. Doubtless the prophetic word is heard by the church in our day. Indeed, it is often heard through the medium of the prophetic writings today. At the same time, however, these writings are open to our analysis, as are all others.

[4] I Kings 22:38; II Kings 21:10-15; Jer. 23:33-40; Hos. 6:4-6; 14:4-8; Amos 1:2–2:8; 9:7-15.

('ehyeh 'asher 'ehyeh), affords an instructive view of the prophetic attitude toward the subject of a developing theology, as it serves also to substantiate what we are here saying relative to the scientific method of observation employed by these men of insight. From the Semitic standpoint, when Moses asked to know God's "name," this was equivalent to seeking for a complete and final theology, for the name stood for the person and all he was. By contrast, therefore, it is likely that the reply Moses received meant, "Not all at once shall you know all that I am; rather I will reveal myself to you in experience throughout the generations that lie ahead, as by deed and word I shall deal with you."

Following out this method of observation the prophets seized upon every notable happening in Israel's history and under the divine afflatus interpreted it in the light of God's overarching sovereignty. In the exodus from Egypt, the conquest of Canaan, the Philistine wars, the fierce battles with Ba'al and his prophets and priests—in every phase of the history of the kingdoms, the exile, and in many other happenings these men of God saw his hand and sovereign rule.[5] At times the divine word which interpreted the event was accompanied by a vision in which the prophet saw the sovereign God high and lifted up. Such was the case with Isaiah and Ezekiel, as it had been with Micaiah ben Imlah before them.[6] This, however, was not essential to his recognition of the concept of God's sovereignty, which the prophet saw in His every act as that act was interpreted to him by its accompanying word. We should not be wrong, therefore, to speak of the prophet's living in what to him was a "sacramental universe"—a universe, that is to say, rendered sacramental for him by the divine word which interpreted all historic events as significant acts of God.

T. W. Manson has shown that the prophet's conception of God's sovereignty differed from that of his contemporaries both within and outside Israel in three significant ways: first, in its

---

[5] To the references in note 4 add Amos 2:9-12; 3:1-2; Mic. 4:1-8.
[6] Isa. 6:1-5; Ezek. 1:1-3:15; I Kings 22:19.

character of *universality*. Israel generally and the surrounding nations likewise held God to be king, but in a more restricted sense.
Yahweh was Israel's God, in their view, even as Melkarth belonged
to Phoenicia and Milcom to Ammon, these and other names of like
form being merely variants of *melek*, "king." Again, for the prophets
God was sovereign in *every sphere of life* and human activity,
whereas for the Semites generally the "god" was restricted in his
influence, as Robertson Smith has shown, to "help against their
enemies, counsel by oracles or soothsayers in matters of national
difficulty, and a sentence of justice when a case was too hard for
human decision." [7] In the third place, for the prophet the sovereignty of God meant that he was quite *independent* of the loyalty
and worship of his people. He could get on quite well enough
without them, though they were always dependent on him for their
well-being. Not so the gods of paganism; they were as dependent
upon their worshipers for the maintenance of their prestige as the
latter were on them for the benefits they were supposed to render.[8]

This problem of the extent of God's sovereign rule is a crux in
any theology, and the solution provides us with an index of its
worth. In any kind of theism worthy of the name, God is all in all.
Therefore it cannot but be deeply significant for our estimate of the
religion of the prophets that from their first emergence on the stage
of Israel's history we find them battling with the popular faiths at
the three points of Manson's thesis. In so far as they held God to
exercise universal sway over the entirety of men's lives, fearless of
loss to himself and devoid of the necessity of finding gain through
their allegiance to himself, by so much the prophets were theists
and, so far as our records go, the first of their generation. That this
high ground was attained by Amos and his successors seems to me
beyond dispute, and I see no reason why Professor Albright's view
that Moses was a monotheist may not be correct. For his definition
of that term accords remarkably with the three points of Manson's

[7] *Religion of the Semites*, p. 64.
[8] T. W. Manson, *The Teaching of Jesus*, pp. 142 ff.

statement. Professor Albright says that he means by the word one who holds to

the existence of only one God, the creator of everything, the source of justice, who is equally powerful in Egypt, in the desert, and in Palestine, who has no sexuality and no mythology, who is human in form but cannot be seen by any human eye and cannot be represented in any form.[9]

This, I agree, is monotheism; and the only problem remaining is whether the evidence proves Moses to have believed these things. In any case, that the Hebrew prophet generally differed from his popular confrere in Israel on this crucial matter of the radical sovereignty of God there can be no doubt.

The Righteousness of God

The sovereignty of God was interpreted along ethical lines by the prophets of Israel who appeared on the scene after the middle of the eighth century B.C., and they assumed the task of spiritualizing, of ethicizing, and so in the end of universalizing the popular conception of God as Sovereign Lord of men. This task became a necessity laid upon their conscience by the degrading and immoral practices associated with the local ba'alim of Canaan. These presented a striking contrast with the "sober hues and stern morality of Yahwism" as preached by an Elijah, an Amos, and an Isaiah.[10] It is probably correct to say that it is this prophetic concept of morality as definitive of God's nature which more than any other serves to distinguish prophetism from the popular religions of the prophets' day. It is this ethical difference which underlies and serves to explain the three points of disagreement noted by Manson relative to God's sovereignty. For it ought to be obvious, one imagines, that only a wholly "good" God could prove a universal sovereign, as such alone would respect and love, and therefore show an interest in the affairs of all men. Equally, only such a God would be worthy

[9] *Op. cit.*, p. 235.   [10] *Ibid.*

44

of the lordship over all the affairs of any man, including the most remote and otherwise inaccessible areas of his mysterious "personality"; for unless God were "good," he would have no real concern for the souls of men, for the condition of their moral natures, for their eternal welfare. Moreover, none but a "good" God would have the requisite courage to deal disinterestedly with his people; for courage is a product of the high resolve to serve unselfish ends, and none but a "good" God would entertain such resolve.

The prophetic term which was intended to cover the totality of God's "goodness" was *qōdhesh*, "holiness," a word whose fundamental meaning was "separation," hence "setting apart, consecration, dedication." Because of this original meaning, *qōdhesh* stood as regards God for his "majesty, 'his sacred awe-inspiring personality' " [11] as over against the world which he had made, for that numinous quality in him which inspires man's feeling of awe as he contemplates the divine.[12] It is a great mistake, however, to fail to recognize the fact that the prophets filled this majesty or numinous character of Yahweh with content. At their hands, while no doubt something of the idea of metaphysical distinctness from the world on God's part remained inseparable from the word in view of its etymological meaning, yet it now took on the added sense of ethical uniqueness which it was eminently qualified to bear. This appears from its use in such an ethical passage as Amos 4:2, where the "holiness" of God is set in contrast with the immorality of the "kine of Bashan" and can scarcely fail to have an opposing moral content, therefore. The same may be said for a passage like Isa. 6:1-5; here the "holiness" of Yahweh finds its definition from the contrasting "unclean lips" of Isaiah and his people, as is clearly intended (vs. 5b).[13] And so of many other later passages in the

[11] W. R. Harper, *Amos and Hosea* (ICC series), on Amos 4:2; cf. George Adam Smith, *The Book of Isaiah*, on Isa. 6:3.

[12] Cf. Rudolf Otto, *The Idea of the Holy*, passim; cf. also Burrows, op. cit., pp. 68-69.

[13] Cf. further Amos 2:7; Pss. 15:1; 33:21; *et passim*. See also Bewer, op. cit., pp. 186-88, relative to the non-cultic idea of "holiness" to be found even in the Holiness Code, and see below in ch. v for some discussion of the point.

Prophets and Psalms. For the prophets, then, the pattern, so to speak, of God's majestic personality became what we should call *moral character*; and the term *qōdhesh*, because of its inherent sense of separateness or uniqueness, served their purpose of representing that moral personality, when they had in mind to do so, as a *Ding an sich*. There stood God's *qōdhesh*—his unique Moral Person— over against his universe and over against men as something to be contemplated by his people, to inspire in them the while, not the awe due a pagan deity conjured up by the magic spell of some lewd sorcerer, but rather a wholesome respect for "goodness" as found at its highest and in its perfection in this holy God.

But this holy God was not only to be contemplated and viewed in meditation. Had the prophets been satisfied with this procedure, it would have meant in the end the denial of what we have termed their method of observation or audition. Obviously, a God who is content to remain a *Ding an sich* does not speak to men after any fashion, nor does he ever do anything which they may observe. Both the logic of the situation and the record of their contact with God, therefore, conspire to indicate that before they could contemplate God's "holiness," the prophets had become aware of his activity on the plane of history—an activity of which they among others were the object. For this activity, or rather for Yahweh's impact upon his universe and especially for his dealings with men, they employed the term *tsedeq* (*ts^edāqāh*), "righteousness." Righteousness, then, was God's whole moral character, which in itself the prophet termed "holiness" as we have seen, expressing itself in his relations with mankind.

The prophetic writer responsible for the Song of Deborah in its present form at Judg. 5:11 used the word in this sense.

> There shall they rehearse the righteous acts of Yahweh,
> Even the righteous acts of his rule in Israel.

The same is true of its use in Samuel's address to Israel on the occasion of the setting up of the monarchy under Saul at Gilgal

(I Sam. 12:6-18). Here Samuel begins to narrate Yahweh's faithfulness in his dealings with Israel and that people's often repeated defections, and he says, "Now therefore stand still, that I may plead with you before Yahweh concerning all the righteous acts of Yahweh, which he did to you and to your fathers" (vs. 7). Micah also, calling upon the prophetic category of "memory," rehearses a bit of Israel's history: "O my people, remember now what Balak king of Moab devised, and what Balaam the son of Beor answered him; remember from Shittim unto Gilgal, that ye may know the righteous acts of Yahweh" (6:5).[14]

This "holiness-righteousness"—that is to say, moral character—of God expressed itself in two ways in his dealings with men: as retributive justice and as salvation. The fiery message of Amos, the "stormy petrel" among the Hebrew prophets, was that God's retribution is exercised equally against sinners everywhere, regardless of race or people. "You only," he says in a familiar passage with reference to Israel, "have I known of all the families of the earth: therefore I will visit upon you all your iniquities" (3:2). Amos' associates and successors of the prophetic school, who rewrote the history of Israel and Judah from the prophetic viewpoint, succeeded in producing what is in reality a theological view of history—history, that is to say, written from the standpoint of God's judgment on man's sin. As Yahweh is Lord, he is therefore Judge, both of nations and of individuals; and these prophetic historians with the utmost rigor press home this moral, selecting those incidents in the life of the chosen people which lend themselves to pointing up this fact. Of the Deuteronomists, therefore, who were to a large degree responsible for this prophetic historiography, Professor Albright has written: "For the first time in the records of Israel, as far as we possess them, the concept of theodicy is inextricably interwoven with history."[15]

[14] Cf. further Pss. 96:13; 145:7; Jer. 23:6; Zech. 8:8, and numerous other passages which serve to define Yahweh's "righteousness" as herein indicated.

[15] Albright, op. cit., p. 245. Cf. the uniting of the concepts of "righteousness," "judgment," and the like in such passages as Jer. 4:2; 9:24; 22:3; Isa. 11:1-5; 16:5, et al.; Pss. 50:6; 72:1-2.

But God's retribution is never final, nor does it alone present an over-all picture of his attitude toward men. God desires above all to save men, not to damn them. Accordingly, in Deutero-Isaiah God's "righteousness" is frequently equated with and made to signify the "salvation" which he grants his people. This appears in the remarkable passage at 45:8: "Distil, ye heavens, from above, and let the skies pour down righteousness: let the earth open, that it may bring forth salvation, and let it cause righteousness to spring up together; I, Yahweh, have created it." And in the refrain of chapter 51, "My righteousness is near, my salvation is gone forth" (cf. vss. 5, 6, 8), or its equivalent, the uniting of these two concepts has the effect at the least of indicating that it is out of God's character of righteousness that his saving activity springs.[16] Jeremiah has the same thought of God's saving activity as embraced under the term "righteousness" when he speaks of the messianic "Branch" (23:5) and even of Judah and Jerusalem (33:16) as about to be given the name "Yahweh our righteousness." This thought of God's saving activity as arising out of his essential character of "righteousness" probably had its origin with the great prophets of the monarchy, as when Micah remarks: "But as for me, I will look unto Yahweh; I will wait for the God of my salvation. . . . He will bring me forth to the light, and I shall behold his righteousness" (7:7, 9).[17]

Accordingly it is legitimate to think of the entire series of saving concepts employed by the prophets as arising out of and revolving about this "righteousness" or moral nature of God. For Hosea it expresses itself in terms of "lovingkindness" and forgiveness, for Isaiah in those of the righteous reign of the Branch; again, Jeremiah conceives its effect in terms of the "new covenant," and Deutero-Isaiah in those of the Suffering Servant and the redemptive community. It is because of God's character of righteousness that Hosea sees chastening and moral growth as his objective for his people

[16] Cf. also Isa. 33:5-6; Ps. 24:5, et passim.
[17] Cf. further such passages as show Yahweh's saving "righteous acts" throughout Israel's history, e.g., Judg. 5:11; I Sam. 12:6-18; Mic. 6:5.

when he has "hewed them by the prophets" (6:5) and been "unto Ephraim as a moth, and to the house of Jacob as rottenness" (5:12). Wherefore in all confidence he declares, "Come, and let us return unto the Lord: for he hath torn, and he will heal us; he hath smitten, and he will bind us up" (6:1).

The Will of God

The common man in Israel unquestionably brought together the two ideas of the sovereignty of God and his choice of Israel as his peculiar people, and derived from this conjunction the conclusion that Israel stood in a peculiar position of privilege in God's sight. Not so the prophetic word! Here the conceptions of God as sovereign and God as "righteous" were rather conjoined, and the result spelled moral responsibility for his people. Professor G. Ernest Wright has an illuminating chapter entitled "Obey My Voice," in which he points out that "it was imperative that a man be obedient to the law of God, just as a servant must obey the commands of his master or ruler." [18] The normal term used to describe the worshiper of Yahweh among the prophets, therefore, was ʿebhedh, slave. Jacob was God's ʿebhedh, as were David, Moses, Zerubbabel, Isaiah, and others.[19] In the psalms, imbued as these are with the prophetic spirit, the idea was broadened to take in all of God's children:

> Behold, as the eyes of servants look unto the hand of their master,
> As the eyes of a maid unto the hand of her mistress;
> So our eyes look unto Yahweh our God,
> Until he have mercy upon us. (Ps. 123:2.)

And again,

> Serve the Lord with fear,
> And rejoice with trembling. (Ps. 2:11.)

[18] *The Challenge of Israel's Faith*, pp. 39-40.
[19] Jer. 30:10 and Ezek. 28:25; Jer. 33:21 and Ezek. 34:23-24; Mal. 4:4; Hag. 2:23; Isa. 20:3.

The concept of servantship or slavedom was softened, however, as the first of the above quotations suggests, by the thought that moral responsibility works both ways, involving both master and slave. Such was the teaching of the prophets throughout: God's and man's relationship is one of mutual responsibility, each assuming certain obligations with reference to the other, as is true of every sovereign and people. The relation was made even more tender by the prophet's occasional use of the terms "father" and "son," along with those of "master" and "slave." [20]

The primary duty of the Lord's servant or of his son is to reflect his character of righteousness. Amos is perhaps the first to suggest as much, as he writes: "Seek good, and not evil, that ye may live. . . . Hate the evil, and love the good, and establish justice in the gate. . . . Let justice roll down as waters, and righteousness as a mighty stream" (5:14-15, 24). Following Amos there is a steady succession of prophets and prophet-inspired psalmists who vie with each other in suggesting the need of God's righteous character being reflected in man.[21] Malachi, therefore, several hundred years after Amos sees that before the "great and terrible day of the Lord" the messenger of the covenant "will sit as a refiner and purifier of silver, and he will purify the sons of Levi, and refine them as gold and silver; and they shall offer unto the Lord offerings in righteousness" (3:3).

As some of the above quotations show, this call to righteousness through the prophets came as a divine imperative like that which demanded that man acknowledge God's sovereignty and righteousness. It was in the first instance a universal imperative applicable to all men everywhere, even as God was the universal sovereign of all men. The covenant relationship, however, which Israel sustained to Yahweh was assumed to heighten the responsibility of the chosen people to exhibit God's righteousness in their lives. This was be-

---

[20] Jer. 3:19 (cf. vs. 14); Hos. 11:1; Mal. 3:17.
[21] Pss. 1:5-6; 37:17; Zeph. 2:3; Mal. 3:3.

cause Israel had of her own free will entered into that contract with God. Professor Wright has expressed this idea:

> God chose Israel to be his people, and Israel chose him to be their God. A special contractual relationship was therefore felt to exist between the two parties, a relationship carrying with it certain obligations, the keeping of which meant life and blessing, and the failure to keep, death and a curse (Deut. 30:15 ff.). . . . Righteousness in the Old Testament, therefore, is primarily the doing of those things which maintain the covenant, while sin is its transgression, a breach of legal agreement.[22]

The necessity which is laid upon man of doing God's will by observing and reflecting his character of righteousness requires that that character be manifested to man. Hence we come round the complete circle, starting with the word of revelation which speaks of God as sovereign and as righteousness, which declares that man must obey the will of God and thereby attain to his ultimate purpose relative to man, and which by a series of divine imperatives reveals the content of that will to man. The prophetic word is thus seen to be for man's obedience and salvation. It is Torah, the divine instruction, intended to portray the divine character, that looking into it man may discover the nature of that character, acquire God's spirit, and reflect his likeness. Its issue is not intended to be rote obedience to a series of disrelated commands; such moronic behaviourism is furthest from the minds of the prophets. Hear Hosea, for example, when he pleads for character above observance: "For I desire goodness, and not sacrifice; and the knowledge of God more than burnt-offerings" (6:6). Micah also in a memorable passage remarks: "He hath showed thee, O man, what is good; and what doth the Lord require of thee, but to do justly, and to love kindness, and to walk humbly with thy God?" (6:8). Ezekiel and Jeremiah might be quoted to the same effect,[23]

---

[22] *Op. cit.*, p. 73.

[23] With Jeremiah's "new covenant," "membership of the true people of God will be a matter of disposition and character rather than birth." So T. W. Manson, *op. cit.*, p. 178.

the one with his teaching of the coming age when God will give to his people "a new spirit . . . , a heart of flesh," even his own Spirit (36:26-28), the other with that of the "new covenant" to the same intent (31:31-34). It was a high point in such prophetic insight into the will of God for men when the Deuteronomist summed up the entirety of Yahweh's demands upon man in the words of the Shema': "Hear, O Israel: the Lord our God is one Lord: and thou shalt love the Lord thy God with all thy heart, and with all thy soul, and with all thy might." (Deut. 6:4-5.)

The Prophetic Eschatology

The Hebrew prophets were essentially "this-worldly" in the sense that they had a profound conviction of the "value" or, as Wheeler Robinson has said, of the "actuality" of history.[24] That is to say, they believed that history had genuine significance for God as for man, so that the events of time were recorded in heaven at their face value, the currency of this world passing freely in the other. They would have dismissed the Hindu doctrine that earthly existence is maya (illusion) with a wave of the hand. This was God's world, and it never occurred to them to question either its reality or its value in his sight. They would have sung with fervor Maltbie Babcock's hymn:

> This is my Father's world,
> O let me ne'er forget
> That though the wrong seems oft so strong,
> God is the Ruler yet.[25]

In consequence even the eschatological teaching of the prophets partook of the generally "this-worldly" character of their view. Like all of the prophetic doctrines their eschatology had a twofold origin: on the one hand, what they observed of God's activity, his

[24] Op. cit., pp. xxx ff.
[25] From Thoughts for Every-Day Living, by permission Charles Scribner's Sons, publishers.

judging and his saving, within history; and on the other, the voice
of the Moral Governor of the universe which they heard. They were
deeply impressed with the disparity between "what is and what
ought to be," [26] between what God willed for men and what men
were and did, and they could not believe that the righteous Sovereign would permit this condition to run on indefinitely. Conditioned as they were through such acute moral sensitiveness, it is not
strange that they heard the voice of God speak to them of a
"far-off divine event" when within history there would be a leveling
off of all moral issues and God would finally vindicate his righteous
rule over the affairs of men.

So far as our records go, Amos first spoke of this event, when
God's judgment upon man's sin would be revealed, as "the day of
the Lord." [27] It was not to be a day when Israel would triumph over
her foes as many fondly imagined, saying, "The evil shall not over-
take nor meet us" (9:10b). For this was Yahweh's day in the
peculiar sense that now if ever he must vindicate himself, must right
all wrong, must bring to a summary the total moral score and clear
his books to the satisfaction of his own holy nature. On such a day
he would play no favorites, and even the chosen people would be
brought to book. "Are ye not as the children of the Ethiopians unto
me, O children of Israel? saith Yahweh. Have not I brought up
Israel out of the land of Egypt, and the Philistines from Caphtor,
and the Syrians from Kir?" (Amos 9:7.) But on that day there
would also of necessity be a final display of God's saving grace, in
accordance with the constantly two-sided nature of his righteousness. His day would be one of both final judgment and final salvation. "In that day . . . I will bring back the captivity of my people
Israel. . . . And I will plant them upon their land, and they shall
no more be plucked up out of their land which I have given them,
saith Yahweh thy God." (Amos 9:11-15.) Differing stresses were
placed upon these two features of Yahweh's day by the various

[26] T. W. Manson, op. cit., pp. 244 ff.
[27] Amos 5:18-20; 9:1-10; Hos. 2:18-23; Joel 1–3; Mic. 3–4; Isa. 2–3; 13:6, 9,
13; 34:8; Zeph. 1:7 ff.

prophets, stresses which appear upon examination to be governed by the varying necessities of the hours in which they were severally made. But both elements were rather generally present everywhere, and indeed it seems inconceivable that it should have been otherwise.

In the course of the development of this prophetic doctrine of "the day of the Lord," three great figures emerged upon the horizon of history's close. These were Yahweh himself, the "Anointed One" or Messiah, and the Servant of Yahweh. Amos, the earliest of the prophets to speak of the day of the Lord, spoke of it as a time when the Lord himself would vindicate his righteous rule by a personal appearance on the stage of history: "For I will pass through the midst of thee, saith the Lord" (5:17-20).

Side by side with this teaching relative to Yahweh's coming was the doctrine of an Anointed One who should rule in his name and as his viceroy. This messianic hope has been termed "the central theme of the Bible. It is that which gives to the two Testaments their unity." [28] If the various ramifications of this doctrine are taken into account, this statement will probably be found true. It had a long history which has been traced out with great care, but we cannot give space to a recounting of it here.[29] It includes the prophetic references to the scion of David (Isa. 9:6, 7), the "shoot of the stock of Jesse" (Isa. 11:1-5), Ezekiel's "shepherd" (34:23-24), Zechariah's "Branch" (3:8), and Micah's "ruler in Israel; whose goings forth are from of old, from everlasting" (5:2b).

The last of these three figures to appear on the stage of Hebrew prophecy was the Suffering Servant of Deutero-Isaiah. This figure brings together "two concepts, vicarious suffering and perfection through suffering," concepts never associated with either of the other figures in the prophets or in Hebrew thought.[30] This disparity between the three figures, however, must not blind our eyes to their

---

[28] Hebert, op. cit., p. 39.
[29] See T. W. Manson, op. cit., pp. 228-29, 248-49, 255-56; C. F. Burney, *Outlines of Old Testament Theology*, ch. vii.
[30] Albright, op. cit., p. 254.

essential oneness of conception. For all three in their own ways are intended to elucidate the fact that God, the sovereign of his people, is also their Saviour. The Lord himself is that as the vindicator of his righteous rule, the Messiah as mediatorial leader of his people, the Servant as vicarious sufferer on their behalf. The only real disparity between the three lies in the fact that to the figure of the Servant no thought of retributive justice attaches as it does to the other two, this concept being thrust into the background by that of suffering, which the other figures do not experience.

It has already been noted that the original thought of the redeemed community as embracing a whole people was displaced by the doctrine of the "saving remnant," as it became apparent that the people as a whole were not to be committed to the redemptive task.[31] As this shrinkage of the original conception occurred through the observed necessity of placing it upon the basis of an individual commitment to God's will, it was at the same time expanded to take in like-minded persons of every race and nation. That is to say, the individualizing and universalizing of the doctrine quite naturally and logically went on at the same time and in the minds of the same prophets. These same prophets also elaborated the idea of the Messiah in one form and another. So one may say that the ideas of saving remnant, universalism, and Messiah took shape together under the divine leading.[32]

These three concepts therefore serve mutually to interpret one another—a matter of the greatest possible moment for our understanding of the fully developed prophetic doctrine of salvation. It is permissible to formulate this doctrine in its final form as looking for the approach of a great figure who should prove to be the moral leader of a community—the "saving remnant"—composed of individuals of every race without distinction who should rally round him with a view to accomplishing the salvation God has to give to all the peoples of the earth. Here, save for the development of the

[31] See above, p. 38.
[32] See my *Intention of Jesus*, pp. 72-77; also Mic. 4:2, 7; 5:2-5; Isa. 11:1-16; Jer. 3:14-19; 23:5-8.

parallel teaching on the Suffering Servant, the prophetic word ceased. For it could go no further in revealing the divine mind to man. It was no more divine word, but rather divine act, which man needed for his salvation. Canon Ottley, quoting in part from Pleiderer's well-known Gifford lectures, has phrased what I should wish to say here as follows:

[For the prophets in the end] the Messiah was not destined to fulfil the aspirations of national ambition, but to satisfy the yearnings of spiritual need. . . . Religion is not merely a matter of national obligation, but a personal and individual relationship with Jehovah. A spiritual religion can no longer be a merely national religion. "When religion is thus carried back to its deepest center, to the fellowship of man in his heart with God, the separating limits of the national cults fall away as meaningless; the most inward experience of what is purely human can no longer be a privilege of one people above the others—it must become a thing of the whole of mankind." [33]

The time element involved in the prophet's eschatological picture may be thought of as being the product of tension between his "this-worldly" perspective on the one hand and his necessary sense of the relativity of history on the other. History, as we have seen, had genuine significance for him—but a significance achieved at every point through the creative fiat of the divine word which constituted it real or "actual." God would vindicate his righteous rule; he would judge and save on the historical plane and within time. This he must do, indeed, because he had by his creative act imparted to history a reality which necessitated his staying with it right through to its last dramatic climax. By the same token he must accomplish on history's stage his own final purposes of judgment and salvation, else he would seem to have denied the "actuality" of history, and such to the mind of the prophet was unthinkable. Hence the term "eschatological," which refers to the eschaton or last time in the prophet's nomenclature and not to an eternity outside of or

[33] R. L. Ottley, The Hebrew Prophets, p. 115.

beyond time as such.[34] Hence also the prophet's lack of interest in the doctrine of a future life to be lived in a "heaven" divorced from life on this earth. He cannot have been ignorant of such teaching, for it has been the common property of nearly all primitive peoples, including the contemporary Egyptians, Persians, and Greeks.[35]

Over against the Hebrew prophet's sense of the value of history, however, was his equal sensitiveness to the eternal order surrounding, engulfing, and piercing, as it also transcended, the temporal with which his sense life had to do. It was this sensitivity to the eternal order which kept this very practical realist from degenerating into a materialist, even as his belief in the reality of history saved him from the danger of ever developing an unrealistic theosophy. History had meaning for him only because the divine word imparted meaning to it in the creative act. "Let there be . . . and there was"—such was his view of the power of the word of God. But if that word could create, obviously it could also destroy; and if there was beginning, there must also be ending. God was for the prophet the first and the last, the Alpha and the Omega, and the Living One, and upon his will all things depended (Isa. 44:6; 48: 12). Isaac Watts epitomizes this aspect of prophetic teaching in the words:

> Know that the Lord is God alone,
> He can create, and He destroy.

Hence while the prophet conceived that God's judgment and his salvation must be realized within the historical situation, it was equally clear to him that they would be the end of history as such. As God's first word had been one of creation, so his last would be one of destruction and re-creation. "For, behold, I create new heavens and a new earth; and the former things shall not be re-

---

[34] Cf. "the latter days" (ἐσχάταις ἡμέραις) in the Septuagint rendering of Isa. 2:2; Hos. 3:5; Mic. 4:1, et al.

[35] Examples are to be found in the Papyrus of Ani, the Garō demāna or paradise of Zoroastrianism, and the Greek Hades.

membered, nor come into mind." (Isa. 65:17.) [36] The prophet did not peer beyond this point into the future. The "day of the Lord"—the day of God's wrath and judgment, the day of his power and vindication, the day of his saving goodness—would be the horizon line setting off the old from the new. For God would speak again, and behold, all things would become new! Here the prophet's interest ceased; he could well enough leave the future—the beyond-history—to God, for his own hands were quite full of the concerns and responsibilities of the present life. He had sufficient faith in God to leave it so.

When would that "last great day" occur? The prophet did not know, nor was he greatly concerned to inquire. Of its certain approach he was deeply convinced, and he was concerned that it should serve as a motive to righteousness on the part of God's people. But of the temporal span of the *eschaton* or of its distance from the day in which he wrote he was quite ignorant. His characteristic attitude was that of Deutero-Isaiah as expressed in the words: "Thus saith the Lord, Keep ye justice, and do righteousness; for my salvation is near to come, and my righteousness to be revealed" (56:1). Or again of the psalmist who wrote:

> I will hear what God the Lord will speak;
> For he will speak peace unto his people, and to his saints:
> But let them not turn again to folly.
> Surely his salvation is nigh them that fear him,
> That glory may dwell in our land. (85:8, 9.)

To the prophet's mind God was always about to break into human experience. Professor G. Ernest Wright has phrased this idea as follows:

The prophets had laid hold on a great truth, though their exact formulation of it in time was limited by their perspective; namely,

---

[36] As Gressmann has written, "in Wirklichkeit ist die Endzeit eine Urzeit, freilich die Urzeit einer künftigen, neuen Welt, die kein Ende hat," but the prophet characteristically did not look with great interest into that "Urzeit." See his *Der Ursprung der israelitisch-jüdischen Eschatologie*, p. 199.

that in every juncture of history, in every crisis of personal and social life, there is a Day of the Lord. That Day is always present for those who have eyes to see it, and *yet it is ever about to come.* The judgment of God is always upon us, though we become aware of it when we find ourselves in a crisis.[37]

Accordingly, it was contrary to the prophetic genius to set a time for the advent of the "great and terrible day of the Lord" or of the three great figures who should in one way or another usher it in or have a share in its fulfillment. In a deep spiritual and moral sense those figures were conceived by the prophets as always knocking on the door of each generation of Israel's history.

It is in order, therefore, to enter a caveat against the so-called "prophetic foreshortening of history," which since the day of Franz Delitzsch[38] has been held to characterize their view. According to this theory the prophets are supposed to look for the coming of the "day of the Lord" or of one or another of the eschatological figures in the near future, even in their own lifetimes. This idea is most unlikely in itself, as it is opposed, as we have just seen, to the genius of the prophet's mind and interests. Moreover I believe that on careful scrutiny such passages in the prophets as are supposed to support this theory will be found to yield to one or another of two critical observations. In the first place, some of these represent apocalyptic interpolations into the true texts of the prophets. It is well known that apocalypticism did foreshorten the historic perspective of those who held to its tenets. We shall have occasion to look into this matter in some detail in part IV. This phenomenon was due to the fact that the apocalyptists accepted certain principles of interpretation of the divine working and exhibited in consequence an interest in future events not shared by the earlier prophets of Israel. The prophetic and apocalyptic eschatologies were

[37] *Op. cit.,* pp. 88-89. John Knox in his *Christ the Lord,* apropos of C. H. Dodd's theory of a "realized eschatology," remarks to the same effect: "There are other kinds of immediacy besides temporal immediacy; and Dodd has rendered a great service in making us more vividly aware of that fact." (P. 30.)

[38] See A. B. Davidson, *Old Testament Prophecy,* p. 353.

quite different at this point and ought not to be confused. Among the passages which will be found to yield to this solution are probably Isa. 24–27, Zech. 9–14, and numerous shorter apocalyptic additions like Mic. 2:12-13; 4:6-8; Jer. 23:3-4, et al.[39]

Again, it is to be remembered that the messianic and related concepts had a history and went through various stages of development at the hands of successive prophets. I have referred to this growth in connection with the concepts of the "remnant" and universalism as applied to the doctrine of God's salvation of mankind.[40] It is impossible accordingly to predicate of the Messiah, for example, at one stage what is true of this concept at another, or even to assert that when the prophets use the expression "the anointed one" they have in mind an eschatological figure answering to that name. As H. H. Rowley remarks:

The Hebrew word which is transliterated "Messiah" simply means anointed, and is applied to reigning kinds of Israel, to high priests, and even to Cyrus. There are passages in the Psalms where the term is held to refer to the ideal king of the future, but of these the interpretation is disputed. In any case, the majority of the occurrences of the term in the Old Testament are clearly without the ideal reference. On the other hand, the passages which unmistakably refer to the ideal future leader of the kingdom do not use the term.[41]

It should be axiomatic, then, that it is unwarranted to claim as applicable to the ideal messianic figure any one or other of those accidents which are incidental to its development at any stage along the way. And yet it is on just such identification of the ideal figure with its immature prototypes that the so-called prophetic foreshortening of history is based.[42]

The argument at this point is identical to that advanced by Professor Albright relative to the figure of the Suffering Servant.

[39] Cf. further, Bewer, op. cit., pp. 407-9.
[40] See above, p. 55.
[41] The Relevance of Apocalyptic, p. 25.
[42] The case of Joshua—or alternatively, of Zerubbabel—in Zech. 6:9-15 is a case in point.

After many efforts by Old Testament scholars to interpret the Servant of Yahweh as the people of Israel itself, or as some historical character such as Jeremiah, Jehoiachin, Zerubbabel, Cyrus—or even Moses (E. Sellin)—there has been a pronounced reaction. The figure changes so frequently and so disconcertingly as we endeavor to fix it that we must regard it in all probability (unless we wish to resort to subjective and futile surgical operations on the text) as a standing theme which is differently treated in different poems. In other words, the concept is presumably older than Deutero-Isaiah and it so impressed itself upon his sensitive spirit or seemed so ideally suited to his religious message that he utilized it in various ways.[43]

In each case—that of the Messiah and the Suffering Servant, and I should add also "the day of the Lord"—the fluidity of usage and interpretation stems from fundamentally the same cause: the concept in question has had a history behind it before it came to the hand of the prophet under immediate discussion. In using it, therefore, he felt himself free to mold it into conformity with his immediate needs in order to give adequate expression to the word of revelation which had come to him. But to judge his use of it by its final or total meaning and to say that he had in mind that ultimate sense when he identified, let us say, the "anointed one" with some historical personality, thereby both giving a mistaken identification to the figure and shortening the time of his appearance, is to be guilty of eisegesis. There is no single passage in the Prophets of which it can be said that in prophesying the immediate coming of some historic figure the prophet has in mind that that individual will satisfy the requirements of any one of the three great eschatological figures.

Accordingly, although the prophet's vision was not foreshortened in the sense often asserted—for the reason that the category of "time" was of no interest to him and he had no wish like the apocalyptist to pry into the secrets of the future, whether near or remote—what I have been saying nonetheless is a mark of real limitation on his part. It is also the surest sign of his deep moral and

[43] *Op. cit.,* p. 255.

spiritual insight. His apprehension of the divine categories was slow and characterized by progress, but not in the direction of an expert ability or wish to delve into and resolve fantastic enigmas. The prophet was neither clairvoyant nor crystal gazer. His advance was rather in the direction of a deeper understanding of the nature of God's moral government of and his saving purpose relative to mankind.

CHAPTER

3

Jesus and the Prophets

THE prophets had a doctrine of the *revelation* of the Word of God: it arose out of the divine voice itself, which they were privileged to hear. They had no corresponding doctrine of the *inspiration* of Scripture. This was because it was their function to write Scripture, not to write about it.

As is well known, the Jews spoke of the historical books of the Old Testament—Joshua, Judges, I and II Samuel, and I and II Kings—as the Former Prophets; in this designation they have been vindicated by modern scholarship, which has succeeded in demonstrating that these books were written by men of the prophetic tradition. In addition large portions of the Pentateuch were written by men of like character, and in the Psalms their views are largely determinative of the ethical and spiritual attitudes expressed. It need scarcely be added that, with the exception of certain apocalyptic intrusions like Isa. 24–27 and Zech. 9–14, the prophetical books—the Latter Prophets—were the exclusive product of the men of the revelation of the word.[1]

Jesus' attitude toward these prophetic scriptures is illuminating. He had steeped himself in them from his youth upward, as his numerous quotations from them bear witness. And in spite of the

[1] See above, p. 60.

uncertainties which Form Criticism has introduced into the problem, it may be said that Manson's remark that "his knowledge of the Hebrew scriptures was both extensive and profound" generally stands.[2] Appendix A contains a complete list of passages quoted by Jesus from the Old Testament scriptures. An analysis of this list reveals that our Lord's greatest interest lay with the prophetic writings and those, like Psalms and Deuteronomy, which are so largely akin to them in both letter and spirit. Isaiah, Psalms, and the great nameless Prophet of the Exile were especial favorites with him, though portions of the Pentateuch and more especially the prophetic parts of these five books with their high ethical and spiritual teachings were not far behind in his esteem and affection.

The "voice" from heaven at Jesus' baptism spoke to him in the words of two prophetic passages (Ps. 2:7a and Isa. 42:1; cf. Mark 1:11), a fact which was indicative of the content of his own thought at the time, and surely the use of the three passages from Deuteronomy and one from Psalms at his temptation can be no less so (Deut. 6:13, 16; 8:6; Ps. 91:11-12 [Q]).[3] Jesus used the prophetic scriptures to defend his use of the somewhat obscure method of parabolic teaching (Mark 4:12; Isa. 6:9-10), to describe the condition of men's hearts as he found them (Mark 7:6; Isa. 29:13), to warn cities of coming judgment (Luke 10:15 [Q]; Isa. 14:13, 15), to teach the nature of true prayer (Matt. 6:6 [M]; II Kings 4:33), to describe the character of his own mission (Luke 7:22 [Q]; Isa. 35:5; 61:1), as well as that of the Baptist (Luke 7:27 [Q], Mal. 3:1), to vindicate his cleansing of the temple (Mark 11:7; Isa. 56:7;

----

[2] Op. cit., p. 48, n. 1.

[3] Form Criticism acknowledges the historicity of the events in these and like instances but refuses to attribute the scriptural quotations to Jesus. These represent rather the interpretation placed on such incidents by the later church in the view of these critics. Cf. M. Dibelius, The Message of Jesus Christ, pp. 183, 185, for example. I have argued, however, in The Intention of Jesus that the church's interpretation at these points, if such it be, serves to give meaningful unity to Jesus' ministry as a whole. If, then, this ecclesiastical interpretation of the mind of Christ is mistrusted, it is incumbent on the form critics to suggest another that will better serve to make clear to us what his mind was relative to his ministry. William Manson in Jesus the Messiah has some illuminating remarks to make on these passages; see pp. 138-39, 147-48, 155-56.

Jer. 7:11), and to indicate his position of sonship in the kingdom (Mark 12:1, 10; Isa. 5:1-2; Ps. 118:22-23).

This list is not intended to be exhaustive. But it serves to make evident how extremely varied and crucial was his use of the prophetic scriptures. On them he stayed his spirit in the darkest hours of his earthly life; he sought them in time of temptation; he interpreted to himself and others by their use the nature of his ministry, and in the agony of the cross he found them his sure support (Mark 15:34; Ps. 22:2). The theology of crisis has laid hold of a sound psychological principle in suggesting that it is in the crises of life that the forces which dominate our lives are laid bare. In Jesus' case there can be no doubt that one of these was the prophetic scriptures upon which he had nourished his soul. Surely, then, Matthew's special source gives us a true picture of his mind relative to his mission when it reports him as saying, "Think not that I came to destroy the law or the prophets: I came not to destroy but to fulfil" (Matt. 5:17), a passage in which both prophetic elements of the Old Testament scriptures are brought together.[4]

Jesus' Use of the Prophetic Literary Models

The prophets were men who translated the divine word which came to them into the terms of a devastating rhetoric calculated to bring fear to the heart of a king or to implant hope in the breast of the "poor in spirit." When the need arose, moreover, they could support their claim to be in touch with the true and living God with authenticating deeds. Witness Elijah's activities, particularly those on Mt. Carmel and the restoration of the son of the widow of Zarephath (I Kings 17:8-24), and Elisha's healing of Naaman the Syrian (II Kings 5:1-19). Jesus' ministry was characterized by these same two features of word and deed, and it is impossible to resist the conclusion that therein he was consciously following in the prophets' train. The gospel sources contain several passages in

[4] See also Matt. 7:12 (M); 22:40 (M); Luke 16:16=Matt. 11:13 (Q); Luke 24:44 (L).

which he is reported to have described his ministry in terms of this twofold prophetic function (Luke 7:18-22=Matt. 11:1-5 [Q]; Luke 4:12 ff. [L]; Mark 2:1-12).

Particularly striking is our Lord's adoption of the prophetic literary models, such as the prophetic sermon, the doom song, and the māshāl (both proverb and parable) with its counterpart in the realm of action, the acted parable. The sermon was the commonest of all the prophetic literary devices, and it has become the model of the church's principle literary activity.[5] It was oracular in form with the prophets as we have seen, usually beginning with some such phrase as "Thus saith the Lord." The two sermons on mount and plain (Matt. 5–7; Luke 6:17-49 [Q]) are the outstanding examples in Jesus' teaching; others are the kingdom parables in Mark 4:1-34, the eschatological discourse in Mark 13, and the encomium on the Baptist in Luke 7:18-35.

The doom song was a "prophetic utterance directed against some particular city, nation or country." [6] At least two examples of its use occur in Jesus' teachings, both from the source common to Matthew and Luke: the upbraiding of the Galilean cities in Matt. 11:20-24=Luke 10:13-15 and the lament over Jerusalem in Matt. 23:37-39=Luke 13:34-35. Perhaps to these should be added also the four woes of Luke 6:24-26 (L?).

The Hebrew word māshāl and its Aramaic equivalent, methāl, were used to cover a variety of literary forms, chief of which were the epigram or proverb and the story parable. These are so common in Jesus' teaching as not to require illustration here. The significance of the work that has been done by scholars on the māshāl in Jesus' usage lies in two directions. First, the very forms in which much of this material is cast are suggestive of its originality with Jesus himself. This applies to the epigrammatic type of māshāl which is usually in poetic form. Albertz, Dibelius, B. S. Easton, Vincent Taylor, Basil Redlich, and numerous others—including from

---

[5] Isa. 1; Jer. 10:1-16; Ezek. 34.
[6] R. G. Moulton, *Literary Study of the Bible*, p. 353. See Amos 1–2.

a slightly different point of view, C. F. Burney—who have worked over this material are convinced that there is an unmistakable cadence and poetic structure in much of Jesus' teaching suggestive of the work of a single hand.[7] The materials involved in this statement come from all the Synoptic sources (Mk, Q, L, M), and it is hardly to be supposed that these would converge on a single conclusion—namely, that Jesus was in the habit of uttering his teachings in the epigrammatic poetical form—unless this were indeed true. Easton, indeed, concludes that "the earliest content of the tradition He Himself required His disciples to commit to memory" as it fell from his lips,[8] while T. W. Manson writes that "this strophic parallelism" of Jesus was "the most distinctive characteristic of his poetry and his special contribution to the forms of poetry in general."[9] From such study, therefore, the rather startling result emerges that most, if not all, of Jesus' sayings and poems do not conform to any traditional forms in the sense in which Form Criticism uses the term—i.e., of material rounded and molded in the course of tradition into a standardized pattern. Rather they conform to literary forms of a type elaborated by our Lord himself and through which he expressed something of the creative genius which was native to his mind.

Again, in adopting the māshāl in its story form (the story parable) our Lord was following in a literary tradition which goes back to the prophets for its beginning or at all events for its classical expression in the Hebrew scriptures. Of the nine to eleven examples of parables in the Old Testament, all come from the prophetic writings, and of these all but two are said to have been uttered by prophets.[10] Though Jesus therefore was par excellence the master of the parable of this story type in the Hebrew tradition, he was

---

[7] Cf. by way of example on this extensive subject Dibelius, op. cit., pp. 156 ff.; V. Taylor, The Formation of the Gospel Tradition, pp. 88 ff.; E. F. Scott, The Validity of the Gospel Record, pp. 127-28.

[8] Christ in the Gospels, p. 41.

[9] Op. cit., p. 56.

[10] II Sam. 12:1-14; 14:1-11; I Kings 20:35-40; Isa. 5:1-7; Ezek. 15–17; 19:2-9, 10-14; 21:1-5; 23; 24:3-5.

once again simply falling into the prophetic line in adopting and elaborating it for his own purposes.

But even more significant is our Lord's use of the characteristic prophetic *acted parable* or *emblem prophecy*. This is a parable in act or deed, one which "has for its texts . . . visible things or actions." [11] Examples of this in the Old Testament prophets are: Jeremiah's use of the linen girdle (ch. 13), the potter's clay (18:1-17), and the basket of figs (ch. 24), Ezekiel's mimic siege of Jerusalem (4:1-5:4), and Hosea's marriage to an adulterous wife (chs. 1-3). In such emblem prophecy either the acted parable itself or its author was intended as a "sign" or memorial of the working of God in the midst of his people.

That our Lord consciously employed such acted parables as "signs" or memorials there can be no doubt. Examples of this are: his selection of the "twelve" as a memorial of the presence and saving activity of the remnant,[12] his entry into Jerusalem as a memorial to the people of Israel and particularly to the rulers that the Messiah had come,[13] the Lord's Supper as a sign of his approaching death as the Suffering Servant,[14] the foot washing as a memorial of the humility properly belonging to the Servant,[15] and the cleansing of the temple as a sign of his lordly relation to it. [16] There can be no doubt also that the miracles were intended as "signs" in this high sense of a memorial that God was at work among his people. Alan Richardson has alluded to this fact in striking fashion:

There can be little doubt that the makers of the Gospel tradition understood the miracles of Jesus as "signs" or symbolical acts which convey in a dramatized form essential Christological teaching. They were enacted parables, not mere "wonder-stories," or occasional works of charity undertaken from motives of compassion in response to a particular and immediate need, or mere historical reminiscences, or yet decorative appendages to the main preaching and teaching material. . . .

[11] Moulton, op. cit., p. 336.
[12] See *The Intention of Jesus*, pp. 210-18.
[13] Mark 11:1-10.

[14] Mark 14:22-25.
[15] John 13:12-17.
[16] Mark 11:15-18, 27-33.

So, in fact, the historical tradition of the Christian Church from New Testament times has interpreted the miracles of Jesus as the *Gesta Christi*.[17]

Jesus' reference to "the power of God" and his "kingdom" in connection with the Beelzebub controversy is certainly intended to give us the key to the meaning of the miracles as a whole: they are signs of the presence of God's working in his people's midst.[18] I have suggested elsewhere that the miracles are from this point of view to be considered parables in action, as the parables are miracles in word.[19] Finally, our Lord's comparison of the "greater somewhat" in himself with that which functioned in Jonah and his reference to both as "signs" are doubtless to be understood in this same way.[20]

Far more than by his use of the prophetic scriptures and his imitation of the prophetic literary models, however, our Lord showed his allegiance to the prophetic word by certain unmistakably decisive acts and attitudes. At this point it is relevant to remark only on his response to the prophetic "voice" on the banks of the Jordan and his determination to share in what Bultmann has well termed the "eschatological sacrament" instituted by the new prophet, John the Baptist.[21] Here was evidence that he proposed to ally himself with this new phase of the prophetic movement. Moreover, that he should have experienced an inaugural vision in conjunction with his baptism was in line with those of the prophets who were before him and is an indication that he shared the same Spirit which animated them.[22] Two of our best sources (Mk and Q) elsewhere bear testimony to our Lord's reference to John in terms which sug-

---

[17] *The Miracle-Stories of the Gospels*, p. 57.

[18] Luke 11:20. It is to be noted that Jesus' miracles were never objective "signs," i.e., standing alone they never proved anything; only as understood in relation to his person by one who had faith in him did they constitute "signs." See *The Intention of Jesus*, pp. 110-14, 174-75.

[19] See *The Intention of Jesus*, p. 114.

[20] *Ibid.*, p. 175.

[21] *Jesus and the Word*, pp. 23 ff.

[22] For the difference between the prophetic vision and that of the apocalyptist see below, pp. 203-7.

gest that he thought of the Baptist as at once of the prophetic line (Mark 11:30) and the inaugurator through baptism of the movement for which he himself stood (Luke 7:26-28=Matt. 11:9-11 [Q]).

It is instructive to notice that form critics—notably both Bultmann and Dibelius, representatives of the left and right wings of the movement respectively—maintain the historicity of the relation of Jesus to John the Baptist. Dibelius speaks for New Testament scholars rather generally when he remarks, "No Christian would have invented, in Jesus' honour, a tale in which the Master himself was a recipient of John's baptism." [23] Only an unreasonable scepticism, therefore, would have the hardihood to deny this relationship. These critics pronounce both movements "prophetic," "eschatological," "messianic" in the best senses of those terms and find in the connection indicated the only means of understanding Jesus and his ministry. Bultmann, for example, whose generally radical position is well known, after showing that the two movements are essentially one as indicated by this connection, concludes, "At least there can be no doubt that Jesus like other agitators died on the cross as a Messianic prophet." [24]

It seems necessary to add to such testimony but one further item. This is the frequently remarked tendency of the Gospels to pronounce in favor of the superiority of Jesus and the kingdom message which he represented in connection with the conflicts reported between the disciples of these two great teachers. Here, it would seem, is the best possible evidence that in its earliest days the church had to struggle to counteract teaching which would not only associate the two but even tend to subordinate Jesus to the Baptist in view of the former's baptism at the latter's hands.[25] There can be no doubt, therefore, that Jesus allied himself with the prophetic move-

[23] *Op. cit.*, p. 183.
[24] *Op. cit.*, p. 26.
[25] *Ibid.*, p. 24. On the relation of Jesus with the Baptist, cf. W. F. Howard, *The Fourth Gospel in Recent Criticism and Interpretation*, pp. 24-25; R. H. Strachan, *The Fourth Gospel*, pp. 111-12; F. C. Burkitt, *Church and Gnosis*, pp. 100 ff.

ment represented by the Baptist and thus committed himself to the prophetic view generally.

The Freedom of the Word

Again, it is striking that the unmistakable sense of freedom born of the assurance that the word of revelation had come to them, so characteristic of the prophets, appeared also in Jesus. Because of this sense of freedom the Hebrew prophets had roundly criticized the ethical attitudes of kings, priests, and people of Israel. They had even questioned the validity of the ritual worship of the temple. They had scathingly rebuked the contemporary forms taken by the paganism surrounding them. And they did all this in the name of the Lord whose word spoke through them and whose media of expression they claimed to be—a word which on its own claim transcended every human institution, office, and person.

Our Lord has been styled the "incarnate Word" from the end of the first century, beginning with the Fourth Gospel's teaching, "The Word became flesh." And there can be little doubt that Hoskyns and Davey are right in tracing this prophetic conception and conviction back to our Lord himself.[26] It is the creative and re-creative power of the word that John has more particularly in mind in his prologue (1:1-5, 12-14). "Behold, I make all things new" is the keynote of the conception. Paul had it before John, though he expressed the idea somewhat differently: "image of the invisible God," "firstborn of all creation," "the power of God," and "the wisdom of God"—these were his terms (Col. 1: 15 ff.; I Cor. 1:18 ff.), but the idea was substantially the same as with John. For both Jesus was the creative medium used by God in fashioning his world. The author of Hebrews was also familiar with this conception, his terminology being at this point as at some others closer to Paul than to John, though there is little if any change in the fundamental thought: "God . . . hath spoken unto

[26] *The Riddle of the New Testament*, particularly ch. x, pp. 246 ff. See also Bell and Deissmann, *Mysterium Christi*, ch. ii–v, pp. 31 ff.

us in his Son, . . . through whom also he made the worlds; . . . the very image of his substance, . . . upholding all things by the word of his power" (1:1-3 A.S.V.).

There is in this terminology a fluidity, an ease and grace of movement which suggests that the New Testament writers were conscious of writing on a subject of common knowledge in the church. It matters little about the exact words used to describe a phenomenon about which all are conversant already. In this instance that subject was the creative power that had been at work in and through the historic Jesus, as well as that still in operation by the resurrected Christ or his Spirit. What was this creative power, and whence arose the idea that it emanated from Jesus?

The answers to these questions appear to be found in a variety of Synoptic passages in which Jesus is said to have testified to a new creative power that had come with himself onto the historical plane. Thus in a verse interpolated by "Matthew" into the grain-field episode Jesus speaks of it as a "somewhat greater than the temple" (Matt. 12:6). The same terminology is employed in Q at another passage (Luke 11:31-32=Matt. 12:42), where this thing which came by Jesus is termed "a greater somewhat than Solomon," a "greater somewhat than Jonah." No doubt our Lord is thinking of the same "somewhat" when again in Q he claims that his casting out of demons is due to the "finger [Matt.: Spirit] of God" (Luke 11:20=Matt. 12:28), and that this indicates the "kingdom of God" to have come upon his generation. Again, in the Marcan passage (2:23-28) in which the above-mentioned Matthaean interpolation occurs the whole tenor of the passage suggests the presence in Jesus of a unique authority. The argument runs: David was able to validate for his followers an action which the common man could not do, the assumption being that he could do so because of a unique authority which resided in him; in the same way Jesus is able to allow his disciples to do what for the ordinary individual would constitute a breaking of the law of the Sabbath. The conclusion naturally follows: "The Son of man is lord even of the sabbath" (v. 28). It is striking that, though modern critics have endeavored to remove or to explain away this verse, and to find the point of the incident rather in verse 27, its authenticity is supported by both Matthew (12:8) and Luke (6:5). Moreover, not only is verse 27—which enunciates the principle, "The sabbath was made for man, not man for the sabbath"—lacking in both Matthew and Luke as though considered by them irrelevant to the main point at issue in the discussion, but it actually appears to be a quotation on Jesus' part from the current stock of proverbs employed especially among the Pharisees.[27]

But there are several passages in the Synoptic Gospels where an even closer approximation is attained to the terminology of the Johannine teaching than in those just cited. Thus in Q the man "who hears my words and does them" is like the man who builds upon the rock (Luke 6:48=Matt. 7:24), while the man who does not, builds upon "the ground" or sand. In this passage the signal importance of Jesus' "words" is quite in accord with that attached by the prophets to the word which they heard. Again, in an eschatological passage in Mark (8:38) our Lord states that it is by their attitude to him and his "words" that men will be judged at the coming of the Son of Man. Similarly in Mark 13:31 in a passage generally conceded to be from Jesus' lips he remarks, "Heaven and earth shall pass away: but my words shall not pass away."

From all this it appears evident that Jesus was conscious of a unique spiritual force which welled up within him and which gave creative power to his utterances. By contrast the prophets were even more objective in their treatment of the word which they heard, for with them it was always a word *from without* which validated itself to them so that they could say, "Thus saith the Lord." In Jesus' case on the contrary it was something *from within* which empowered him to speak. Accordingly he spoke with an unwonted tone of authority that, on the testimony of several sources, startled his hearers and challenged them to inquire its source and nature

[27] See further below, p. 116, and see G. M. Moore, *Judaism*, II, 31.

(Mark 10:24; Luke 4:32 [L]; Matt. 7:29 [M]). And moreover he demanded that his listeners adopt toward his message the same technique of listening or "audition" that the prophets observed toward the divine word. "If any man has ears to hear, let him hear." (Mark 4:23; cf. 8:18.) It is true that of the available sources only M reports the striking words as from his lips, "You have heard that it was said. . . . But I say to you" (Matt. 5:21, 27, 33, 38, 43). But the authenticity of this refrain seems guaranteed, as Dibelius observes, by the purity of the metric form in which it is cast.[28] And the sense is nearly conveyed by another mode of expression which appears to have been habitual with Jesus: "Verily [verily, verily—John], I say unto you" (Mark 3:28; 9:1; 10:15; 12:42; Luke 4:24; 23:43 [L]; Matt. 6:2, 5, 13, 16 [M]; John 3:3, 5, 11—A.V. and A.S.V.). Accordingly William Manson concludes: "The claim not merely to supersede the tradition of the elders, but to set his own interpretations upon the commandments of the Torah ($\dot{\epsilon}\gamma\dot{\omega}$ $\delta\dot{\epsilon}$ $\lambda\dot{\epsilon}\gamma\omega$ $\dot{\nu}\mu\hat{\iota}\nu$) and to offer these not as matters of opinion but as authoritative declarations of the Will of God" is clearly the intent of the tradition.[29]

The entire series of arguments between Jesus and his enemies is also relevant here—the Sabbath controversies, and those regarding forgiveness of sins, eating without washing of the hands, and the cleansing of the temple—as are also "the consciousness of performing his mighty works by divine inspiration ($\dot{\epsilon}\nu$ $\pi\nu\epsilon\dot{\nu}\mu\alpha\tau\iota$ $\theta\epsilon o\hat{\nu}$), so that to indict him as a sorcerer is to blaspheme against the Holy Spirit," and "the sense of authority not only to summon men to follow him, but to pronounce their salvation conditional upon their acceptance of what he reveals." [30] In all of these instances Jesus claimed an authority which went beyond anything his auditors had ever known. It suggested to them, therefore, the old category so well known in Israel but so long without an apposite example of

[28] Op. cit., pp. 73, 158.
[29] Op. cit., p. 139.
[30] Ibid.

its functioning, that of "prophet"; and it is little wonder that the common people thought of him in this way.[31] For he spoke to them with the same note of authority that had characterized those men of old who had interpreted the ways of God to Israel.

A Unified Theology and Ethics

The term "ethic(s)" does not occur in our English Bible, and "moral(s)" only at I Cor. 15:33, where Paul is quoting from the Thaïs of Menander. The very good reason for this is that Hebrew had no exact equivalent for these words, while as for the Greek writers of the New Testament, though they wrote and thought in Greek, their thought-frames and concepts were of the prophetic strand within the Semitic tradition.[32] The further reason for this phenomenon in the biblical scriptures is the absence of that religio-ethical dualism which is normative for us in the West, where the Greek—that is to say, pagan—tradition has been the dominant influence. In this tradition—as in that of the Far East (in Confucianism, for instance)—and as the very Greek and Latin words (ethos, mores) imply, ethical conduct is simply customary action which derives its sanction from the class, caste, race, or other affiliation under consideration. It has, therefore, no necessary relation at all with religion, which is restricted to the worship of the gods. These latter are anthropomorphically conceived and partake of the passions and sins of men rather than serve as a pattern of ethical conduct for them.

The prophetic word, whose content we have spoken of as an ethical theism, is diametrically opposed to this pagan tradition. That word assumes a theology whose God is Sovereign of all of man's life and man's ethical prototype because the pattern of his personality is ethical character. Here man is to be made "in the image of God" and not the reverse as in the pagan tradition where

---

[31] See table and discussion in my Intention of Jesus, pp. 131 ff.

[32] See Dibelius, A Fresh Approach to the New Testament and Early Christian Literature, pp. 16-17.

the gods are made in the image of man—the true anthropomorphism.

That "image," be it noted, in the prophetic thought is not reason or intellect as in Greek thought—for example in Stoicism, where God is conceived as *logos*, the divine reason, diffused through all existence—but rather character or "righteousness." And this when broken down into its parts is seen to be composed of justice, truth, kindness, mercy, love, goodness, and the like. Man's "chief end" according to the prophets is to reflect this image. Accordingly they foresee the setting up of a new covenant between God and man under which the law of God will be written on men's hearts in this sense (Jer. 31:31-34).

Jesus' teaching was in direct line with this prophetic revelation. He began his ministry with a call to repentance after the true prophetic tradition—that is, with the demand that men return to God in view of the near approach of his rule in the affairs of men (Mark 1:14; cf. Joel 2:12-14). This was at once the language of the prophetic eschatology and of the prophetic theism. As the sequel showed, it meant that the *eschaton* was to be realized through the achievement on man's part of a right attitude toward God and one's neighbor. "Truly, I say to you, whoever does not receive the kingdom of God like a child shall not enter it." (Mark 10:15 R.S.V.) To "receive" the kingdom, as the Mishnah clearly shows, was to accept God's rule over one's life, while to "enter" the kingdom meant to have the *eschaton* realized in one's experience.[33] Both things are accomplished by the adoption of a right relationship of childlike humility and trust accompanied by obedience to God.

In such teaching as this there can be no doubt that Jesus was as truly "this-worldly" as the Hebrew prophets. The kingdom of heaven was realized on the plane of human history when he stepped upon its stage, first because he was himself everything he taught, and again because in calling men to "follow" him, to "take up the cross" and do the Father's will, to become "sons of your Father

[33] M. Berakot 2:2.

who is in heaven," he was challenging them to realize the *eschaton* on the human plane. The rule of God, he affirmed, was already at work in their midst through him (Luke 11:20=Matt. 12:28 [Q]), and the "men of violence" were momentarily entering into it (Luke 16:16=Matt. 11:12 [Q]); that it would be realized, therefore, "in power" in that generation he had no doubt (Mark 9:1). Our Lord's eschatological teaching will come up for treatment at a later stage; for the moment I should like to record my conviction that this combining of the eschatological with the ethical is one of the great contributions of Jesus in the field of religion, and moreover that in doing this he was carrying through the prophetic line and spirit to its logical conclusion.[34]

Jesus' Fulfillment of the Prophetic Concepts

This leads us naturally to the last consideration suggestive of Jesus' identification of himself and his teaching with the revelation of the word. This is his intentional activity relative to the major prophetic concepts. There is a close connection between these two things to which hitherto insufficient attention has been paid by biblical scholars. The Hebrew prophets dealt with ideas or concepts about God, but never in the history of the Old Testament worthies had the prophetic word been clothed in flesh. It remained for the church of the New Testament to testify that the prophetic concepts had received concrete expression in the life and work of Jesus (Heb. 11:39-40).

Orthodoxy has always made the mistake of maintaining that this fulfillment was to be found by checking over point for point the details of the prophetic imagery against like details in the ministry, death, and resurrection of our Lord. In so doing it has been unmindful of the fact that these details were intended by the prophets as so many "props" for the support of the great concepts with which they were laboring and to which, as the core of the divine revelation, they were endeavoring to give expression in intelligible human speech. To look for such minutiae of fulfillment is to seek for "signs" after the analogy of a people trained in the school of Pharisaic pedantry. It carries with itself as a method its own refutation, for any tyro in the study of the prophets can point out many more "props" which find no counterpart in the fulfillment provided by the picture of Jesus in the Gospels.

And yet the keynote of the New Testament is fulfillment, as that of the Old is promise. "I came," says Jesus according to Matthew's special source, "not to destroy, but to fulfil" (5:17b), and every source of the gospel tradition without exception bears out this statement. Moreover there can be no doubt that what our Lord fulfills—to the mind of the primitive church at all events—is the prophetic concepts about which I have been speaking, particularly those of the Messiah of the remnant, the kingdom of God, the Suffering Servant.[35] On this point there is, one is led to believe, unanimity among New Testament scholars at the present day. The questions which remain to be solved here, therefore, are two: first, how far the church was right in so interpreting the work of Jesus; and second, whether to fulfill these prophetic concepts was a part of Jesus' own purpose. It would seem that the answers to these two questions ought to approximate each other. For it would appear to be an anomaly that Jesus should have accomplished unwittingly or involuntarily what he had not thought of doing, that is—to put the matter very bluntly indeed—that he should have become the Redeemer of and Lord over men's lives without either intending to be such or even realizing that he had done so. The alternatives appear, therefore, to be: either the church was right and Jesus intended to fulfill the prophetic concepts to which reference has been made, or contrariwise the church was wrong and he entertained no such purpose.

In the United States, however, a school of thought is fast matur-

[35] Cf. C. H. Dodd, *The Apostolic Preaching and Its Developments;* Floyd V. Filson, *One Lord, One Faith;* William Manson, *Jesus the Messiah,* and numerous others.

ing among New Testament scholars which is unwilling to accept this simple statement and solution. Its members are influenced severally by a parallelogram of forces, among which I should list: Wilhelm Wrede's theory of the "messianic secret," the work of the form critical school with its theory that the church read back into the mind of our Lord its own thought and desires, a technique in the handling of the written sources of the Gospels which results in their canceling each other out rather than in their supplementing one another, and the "exaggerated theory of the social origin of knowledge" to which reference has already been made.[36] This school holds that no degree of trustworthiness attaches to the church's witness regarding our Lord's consciousness and motivation. In varying degrees, therefore, its members urge that the church was right in acclaiming Jesus as one through whom men are brought nigh to God, but that the church's categories were inadequate to express the nature of his work as conceived by Jesus himself. As to how our Lord did conceive of his lifework we have no certain knowledge and unfortunately no means of ascertaining, because either he would not have disclosed such a mystery or the disclosure has been covered over with such a hoary mass of ecclesiastical tradition that it is no longer possible for us to search it out. These considerations, however, need not alarm us. What Jesus succeeded in doing for us is of infinitely more importance than either what the church thought he did, on the one hand, or what he may have intended to do, on the other. Of this we are assured through our own experience of his saving power in our lives.

This modern position represents a curious reversal of the old "back to Jesus" movement. In that we were told that the church had so covered over the real Jesus with its various doctrinal teachings about him that our task must be the stripping off of the thick layers of doctrine with which he had been embalmed with a view

---

[36] Cf. S. J. Case, Jesus—A New Biography; F. C. Grant, The Gospel of the Kingdom and The Earliest Gospel; John Knox, The Man Christ Jesus and Christ the Lord; Clarence T. Craig, "Jesus and the Suffering Servant," Journal of Religion, Oct., 1944, with my reply in Jan., 1945.

to exposing the simple Jewish rabbi whom we should discover beneath. Now it seems that these layers are far too thick. The task can never be accomplished, and we shall never hope to know what Jesus really thought about himself and his mission. We might as well, therefore, rest content with either what the church has found Jesus to be or our own experience of him.

It is not clear, however, in what sense a Christian is to conceive of Jesus as Lord and Saviour if it is not against the background of the rich heritage which the church possesses in the prophetic categories with which we have been dealing and which we are told are inadequate to express what Jesus means for human life. And moreover it seems strange that the church should have found these categories so far adequate to its understanding of the meaning of Jesus for its own life as mistakenly to have read them back into his mind about himself. For this would mean that between the prophetic word and the experience of the church there is a continuity and a harmony of spirit which Jesus did not share. And yet on the church's own testimony it was he who created that continuity and that harmony by living up to and fulfilling the requirements of the prophetic categories on which these depend.[37]

Professor C. H. Dodd in *The Apostolic Preaching and Its Developments* succeeded in exhibiting the continuity in the witness of the church relative to the significance of Jesus from Pentecost through the apostolic age. The importance of this work lay in the demonstration of the unanimity of the early church's testimony as to its conception of the person and work of Jesus, in spite of the well-known diversity in the terminology which it employed to express that conception. Professor Dodd succeeded in showing that the church's witness to Jesus followed the pattern of, and was essentially one with, the prophetic promise of the Messiah—in

[37] At least two other factors have deeply influenced the New Testament school in the United States: namely, the work of the *Religionsgeschichtliche Schule*, with which ought to be included perhaps the development within the present generation of a vital psychology of religion; and that of the school of consistent eschatology as represented particularly by Albert Schweitzer. There is, however, much disparity among the members of the school here as regards the influence of these factors.

other words, that there was genuine continuity between the concepts used by the prophets and the observations of the church relative to Jesus.

This contribution of Professor Dodd was a first necessary step in the reconstruction of a real continuity between the Testaments. But it was not enough to satisfy either the mind of the church or the manner of the Spirit's working in the revelation of the word. The church from the beginning exhibited its dissatisfaction with its sole witness by making the claim that Jesus himself acknowledged his messiahship, his awareness of fulfilling the Suffering Servant concept, his title to be the Son of Man. The church of course wrote the Gospels; and they contain its theology, its witness to Jesus, the record of its spiritual pilgrimage. But the church did not remain content merely to write up its testimony to Jesus; rather it incorporated in the Gospels his own acknowledgment of the truth of its claims. That there are varying levels of assurance regarding the authenticity of these claims of the church will be at once acknowledged. But this is no argument against the church's sense of need that such claims be established, rather the reverse. For it is exactly out of such sense of need that an interpolation is made here, the language strengthened there, a substitution of word or phrase inserted in a third instance.

But neither is the existence of such levels of assurance subversive to the church's conviction that Jesus exhibited continuity with the prophets in his thought about himself and his mission. For the continuity between prophets and church is a continuity, not of identity, but of selection. That is to say, it is not the only continuity that could have occurred. It curiously passes over some prophetic concepts and fastens on others, and it makes combinations of the concepts which it does adopt of a sort not immediately suggested by the writings of the prophets themselves. Moreover, of the three terms—Messiah, Suffering Servant, and Son of Man—applied to Jesus in the tradition of the church, the two latter ones almost immediately dropped into abeyance, only Messiah continuing to be used widely, though it was admittedly modified in meaning in the direction of the other two concepts.[38] And yet of the three Messiah seems least adequately to represent Jesus' own interpretation of his mission on the church's testimony and is perhaps least certainly to be attributed to his teaching. *From these considerations it seems reasonable to suppose that the selection of prophetic concepts for defining Jesus and his mission was made, not by the church in the first instance, but by Jesus.* And it accords well with this conclusion that Jesus' intentional activity appears on close examination to be directed toward the fulfilling of the requirements of these same prophetic categories.

The discovery of such a selective continuity from the prophets, through Jesus, to his church will not come as a surprise to anyone who believes in a divine purpose in history. Nor will it seem in any way exceptional that Jesus should add his (the divine) word of revelation to the divine act which he incarnated. We have already seen that this was always the way of genuine revelation, which was never complete if either element was lacking. There was never a final revelation in the saying "Thus saith the prophet," nor is there such in the like "Thus saith the church." Through both media God himself must speak—through one the word of revelation, through the other the Incarnate Word, Jesus himself. Consequently only as in the Gospels we hear Jesus himself speaking to us are we reassured and led to believe the witness of the church.

The evidence that in the Gospels Jesus does speak and not the church only, and that the intention to fulfill the prophetic concepts is, indeed, his own in line with the above argument, has been collected and presented by William Manson in his *Jesus the Messiah* and in my own *Intention of Jesus*. It is the endeavor of these two books to build upon the contribution of Professor Dodd and to carry the argument back one stage, thereby filling in the final gap from the prophets to the church and exhibiting the real con-

---

[38] See for the evidence here the materials presented in the articles by Clarence T. Craig and myself referred to in n. 37.

tinuity represented by the steps: prophets, Jesus, primitive community, Paul and the other theologians of the apostolic period. Here, therefore, I shall rest the case for Jesus' attachment to the prophetic message, merely registering my personal conviction that the case for Jesus' intentioned fulfillment of the prophetic concepts is as nearly demonstrated as the present condition of the evidence will permit.

PART

II

And the altar shall be most holy.
—Exod. 29:37

Having then a great high priest . . . ,
Jesus the Son of God, let us hold fast our
confession.—Heb. 4:14

JESUS and
THE RELIGION of the ALTAR

Synopsis

Chapter 4:—The revelation of God's word to man calls for a "response" on the latter's part. Such a response is what men call RELIGION. Historically within Judaism the first religious response to the prophetic revelation was that of the priests. The priest's AUTHORITY for the form which he gave to his religion was that of hereditary or tribal CUSTOM, or at most of the UNCTION or INVESTITURE which he had received. His priestly FUNCTION proceeding from this authority concerned the performance of a set ritual from day to day, the observance of "times and seasons," and the keeping of certain ceremonial laws such as those of "clean and unclean." The climactic event of his career was that SACRIFICE which he held brought salvation for man. Accordingly the INSTITUTIONAL PRODUCT of his efforts as a religious leader was the TEMPLE in which such sacrifice was performed.

Chapter 5:—The postexilic altar religion was by no means what Israel's ancient cult religion had been. For the former was a real endeavor to constitute a right religious response to the prophetic revelation which had intervened. This appears from a study of the priestly writings, canonical and extra-canonical.

Chapter 6:—Jesus was not antagonistic to the altar religion as such. He showed annoyance only at the priests' failure to measure up to the high ideals of their office and to the aims of the temple worship. For himself, however, he was not concerned to perpetuate the religion of the altar through the inauguration of new rituals. The Lord's Supper is prophetic in its teaching content.

CHAPTER

4

The Religion of the Altar

THE Judaism of our Lord's day was the product of a curious blending of paradoxical and even contradictory elements. It is true that by and large the religious culture of postexilic Judaism stemmed from the prophetic revelation of the word. But centuries before the Christian era forces extraneous to the faith of the prophets began to impinge on that culture. These forces in time gave rise to three abortive attempts to implement the prophetic word and to give it concrete expression after a fashion intelligible to the common man. These attempts were successful about to the degree that all such endeavors to reduce a spiritual movement to the level of popular interest and expression may be thought to be so. They proved abortive in the end, however, for the reason that popularization or rationalization is an inadequate method of implementing a prophetic faith, which requires rather fulfillment of divine word by divine act for its historical realization, and this was provided in Christianity. The scriptural formula which follows the line of the prophetic revelation is: divine instruction (Torah) came by Moses and the prophets, whereas divine love and faithfulness answering to and rendering effective the revelation came by Jesus Christ (John 1:17). Meanwhile by Jesus' day the three attempts referred to had flowered out into three popular

87

expressions of religious zeal—what we may term the religions respectively of the altar, of the book, and of the throne.[1]

Historically the first of these three *people's religions* to take shape was that of the altar. The prophet was succeeded in Israel by the priest, the divine word by the human rite, as the "faith of Israel" became crystallized in Judaism's religious formalism. I have no wish, of course, to deny that many of Judaism's religious practices antedated the beginnings of the prophetic writing toward the end of the tenth century B.C. It is a matter of common knowledge among students of religious phenomena that rite often precedes the doctrine which is put forth as its explanation. The development of the cult ritual in the old Israelitish religion followed this pattern.[2] We are concerned here, however, not with the preprophetic cult of Israel, but rather with the reformed cult religion which succeeded the exile and which by reason of the prophetic movement that intervened presents a pattern unique in the history of religions of ritual. For the doctrine which we find in the priestly writings beginning with the Deuteronomists in approximately 621 B.C. is the teaching of writers concerned to give a description of the cult in the light of the moral and spiritual impact which the prophets had made upon it.

The Priest's Authority—Heredity and Unction

The origin of the priesthood in Israel's early history is obscure. It has been suggested that the priest "may have been originally in Israel, like the 'kahin' among the Arabs, the soothsayer or giver of oracles" and guardian of the local shrine or altar as these were established throughout Canaan.[3] Moses himself was accounted

---

[1] No account is taken of the sect known as the Essenes in these chapters as they did not represent "normative" Judaism in any of its expressions. This group and its Egyptian counterpart, the Therapeutae, veered so far to the left in the direction of paganism that neither sect greatly influenced the development of ongoing Judaism. For our present purpose, therefore, they may be ignored. Neither was even so much as mentioned in the Christian Scriptures.

[2] See McFadyen in *The People and the Book*, pp. 205, 208-10.

[3] Lofthouse in *ibid.*, p. 246.

Israel's first priest after her deliverance from slavery into real nationhood (Ps. 99:6-7), and in this capacity he had given out *toroth* or oracles of God (legal decisions) and had served also as guardian of the Tabernacle in the Wilderness, so fulfilling the two priestly functions indicated.[4] Moses had, however, initiated the Levitical priesthood into which one must be either "born" or "adopted," and this continued to be the rule until the exile.[5] Then with Ezekiel the "sons of Zadok," who alone among the priests had refused to sacrifice at the local shrines scattered throughout the land, remaining true to the one sanctuary in Jerusalem, were allowed to continue as priests, while the rest of the Levitical clan were degraded to the performance of menial tasks because of their inconstancy.[6]

This brief history of Israel's priesthood serves to demonstrate the fact that, unlike the prophet, the priest traditionally had no word from God to communicate to his people. Originally he may have made a claim to have an "oracle from the Lord," and Moses' dual function as priest and prophet no doubt is intended to suggest that historically both figures on Israel's religious horizon had the same divine origin. But with the hardening of the priestly office along family lines as indicated above, the priest ceased to be known as a man who had a word from God, and the prophet became by definition one possessed of this word. Neither did the priest share the prophet's sense of a divine "call" to undertake the responsibilities of his office, and for a like reason. His standing in the priesthood and his ultimate authority as a religious leader depended, not upon moral and spiritual considerations, but upon the single incident of family or tribal affiliation for the ordinary priest, and additionally in the case of the high priest upon the rituals of anointing and investiture.

This is not to say, of course, that a priest might not receive the

---

[4] Exod. 33:11 says Joshua was. But cf. G. Buchanan Gray, *Sacrifice in the Old Testament*, p. 205.

[5] See Albright, *Archaeology and the Religion of Israel*, pp. 109-10.

[6] See Pfeiffer, *Introduction to the Old Testament*, p. 557.

prophetic "call" and become a genuine prophet, as could any man of every calling or profession in Israel. Similarly the priestly writings are by no means devoid of real prophetic elements. Ezekiel and Jeremiah are outstanding examples of priests who were also prophets. The point to observe here, however, is that no divine afflatus was required or claimed by the priest to confer on him the standing pertaining to his office, the contrary being invariably true of the Hebrew prophet. The rule laid down for the guidance of Moses and Aaron in their mutual relations, as reported by the prophetic writer at Exod. 4:10-31 (J), is no doubt intended to set forth the principle generally that in both pre- and postexilic Judaism the prophet was to the priest "a mouth" and "as God," while the priest's function was to perform "the signs"—and so later the cult ritual in acknowledgment of the presence of God—"in the sight of the people," with a view to the practical expression of the revelation on a level the people could understand and appreciate.

In the postexilic period the position of the high priest became a pre-eminent one, as in the absence of a king he frequently assumed the headship of the Jewish people.[7] Under John Hyrcanus (135-105 B.C.) a small group developed among the Zadokite priests to become known as Sadducees (Zaddukim) from the priestly family out of which they sprang. These Sadducees from the first were characterized by religious conservatism and adherence to the written Torah and the prophetic writings to the exclusion of the so-called "oral traditions" developed in postexilic times, as well as by their adoption of many elements in the surrounding Hellenistic culture.[8] This group constituted itself the nobility of the temple and was largely limited in New Testament times to the patrician priestly families from which the high priest was chosen. In the time of our Lord, therefore, as Finkelstein has shown, the temple was served by three cultural groups: the Sadducees or temple nobility, the commonalty of priests who were middle-class Shammaites in

---

[7] See Oesterley in The People and the Book, p. 349.
[8] See Josephus Antiquities XIII. x. 6; cf. Finkelstein, The Pharisees, I, 4-5.

the main—that is, Pharisees of the stricter and somewhat more aristocratic sort—and the Levites from the lower classes who were usually to be counted among the followers of the more lenient and democratic Hillel.

After the exile at least, the high priest, in addition to his tribal affiliation, was required to be set aside by the ritual of anointing. He was termed, therefore, to distinguish him from the lower priests, "the anointed priest" (Lev. 4:3, 5 [P]), a practice to which both Mishnah and Talmud also bear testimony.[9] Unction, of course, was common custom in ancient times in Israel, and we read of its early use in connection with *things* (Gen. 31:13 [E]; Exod. 29:36 [P]), with a *prophet* (I Kings 19:16), with even the *lower priests* (Exod. 29:21; 30:30 [P]), and above all with the *king* (I Sam. 9:16; 15:1; 16:3, 12 [J]). But Wellhausen and Gray have argued cogently for the high priest's becoming "the outstanding, even if not the only, anointed person" after the exile, even as the king before the exile had been "*par excellence*, 'the anointed of Yahweh.'"[10] At a later period the high priest who was "anointed with the oil of unction" was distinguished from him who was "dedicated [invested] by the many garments," pointing no doubt to the discontinuance of the older custom.[11] But however the ordinary priest and the high priest were set apart—whether by reason of tribal affiliation, by anointing, or by investiture—it is clear that the authority for both their ministries depended upon the sanction of tradition rather than upon a moral or spiritual principle akin to the prophet's "call" through the divine voice.

The Priest's Function—Ritual of the Temple

The artificiality which characterized the manner of the appointment of the priest to his office was matched by the materialistic nature of the means which he employed in furthering the functions

[9] M. Meg. 1:9; Makk. 2:6; Shebu. 1:7; Hor. 2:1; *et al.*
[10] Gray, *op. cit.*, p. 259.
[11] M. Meg. 1:9; Hor. 3:4.

of the office. Professor Bewer has summed up the priestly attitude toward religion thus:

> The priests had ultimately the same aim as the prophets. They wanted to make the people acceptable to God. But while the prophets insisted that this could be done only by morality, the priests believed it could best be accomplished by ritual holiness. In and through the cult they sought to educate the people in obedience to Yahweh. . . . A purely moral and spiritual religion was too high and exacting for the mass of the people [to the priests' way of thinking, of course].[12]

Accordingly, with the exceptions noted at the beginning of this chapter due to the impact of the prophetic revelation, the priestly writings were concerned only with instructions for the acceptable manner of worshiping God through sacrifice and ceremony. Sin, trespass, meal, and whole burnt offerings consumed the priest's interest. The use of proper vestments, the observing of "times and seasons" and of feasts and fasts, the laws of "clean and unclean," anointing, bathing, the maintenance of the fires of incense and offering—attention to these and the like regulations and rubrics made up his day. The priest was indeed as much of a legalist in his care for the proper techniques pertaining to the cult ritual as we shall see the rabbi later to have become in the maintenance of Torah as the instrument of God's sovereign rule among his people. Both at all times were in grave danger of, if they did not actually succeed in, forgetting that Torah in the prophetic sense stood for God's *living revelation* of himself and his will to his people in the multifarious crises of daily living under the divine rule.

It is instructive to see how this priestly modification of the prophetic view of religion worked out in practice. It will be sufficient to take by way of illustration the change it effected in the definition of the prophetic concept of "holiness." For the prophets, as we have seen, this term stood for the moral separateness of God's person from all contamination with sin and the consequent insist-

[12] Op. cit., pp. 266-67.

ence that his servants must be equally separate therefrom. The priest stepped down the concept to the lower level of ceremonial and taught the people that it had to do, not with "moral perfection," but with "the separation from everything tabooed by the religion of Yahweh." [13] This is clear from such a quotation from the priestly writings as this: "And ye shall be holy unto me: for I, Yahweh, am holy, and have set you apart from the peoples, that ye should be mine." (Lev. 20:26 [H].) In this, as the context shows, to be *holy* means to observe the laws relating to "clean" and "unclean" beasts, eating the one and not the other, and by so doing to maintain that ritual "holiness" without which Yahweh may not be served or worshiped. Similarly, according to the priestly code (P), Moses was commanded by Yahweh to speak to Eleazar the priest to the effect that he should take the censers used by the wicked Korah and his 250 associates and make them into "beaten plates for a covering of the altar" (Num. 16:38-40). "For they offered them before the Lord"—that is, set them apart ritually for the service of God—and, therefore, though Korah's action was wrongfully conceived in a spirit of rebellion against Moses, the censers were ceremonially "holy" and could be put thenceforth to no "unholy" use. "Holiness" in such contexts is obviously not the perfection of moral character to be acquired through fellowship with a moral God, but a function of "physical" or ritual separation from certain tabooed objects—particularly the pagan deities and all things associated with their worship, including their worshipers—to be preserved by the sanctioned ceremonies.[14]

The difference between the prophet and the priest at this point was that which always is found to pertain between the man of vision and his fellow of practical sense or worldly prudence, between the statesman and the politician, the architect and the draftsman, the landscape artist and the gardener, the sculptor and the stonemason. The priest, like the later rabbi, wrote the prophet's sym-

[13] *Ibid.*, p. 184.
[14] Cf. Isa. 6:5; Wright, *op. cit.*, pp. 56-57.

phonies in a lower key where they could be appreciated by the so-called "man in the street" and stepped down the required obedience to the divine will, which for the prophet involved personal sacrifice, to the level of the offering of the personally-owned animal that had a monetary value rather than a moral one. Like the rabbi of the later day the priest would have justified his method by the claim that only thus could the Torah and the prophets be made intelligible and therefore workable within the historical situation.[15] We are not concerned here to criticize this view, but only to state it. And let it be observed that clarity in the latter respect is vastly important. For unless we see clearly how fundamental was the temperamental and moral cleavage between the prophet and the priest in Israel, we shall never be able to appreciate the conflict that ensued or to evaluate the issue of the conflict for the cause of true religion.

The Product of the Ritual—Salvation by Sacrifice

It was in connection with this priestly law of "holiness" that the element of sacrifice in the temple worship was to find its rationale. The required ritual cleanness could be forfeited through contact with an object tabooed by the divine Torah. When this occurred, the person thus rendered "unclean" was debarred from the cultic worship as a sign of Yahweh's displeasure. "Sin" was for the priest an act of disobedience against a command of Yahweh, and to become "unclean" was the result of an offense against the ultimate command of all—that respecting Yahweh's unapproachable "holiness." It is true that the priest, along with the later rabbi, "recognized the distinction between acts which the common conscience of mankind condemns as morally wrong and such as are wrong only because they are made so by statute; but," as George Foot Moore has pointed out, "the former are not the more properly sin because of their moral quality nor the latter less so because in themselves

[15] See Pfeiffer, op. cit., pp. 179-80.

they are morally indifferent. The sin is in either case the same, violation of the revealed will of God." [16] So must it always appear to one of legalistic mind, whether priest or Pharisee or any other.

In view of this legalistic view of what constitutes sin it need not strike us as strange that the Priestly Code recognized two possible attitudes of the offender toward his transgression and two corresponding methods of redressing that transgression. One might sin "unwittingly," that is, transgress against a law of whose nature or even existence he did not know, or contrariwise "with a high hand" of set purpose and intent through indifference to God's will as expressed in a particular command.[17]

For the latter—voluntary transgression—there could be no mercy shown; whether the sin were of a moral or ceremonial nature, the offender was equally to be "cut off out of the midst of his people." [18] In the end, however, repentance and the "scapegoat" on the Day of Atonement would effect atonement for these as well as for the other category of sins.[19] For the unwitting offender, on the other hand, expiation might be effected at once by means of sacrifice; and if offered, such sacrifice spared such a one the punishment which he should otherwise have undergone.[20] Two passages in the Mishnah summarize for us the rabbinic rules on the subject which represent the practice of the postexilic priests:

For uncleanness that befalls the Temple and its Hallowed Things through wantonness, atonement is made by the goat whose blood is sprinkled within the [Holy of Holies] and by the Day of Atonement; for all other transgressions spoken of in the Law, venial or grave, wanton or unwitting, conscious or unconscious, sins of omission or of commission, sins punishable by Extirpation or by death at the hands of the court, the scapegoat makes atonement. (M. Shebu. 1:6.)

The Sin-offering and the unconditional Guilt-offering effect atonement; death and the Day of Atonement effect atonement if there is

---

[16] Op. cit., I, 462.
[17] Cf. Lev. 4:5; Num. 15:22-31; Deut. 17:12 (all P).
[18] Ibid.; cf. Moore, op. cit., I, 463, n. 7.
[19] Cf. Lev. 16:29-34.
[20] Cf. Num. 15:27-29.

repentance. Repentance effects atonement for lesser transgressions against both positive and negative commands in the Law; while for graver transgressions it suspends punishment until the Day of Atonement comes and effects atonement. (M. Yoma 8:8.) [21]

In the light of these quotations it is obvious that for both types of sins, witting and unintentional, as Moore observes, "repentance is . . . the *conditio sine qua non* of the remission of sins." [22] This, it may be added, has been the view of Judaism throughout the centuries, and it is possible to quote from both rabbinic and priestly sources passages in which the worshiper of Yahweh is cautioned not to rely on the efficacy of sacrifice alone.[23] Moreover, although the Priestly and Holiness Codes never speak of repentance, the Deuteronomic legislation does contain this prophetic note; [24] and the two former codes at all events make much of confession of sins, which if conceived on an ethical level is, of course, an element in repentance.[25]

Nonetheless the priest pertained to the altar and to sacrifice which was its necessary accompaniment, and there can be no doubt that the priest considered sacrifice to effect the end for which it was intended.[26] The essence of the priestly view was, therefore, that salvation is the product of the right (i.e., "clean" or "holy") performance of certain ceremonial practices, as that of the prophets was that it is a gift of God's mercy to the people of his choice. That the priest advanced no theory as to how sacrifice could serve this end is no argument against his having believed in its real efficacy, rather the reverse. Moore here has said the final word as on so many other subjects in this field:

A theory of the way in which sacrifice and other rites expiate sin is in a revealed religion a superfluous speculation. God has attached to certain cases certain conditions on which he promises to remit sins.

[21] Cf. Lev. 4:27-35; 5:15; 6:6-7; 16:22, for like teaching.
[22] Op. cit., I, 498, 508.
[23] Cf. M. Yoma 8:9; Ecclus. 5:4-7.
[24] Cf. Deut. 4:30; 30:2-3, 8, 10; Num. 14:43 (JE).
[25] Cf. Num. 5:6-7; Lev. 16:6-11, 21; 26:40-45; cf. Moore, op. cit., I, 511-14.
[26] Cf. Num. 18:7 (P).

The essential condition is the use of the means he has appointed, whatever they are. To neglect them because a man does not see how they can be of any effect, is itself deliberate and wilful sin, vastly graver than the original offense. Judaism had, therefore, no motive for discussing the *modus operandi* of sacrificial atonement, and never even raised the question![27]

The Altar's Distinctive Institution—The Temple

The distinctive institutional product of the religion of the altar was the temple. This needed never be larger than the necessities of the service of the altar and its sacrifices required. In general the temples of the pagan cults have been small affairs, or at all events have not been built with a view to the congregating of large numbers of people for the purpose of communal worship.[28] In Canaan the typical pagan "highplace" was usually a small edifice capable of admitting but few and intended, not as a center of corporate worship, but as the dwelling place of the "god."[29] When the worship of Yahweh succeeded that of the local deities in these small sanctuaries, the essential nature of the holy place as a spot where God chose to make himself known or to "put his name there" persisted.[30] The *haekel* was "God's house" and was made as sumptuous as conditions permitted with a view to glorifying him.

The peculiar sense of *community*, however, fostered by the prophets to whom Israel was the "chosen people" of God—a concept going back certainly to Moses—was responsible for the parallel development of the idea of corporate worship. This obviously could be achieved only in a temple large enough to hold the worshiping assembly. Israel's successive temples accordingly were capacious structures permitting the development of a communal worship service of an elaborate sort, though at the same time they

[27] *Op. cit.*, I, 500.
[28] See Wright in *The Biblical Archaeologist*, Dec., 1944, p. 66.
[29] *Ibid.* The same is true today of the temples in North India. The great ones of South India are the exception, not the rule. See also Albright, *Archaeology*, pp. 105-7.
[30] Wright, *op. cit.*, p. 71.

allowed for private sacrifice and worship.[31] Corporate worship, however, was by far the more important type carried on in the temple at Jerusalem on behalf of Jewry at large. This was because only the immediate residents of the city were physically able to attend the temple ritual with private offerings and for private worship except at widely separated intervals.[32] The distinctive institutional product of the priestly cult religion, the temple, together with the worship services conducted in it, was therefore modified in Israel by the prophetic concept of the "chosen people" and was to that extent prophetic in character.

[31] Albright, op. cit., pp. 142-56.   [32] Moore, op. cit., I, 499.

CHAPTER

5

A Sacrifice Acceptable and Pleasing to God

JOHN W. LIGHTLEY has re-
marked: "The Sadducees, alas! have almost no advocates in these
days. Nothing too bad can be said of them, apparently, and the
modern Jew appears to be quite indifferent to their fate at the
hands of the investigator." [1] There is, of course, a discernible
reason for this. The religion of the altar within Judaism passed out
of existence as a separate entity, and the Sadducaic party as such
became an impotent sect which disappeared entirely from the
scene in time, the devastating cause of these calamities being the
destruction of Jerusalem at the close of the First Jewish War in
A.D. 66-70.[2] The rabbinic Judaism which persisted from that date
forward was and remains today the legitimate child of Pharisaism—
the religion of the book. Witness the "Act of Affirmation" of a
Jewish magazine recently started, Commentary by name: "As the
people of the Book we believe in study—as a guide to life, for the
wisdom it brings to the counsels of men, and for its own sake." [3]

In consequence every Jewish writer from Josephus and Yahudah
ha Nasi, the compiler of the Mishnah, onward has delighted in

[1] Jewish Sects and Parties in the Time of Christ, p. 108.
[2] Moore, Judaism, I, 85-86, 100, 166.
[3] Edit. statement, first issue (Nov., 1945).

berating the Sadducee for his severity in judgment,[4] his infidelity, particularly in view of his denial of the Oral Law,[5] his profligacy,[6] and his political opportunism.[7] The latest phase of this antipriestly diatribe appears in Sholom Asch's *The Nazarene*, a popular work which ought not to be taken too seriously except as a symptom of current tendencies.[8]

It is easy to form a superficial judgment on the merits of the controversy that proceeded for centuries between Pharisees and Sadducees. Eduard Meyer pointed out that the Sadducees belonged to the patrician stock within Judaism, while the Pharisees were plebeians.[9] The conclusion might very well be drawn, therefore, that the hostility between them had principally, or even exclusively, a social and not a religious basis. And indeed there can be no doubt that sociological status was a factor of great importance which determined to some extent the attitudes which these groups assumed toward each other and toward problems of law and custom of interest to both.[10]

This social animus may very well have colored the extant reports of rabbinic writers regarding Sadducean beliefs. But as Moore and Finkelstein have pointed out, it is the "unanimous testimony of the sources" that there were undoubted theological differences between the two groups [11] and that these went beyond the series

[4] Cf. Finkelstein, *The Pharisees*, I, 83; Joseph Klausner, *Jesus of Nazareth*, pp. 334-35; G. F. Moore, *op. cit.*, I, 67, 280, and II, 141, 186; also Josephus *Antiquities* XIII. x. 6, and XX. ix. 1.

[5] The Mishnah has "Sadducee" and "infidel" interchangeably in its various manuscripts; cf. M. Ber. 9:5n; Yad. 4:8n (Danby's edit.), and Danby's note on p. xv (n. 1); also Josephus *Wars* II. viii. 14, and *Antiquities* XIII. v. 9, and x. 6, also XVIII. i. 3; Moore, *op. cit.*, I, 58, 67, 279-80.

[6] See Finkelstein, *op. cit.*, I, 193.

[7] See Klausner, *op. cit.*, p. 336.

[8] In recent years the endeavor has been made to relieve the Pharisees more especially of all complicity in the death of Jesus. At times the guilt is laid at the door of the Sadducees, at times upon the Romans—as though it were a matter of any concern who crucified Jesus in the first century, and not rather lest we, Jews and Christians alike, shall do it again in the twentieth. John Knox has a very sane note on this matter in his recent book *Christ the Lord*, p. 21, n. 13.

[9] *Ursprung und Anfänge des Christentums*, II, 293.

[10] See Finkelstein, *op. cit.*, I, 83.

[11] Cf. Moore, *op. cit.*, I, 70; Finkelstein, *op. cit.*, I, 101-44, *et passim*.

of mere theological negations usually attributed to the Sadducaic party. In such matters of belief the cleavage between Pharisees and Sadducees concerned the authority of the Oral Law and the dogmas which were related to it. The Sadducees were the champions of the written Torah as opposed to the "traditions of the elders" which had grown up as a "hedge" about it; to this fact all of our sources are witness either explicitly or implicitly.[12] And this means, of course, that the Sadducees were staunch supporters of and adherents to not only the priestly elements of the Pentateuch but the prophetic literature as well.

This fact may strike us as strange at first, for our natural inclination is to suppose that the Sadducees by virtue of their calling would be concerned only with the *ritual* (i.e., priestly) portions of the Law and that they might very well indeed have passed over the prophets altogether. However paradoxical it may appear, this was not the case. And what is more, the lesser orders of priests, being Shammaites in the main as we saw in chapter 4, in spite of their profession and its necessary attachment to ritual and ceremony were also by reason of their theological affiliation loyal to both Law and Prophets.

The resolution of this paradox in the case of both Sadducees and lower priests is to be found in the fact to which reference was made in chapter 4: the reformed cult religion of Judaism was by no means the same as the preprophetic religion of ancient Israel. All priests, high and low, in Jesus' day, whatever else their affiliation may have been, at all events gave their allegiance to both the prophetic scriptures and the priestly writings of their people. And in doing so, one imagines, they saw no disparity between the one and the other for the reason that centuries earlier the priestly writings had been greatly influenced by the prophetical teachings and had incorporated much of their spirit and doctrine. It will be well for us at this juncture to examine the priestly writings, canonical and extracanonical, with a view to discovering how far this statement is to be accepted.

[12] Cf. Mark 7:3 with 12:18, 24-27; Josephus *Antiquities* XVIII. i. 4.

The Canonical Priestly Writings

The earliest of the documents in the Old Testament pertaining to the religion of the altar is Deuteronomy (621 B.C.), which scholars are agreed rather generally was in some form the Book of the Law discovered by Hilkiah in the temple in the eighteenth year of King Josiah.[18] Of this priestly source book Canon Box remarks: "The whole spirit and teaching of the Book presuppose the work of the prophets of the eighth and seventh centuries B.C. The Book of Deuteronomy itself represents an alliance between prophecy and priesthood." [14]

An excellent example of the prophetic influence on this priestly document is the well-known change introduced into the fourth commandment, wherein the social obligation for resting on the Sabbath day, rather than the religious one of Exod. 20:10-11 (E), is enjoined in the words: ". . . That thy man-servant and thy maid-servant may rest as well as thou. And thou shalt remember that thou wast a servant in the land of Egypt" (Deut. 5:14-15). In commenting on this combination of prophetic and priestly elements in Deuteronomy, Pfeiffer remarks that "the spiritual religion and exacting morality of the prophets was codified in a series of concrete enactments" by the compiler.[15] Amos had made much of the demand of God that *righteousness* should roll down "as a mighty stream" (5:24), but the Deuteronomist defined righteousness, "which for Amos was merely a principle, as observing to do 'all these commandments before Jehovah our God, as he has commanded us' (6:25)." [16]

A somewhat later priestly writer (ca. 570 B.C.), the author of the Holiness Code (Lev. 17–26), at times closely akin to the Deuteronomist(s) in spirit, however laid special stress on the holiness of Yahweh and on his requirement that his people like him should be

---

[18] II Kings 22:8; cf. R. H. Pfeiffer, op. cit., pp. 52, 181.
[14] A Short Introduction to the Literature of the Old Testament, p. 51.
[15] Op. cit., p. 180.
[16] Ibid.

"holy." As has already been remarked, "this holiness was primarily physical, it was not moral perfection but especially the separation from everything tabooed by the religion of Yahweh." [17] And yet the writer of the Holiness Code was not without ethical interest, particularly in the direction of social ethics. For it was he who wrote: "Thou shalt not hate thy brother in thy heart. . . . Thou shalt not take vengeance, nor bear any grudge against the children of thy people; but thou shalt love thy neighbor as thyself: I am the Lord" (Lev. 19:17-18). Bewer's comment on this passage bears testimony to the rich prophetic influence found here: "This is the highest point in the ethics of the Old Testament, where the inner disposition, the heart, not only the outward deed counts." [18] This same nineteenth chapter contains also the stipulation regarding righteous dealings in bartering, "Just balances, just weights, a just ephah, and a just hin, shall ye have" (vs. 36); regarding the giving of vexation to "a hired servant" by keeping his "wages" back "with thee all night until the morning" (vs. 13); against "unrighteousness in judgment" (vs. 15), which should manifest itself in "respect" of "the person of the poor" or "honor" to "the person of the mighty"; together with other laws of like nature. The twenty-fifth chapter of the same book contains laws of equal social value, particularly those centering in the "year of jubilee" (vs. 13), which were intended to ameliorate the condition of the poor within Israel. The prophetic influence is clearly evident in these emphases, so much so that it has been seriously proposed—though of course this view no longer prevails—that Ezekiel was the author of this code. Its writer was in any event the "spiritual kinsman" of that prophet.[19]

The return of the Jews from exile gave the priest his great opportunity to capture the interest of the people in the cult religion. Ezekiel's vision of "the Holy Land laid out like a Dutch garden," [20]

---

[17] So Bewer, op. cit., p. 184.

[18] Ibid., pp. 186-87.

[19] Ibid., p. 187; see also Pfeiffer, op. cit., pp. 241-42, for a useful summary of the opinions on this question.

[20] This happy phrase is T. W. Manson's; see his Teaching, p. 250.

with the temple at Jerusalem as the center of its religious life and interest, was realized to some extent through the efforts of prophets like Haggai and Zechariah. As Bewer remarks, "Ezekiel had seen that the restoration of Israel and its religion must centre around the temple. When the Jews came back from captivity, they found that this was true: the temple was the rallying ground of the new community." [21] Prophet and priest therefore joined hands in the new movement. And the so-called Priestly Code (P), which dates from this period (ca. 500 B.C.), accordingly reflects the decline from the high, pure, spiritual ideals of a Hosea and an Isaiah in favor of a religious life dominated by the cult and the sacrificial ritual of the temple.

To a degree, then, the Priestly Code reverses the proportions of prophetic and priestly influence found among the Deuteronomists. Even here, however, an interest in moral and social values is not lacking, so that the prophetic influence is still felt. The monotheism of the prophets is also prevalent throughout the Priestly Code, where contamination of Yahweh with the pollutions of pagan idolatry is as abhorrent as it was to the author of the Holiness Code.[22] Still, as Pfeiffer says, "P shifts the emphasis from ethics to the cult and is only interested in one sphere of life: religion understood as recognition of the rights of God. . . . It presents in its purest form the priestly point of view." [23]

The last of the priestly writings incorporated into the canon of the Old Testament is the work of the Chronicler who, it is agreed, compiled the books of Chronicles and Ezra-Nehemiah (333-250 B.C.). This author was in all likelihood a "Levite and a member of the Temple choir," [24] as his interest in the Levitical singers and musicians suggests. He was naturally, therefore, an ardent adherent to the Priestly Code in principle. At the same time he was "pro-

---

[21] Op. cit., p. 259.

[22] Cf. Lev. 25 with its institution of the "year of jubilee" for the social interest (in PH) and Gen. 1–2:4a for that in a strict monotheism.

[23] Op. cit., p. 260.

[24] So Bewer, op. cit., 288 ff., and Box, op. cit., p. 86. For a discussion of the identity of the Chronicler, see Pfeiffer, op. cit., pp. 824-25.

foundly interested in the prophetic-deuteronomic theory of retribution and showed how all through history piety and goodness were rewarded, idolatry and wickedness were punished." [25] Driver writes, therefore, of his "tendency to refer events to their *moral causes*"— a marked proof of the prophetic influence on his thinking.[26]

Before closing this section mention must be made of the *rapprochement* made by certain of the prophets themselves in the direction of the religion of the altar. The first example of this phenomenon was Jeremiah, himself a priest (1:1), who was in his early manhood at the time of the discovery of the Deuteronomic Code under Josiah (621 B.C.) and already had experienced his "call" to the prophetic office (626 B.C.; 1:2; 25:3). He was disappointed by the character of the reformation that ensued this discovery. He declared "that the Judeans, overlooking the ethical and religious ideals of that Code, had enforced only some of its insignificant regulations about sacrifices (7:21-26). They violated both the spirit (7:23) and the letter (7:6, 9, 17-20, 30; 8:1-3) of Deuteronomy." [27] He looked forward to and prophesied the most profound change in the religion of the chosen people, the creation of a "new covenant" between God and his people, whereby his law would be written "in their inward parts, and in their heart" (31:33). This work of the prophet effected an incalculable result in the realm of personal religion, as seen in his influence upon the psalmists.[28] Nonetheless to the very end Jeremiah did not repudiate the priesthood and its offices for their own sake. When Jerusalem and its temple lay in waste, he foresaw a time when they would be restored, when "neither shall the priests the Levites want a man before me to offer burnt-offerings, and to burn meal-offerings, and to do sacrifice continually" (33:18).[29]

Ezekiel, whom we have already mentioned and whom Professor

[25] So Bewer, op. cit., p. 298; also pp. 293-94.
[26] An Introduction to the Literature of the Old Testament, p. 526.
[27] So Pfeiffer, op. cit., p. 495.
[28] Ibid., p. 514.
[29] Cf. ibid., pp. 484, 517.

Albright designates as "the foremost spiritual figure of Judaism . . . during the exile," [30] is the second of the prophets to have formed, so to speak, a bridge between prophetism and priestcraft. Ezekiel like Jeremiah was, of course, in the first instance a priest (1:3). Unlike Jeremiah, however, his major interest centered in the restoration of Jerusalem with its temple and ritualistic worship (chs. 40–48). And he combined this priestly concern with an earnest desire akin to that of the older prophet to further personal religion of a highly ethical sort (36:22-31). Israel has been from the beginning of her history sinful in the eyes of Yahweh (chs. 20–24). But Yahweh will redeem her, both as a nation and as individuals (36:16-38), and then will the "dry bones" of Israel come to life (37:1-14).

Two other prophets of less stature, Haggai and Zechariah, complete the group from the side of the prophets who endeavored to bring about a restoration of the priestly religion within Judaism while maintaining at the same time contact with the high ethical motif of the prophetic revelation. Haggai's sole interest appears to be in the fact that Yahweh's house "lieth waste" (1:9) and that its "latter glory . . . shall be greater than the former" (2:9). The monotheism of the prophets is his possession (1:12), however, as is also their universalism (2:6-9) and the thought of the need of obeying Yahweh in whatever he commands (1:12). But the strong prophetic emphasis upon ethics is lacking in this short prophecy, which it must be admitted is directed to one specific end for which, as the result showed, it was admirably adapted (1:14). Zechariah, again of priestly lineage (1:1, 7; cf. Neh. 12:16), was more in line with the former two prophets of this group. Like them he was concerned about the maintenance of the temple and its ritualistic worship (1:16-17; 4:9), prophesying its restoration. Like them he was equally concerned to see "true judgment," "kindness," "compassion," "truth" restored among the people of God (7:8-14; 8:14-17).

Whatever, then, the cult religion of Israel may have been before

[30] See *Stone Age*, p. 248.

the exile, it emerged from the captivity an amalgam of cult interest and moral idealism fostered by the prophetic teaching of an unbending ethical theism. In any given writer and in each generation the dominance of one or the other of these elements would depend, to be sure, upon a variety of factors. But both were present and are to be reckoned with in the religion of the altar in postexilic Judaism.

The Extracanonical Priestly Writings

In addition to the canonical writings that partake of the spirit of the religion of the altar there are three books among the Apocrypha and Pseudepigrapha which reflect the same spirit. Box and Oesterley are authority for the view that in Ecclesiasticus Jesus ben Sira has incorporated the priestly outlook of "the first quarter of the second century B.C.," as the "main tendency of his book." [31] There are also other influences at work in this piece of wisdom literature besides the priestly, and Canon Box quotes Edersheim with approval to the effect that "the book of Ben Sira . . . represents an orthodox, but moderate and cold, Judaism . . . before there were either Pharisees or Sadducees"; in one instance at least the former scholar speaks of Ben Sira as "a better Scribe than Sadducee." [32] Nonetheless Box is concerned to argue for the priestly influence as a dominant one in this great work, and he lists nine reasons for thinking so. [33]

It is relevant, therefore, to point out that, as in the canonical priestly literature, so here again in Ecclesiasticus we find the prophetic influence side by side with an interest in cult and ritual. [34] To Ben Sira there is but one God (36:5; 42:21), the "Creator of all" (42:15; 43:33), the All-knowing (42:18-25), the Eternal (18: 1 ff.; 36:17), the "Holy One" (23:9), the "Lord, Father, and God of my life" (23:1), who has made Israel his "portion" (17:17) but

[31] Cf. R. H. Charles, *Apocrypha and Pseudepigrapha*, I, 284, 293.
[32] *Ibid.*, p. 284.
[33] *Ibid.*, pp. 282-83.
[34] *Ibid.*, pp. 303-4.

is at the same time God over all peoples and nations. This last universalistic notion so characteristic of the highest reach of the prophetic revelation occurs in the following passage:

> The mercy of man is [exercised upon] his own kin,
> But the mercy of God is [extended] to all flesh,
> Reproving, and chastening, and teaching,
> And bringing them back as a shepherd his flock.
> He hath mercy on them that accept [his] chastening,
> And that diligently seek after his judgment. (18:13-14.)

In a number of passages Ben Sira exhibits a high sense of the moral flavor of sin akin to that of the prophets, and in at least one remarkable section he couples this with his teaching on the value of sacrifice:

The sacrifice of the unrighteous man is a mocking offering,
And unacceptable are the oblations of the godless.
The Most High hath no pleasure in the offerings of the ungodly,
Neither doth he forgive sins for a multitude of sacrifice. (34:18-19.) [35]

Commenting on this passage Canon Box summarizes its teaching as follows:

The governing thought of the section is that loyalty to God's Law, which is the expression of God's will, demands the offering of many sacrifices. But these are only acceptable if they are offered willingly, from a grateful heart, and if they are combined with high ethical standards of conduct.[36]

We come down another hundred years to the last quarter of the second century B.C. and to the unknown author of I Maccabees to find the next extant priestly writing. Of the origin and character of this writer Oesterley writes that "there are grounds for believing that he belonged to the circle of the Sadducees" and that though he was "a loyal upholder of the Law, his zeal is not characterized by

---

[35] Cf. further 17:25-32; 21:1-10; 23:16-17 et passim, and see Charles, ibid., I, 310 ff.
[36] Ibid., p. 437.

any approach to Pharisaic fanaticism." On the contrary this author's "sympathy for the Jewish highpriesthood is frequently manifested." [37] Once again in this priestly document we find the prophetic influence clearly manifest, side by side of course with priestly elements.

For the priestly interest one should note the stress on circumcision (1:15), the importance attached to the desecration of the "holy place" by Antiochus Epiphanes and to its rededication (1:20-24, 36-40; cf. 2:6-14; 3:45, 50-59, and a host of other passages of like nature), the relation of the cessation of the temple sacrifices and in place thereof the practice of acts that are "unclean and profane" (1:41-53; 2:19-28; cf. 7:42), the establishment of high places and the offering of sacrifices to the "deities of the street" (1:54-56), the destruction of the "books of the Law" and the setting up of the pagan altar (1:57-59), the attitude adopted toward the Sabbath, feasts, and ritual laws (2:39-48, et passim), and the references to the priests and their work (4:42; 5:67; 7:33-34; 10:42; 14:20).

The prophetic element in I Maccabees admittedly is less marked than the priestly and certainly is not so pronounced as in Ecclesiasticus. The author indeed seems rather to exhibit the rugged practical morality and religious interest of the proverbial "man in the street." [38] He looks on life with a firm faith in God who directs the destinies of men, but he speculates about that God's ways not at all. The name of God is never mentioned in the book, and the author's use of "Heaven" as a surrogate for the divine name indicates that the "disinclination, on account of its transcendent holiness, to utter the same has already begun in his day." [39] Still, he believes that "all who hope in Him shall want for nothing" (2:61), that "victory in battle" is determined in heaven (3:18), and that God "redeemeth and saveth Israel" (4:11; 9:46; 12:15). This is good theism, and perhaps the absence of the prophetic universalism may be pardoned in a book whose theme is the struggle of Israel to

---

[37] Ibid., p. 59.　　　　　　　　　　　　[39] So Oesterley in ibid., I, 61.
[38] Cf. especially 2:49-70.

maintain alive her faith in the midst of a sea of Gentile paganism that threatened to engulf her (1:13-15; 2:39-48, et passim). The Coptic Christian Church in Egypt similarly, under the pressure of necessity to maintain her life in the face of the power of Islam, centuries ago ceased to be a missionary church.

The last of the extant priestly documents to be produced is that known as the Zadokite Fragment (18-8 B.C.). The author of this work belonged to the Zadokite sect, a sort of "reformed Sadducee-ism," called also the "sect of 'The New Covenant.'" [40] They "had their origin in the priesthood and formed a party within it," in the opinion of Charles, "but a reforming party, the reformation being due largely to the Apocalyptic side of Pharisaism as is shown by the extreme importance attached to Old Testament prophecy and the advanced views on Eschatology." [41] Of all the priestly literature extant, both canonical and extracanonical, this fragment is undoubtedly closest to the teaching of the New Testament. It has even been seriously entertained that its author was a Christian, though this theory has not proved acceptable to those who have worked extensively on the fragment. Probably the judgment of Canon Charles would commend itself to a majority of New Testament scholars at the present day. Writing of the Zadokite sect generally he says:

For their appreciation of the Prophets—unparalleled in legalistic Judaism; their insistent preaching on the need of repentance; their constant proclamation of God's readiness to forgive the repentant; their expectation of a Messiah (and just at this period) and of a future life—all these beliefs and hopes prepared them to accept Christianity, and accordingly it is most reasonable to conclude that they formed part of the "great company of the priests that became obedient to the faith" (Acts vi. 7).[42]

In view of the foregoing facts it is not surprising to find that this fragment of the Book of the Hago (Sefer ha Hago),[43] as it was

[40] Pfeiffer, op. cit., p. 65.
[41] Op. cit., II, 791.
[42] Ibid., p. 786.
[43] Cf. Pfeiffer, op. cit., p. 65.

called, exhibits in a marked degree the two characteristics of the priestly literature to which we have been referring, namely, the high moral and theological interests of the prophets, on the one hand, and the concern for the cult religion of the temple, on the other. It would be possible to quote almost the entire work in demonstration of the truth of this statement. I shall content myself with a simple tabulation of certain passages illustrative of either side of this equation and chosen almost at random. For the *prophetic element* the following references are of significance:

The "covenant" of God with his people—1:12, 15; 2:1; 4:3, 9; 5:1; 6:6; 7:13; 8:13, 21; 9:11-12, 15, 25
The "new covenant"—9:28, 37, 41, 49; 10:2; 11:2; 16:7; 19:1 ff.; 20:8
The "Messiah"—2:10 (as being "from Aaron and from Israel"—9:29)
The "remnant"—2:5, 9 (cf. the "root of his planting"—1:5)
God's "wrath"—1:5; 4:7; 7:17; 9:22, 40
His "longsuffering" and "forgiveness"—2:3; 5:5; 6:4, 6
Man's "iniquity" and "perfect heart"—1:6, 7
"The Prophets, whose words Israel has despised"—9:7
"Salvation and righteousness" combined as in Deutero-Isaiah—9:43 (cf. Isa. 51:5, 6, 8, *et al.*)

For the *priestly interest* these passages, among others:

"His holy Sabbaths and his glorious festivals"—5:1, 2 (cf. 13:1-9, 13-27; 14:6)
"The charge of my sanctuary"—5:7 (cf. 7:8)
"They shall bring near unto me fat and blood"—5:7 (cf. Ezek. 44:15)
The character and description of "the priests . . . and the Levites"—6:1; 8:11-20.
The description of some as "men of the perfection of holiness"—9:32, 48
"The Book of the Hagu" ("Holiness" from Greek ἅγιος?)—11:1; 15:5
The interest in "uncleanness" and its opposite—14:1 ff.; 15:1-2

Prophet Versus Priest

In the light of the above summary statement of the evidence from the priestly writings of both canonical and extracanonical nature, it is evident that no universal branding of the religion of the altar in the postexilic period, at all events, as unethical and untheological can be justified by the objective historian. The formula "prophet versus priest" represents an oversimplification of the relevant facts and is about as accurate or inaccurate as such popular catch phrases usually are. These two great religious figures were at times in opposition to one another, it is true. But the lines were not drawn as sharply as is popularly supposed, nor does the phrase "ethics over against cult religion" serve accurately to define the nature of the dispute which often arose between them.

The priest who came after the appearance of the eighth-century prophets was by no means the same as the priest who preceded them. The Deuteronomic legislation is the immediate proof of this statement. The opposition of the preexilic prophet, therefore, was by and large directed against the pre-Deuteronomic priest and against the cult as it appeared *in his day* and not as it became in the post-Deuteronomic period. That prophet was led by the word of God which dominated his consciousness to take a determined stand against the cult. For that word, with its high ethical content, would brook no compromise with nonethical forms of worship.[44]

The post-Deuteronomic priest, on the other hand, if we may trust the somewhat scanty evidence at our disposal, was equally prepared to listen to the word which came to the prophet, for he was aware that he had none of his own.[45] But he was at the same time deeply concerned with the religious problem of the common man. And religious stateman that he was, he endeavored to set up a cult ritual that would lead the worshiper nigh to God. This he held would result, not in the worshiper's flaunting the ethical

---

[44] Cf. A. S. Peake, *The People and the Book*, pp. 208-10; Hos. 6:6; Amos 5:24-25; Mic. 6:6-8; Jer. 7:22-23; Pss. 40, 50, 51; Wright, *op. cit.*, pp. 42-45.

[45] See above, p. 89, and Pfeiffer, *op. cit.*, p. 51 and especially note 1.

standards of the older prophets, but in his discovering the need of them as he came into fellowship through worship with a holy God. No doubt the priest, like his confrere the political statesman, was at times swayed by "practical considerations" and the apparent needs of the day in which he lived, perhaps to the detriment of allegiance to the prophetic word. At times also ethical interests would be allowed to drop into the background or to be submerged in view of what seemed to be the strategic importance of strengthening the cult. This probably explains the peculiar emphases and point of view of the Priestly Code. Professor Bewer has remarked relative to this code:

When the question of the organization of religion in the light of the prophetic ideals was attempted, it was seen that a purely moral and spiritual religion was too high and exacting for the mass of the people. External forms were necessary, worship had to be carried on.[46]

But as we have seen, the ethical note was far more to the fore in the work of the Deuteronomists, in the Holiness Code, in Ecclesiasticus, and in the Book of the Hago. On the whole, therefore, it seems fair to say that the post-Deuteronomic priest took advantage of the prophets' deep moral and theological teachings and endeavored sincerely to bring these into contact with, as well as to give them expression in, the cult religion.[47]

[46] *Op. cit.*, p. 267. [47] See Wright, *op. cit.*, pp. 42-45.

CHAPTER

6

Jesus and the Priests

FOR our Lord as for all other Jews of his day the priestly writings of the Old Testament scriptures were a part of the divine Torah, and he cited and quoted them as such, using on occasion with reference to them the usual formula, "It is written," as employed by the scribes in quoting scripture.[1] Needless to say, he was unacquainted with the findings of modern critical scholarship relative to the distribution of the prophetic and priestly elements in the scriptures. It is instructive, however, to note how far he actually employed the writings which are today denominated as "priestly" and what use he made of them. The following table, which includes a mere summary of the passages collected in Appendix A, will serve as a guide for such study:

Priestly Source		Gospel Source				
	Mk	Q	L	M	Jn	Total
P	3		1	1		5
H	2		1	4		7
D[1]	4	3		4		11
D[2]	1		1			2
R[D]	3		2	1		6
Totals	13	3	5	10	nil[2]	31

[1] See p. 175 below.
[2] These data are illuminating in view of the theory that "John" may have had high-priestly connections.

114

An analysis of the material provided in this chart in the light of its subject matter is illuminating. The thirty-one citations deal respectively with matters of: ethics, 17; theology proper, 3; eschatology, 4; law, 1; history, 2; and ritual, 4. This analysis is obviously devastating to a possible thesis that our Lord conceived a profound interest in the essentially priestly factor contained in the writings of the religion of the altar. For even when citing such literature, he chose generally those passages for comment in which the prophetic emphases upon ethical and theological matters were paramount.[3]

Of the four references to passages of a specifically ritual nature, two (Mark 1:44 and Luke 17:14 [L]) relate to the law which specified what a leper should do in order to seek restoration to the rights of the community and of corporate worship in Israel following his being cleansed of his disease (Lev. 13:49; cf. 14:2-3). That Jesus commanded that these unfortunates should do as the law required did not in any way commit him to adherence to the religion of the altar and its viewpoint. To have advised other than he did under the circumstances would have resulted in the continued exclusion of the leper from among his people. Jesus was therefore merely realistic in accepting the necessity imposed by the law of ritual cleansing as a matter of course in such cases. The incident does, however, serve to clear up one point, namely, that Jesus was

[3] When the known interests of the authors of the gospel sources are taken into account, they are seen to have influenced these figures but slightly if at all. Thus Matthew's special source (M), while appearing to suggest an interest on our Lord's part in matters discussed in the priestly writings out of proportion to the length of this source, as compared with the lengths of and interest displayed in the other sources, in reality creates this impression because of its incorporation of the Sermon on the Mount. Seven of M's passages out of its ten belong here. When this is taken into account, the remaining three instances are seen to bring that document more nearly into harmony with the others. This phenomenon, however, suggests the possibility that our Lord's citations of or quotations from the scriptures in formal address may have been more extensive than a study of his teachings generally would lead us to suppose. His use of these scriptures was generally of a haggadic nature, that is, it exhibited a theological, ethical, or devotional interest rather than a legalistic or disciplinary one (halākhāh), as reference to the passages listed in Appendix A shows. Such an interest would naturally prompt the quotation of scripture passages in lengthy discourses and expositions.

no social revolutionary in the accepted sense of that term. His teachings had social implications aplenty, but any changes in the social structure required by them would come by indirection so far as he was concerned and could well await a thoroughgoing understanding of his gospel and its acceptance by men generally.

The other two citations referred to are of even more value for determining our Lord's attitude toward the ritual laws of the Torah. Both are found in a single passage (Mark 2:25-28) and relate to the law of the shewbread (Lev. 24:5-9) and to David's disregard of it as reported in I Sam. 21:2-7. Israel Abrahams has pointed out that the rabbis had a saying almost identical with the one placed here on our Lord's lips: "The Sabbath is delivered unto you, ye are not delivered unto the Sabbath." [4] It may be, indeed, that Jesus was merely repeating a formula well-known to his hearers. Matthew and Luke, as I have mentioned above (p. 73), do not even reproduce it, and in Mark it is dropped by the Western text in what may have been its earliest form.[5] But even if it is allowed to stand, the teaching of the passage as a whole will be: Jesus like David, whose overruling the law of the shewbread he cites with approval, by virtue of his transcendent position as Son of Man can overrule a command of the Priestly Code, and he will do so moreover when the needs of men necessitate his adopting this course.

There can be no doubt that these two incidents give us something of Jesus' fundamental attitude toward the religion of the altar. He was prepared to allow its claims when it appeared expedient to do so; but when these conflicted with the rights and needs of men, they were to be disregarded as detrimental to higher interests.

Jesus' Knowledge of the Apocryphal Priestly Writings

There is some evidence in favor of our Lord's having known and used the extracanonical priestly writings which were in circulation

[4] *Studies in Pharisaism and the Gospels*, I, 134.
[5] Codex Bezae and the Latin manuscripts a c e ff i omit the entire verse (vs. 27), and Codex Washingtoniensis and the Sinaitic Syriac omit its second clause.

among the Jews of Palestine in his day.[6] This consists less of verbal similarity suggestive of direct quotation than of general likeness of terminology and teaching. Charles, for example, somewhat hesitatingly following Nestle suggests that Matt. 6:14 resembles Ecclus. 28:2, which reads: "Forgive thy neighbor the injury [done to thee], and then, when thou prayest, thy sins will be forgiven." [7] The passage may be even nearer in form to Mark 11:25, which is perhaps the original of the saying in M. Nestle also calls attention to the close accord between Matt. 6:19-20 (M) and Ecclus. 29:12, "Store up almsgiving in thy treasuries, and it shall deliver thee from all evil." [8] Once again it seems that Luke 12:33 (L), which may be the source of the M saying, is nearer to Ecclesiasticus than Matthew, as "almsgiving" is enjoined in both Ecclesiasticus and Luke here, but not in Matthew. To these Charles also adds Ecclus. 31:3 and 11:18-19 as like the parable of the rich fool (Luke 12:15-16 [L]). The latter of the two passages from Ecclesiasticus reads: "There is that waxeth rich from self-denial, and this is his allotted reward. What time he saith, I have found rest, and now I will enjoy my goods, he knoweth not what lot shall befall; he shall leave [them] to others and die."

On the other hand, there is a passage in the Zadokite Fragment which appears to bear a peculiar significance by reason of its being the direct opposite of our Lord's teaching on the subject. It runs: "And if it [an animal—vs. 22] falls into a pit or ditch, he shall not raise it on the Sabbath" (13:25). This is followed in verse 26 with the saying: "And if any person falls into a place of water or into a place of . . . , he shall not bring him up by a ladder or a cord or instrument." The first of these sayings is opposed by M. Betzah 3:4 of a much later day: "If a Firstling fell into a pit, R. Judah says: Let a skilled person go down and look at it; if it has incurred a blemish let him bring it up and slaughter it; otherwise it may not

---

[6] On the popularity of Ecclesiasticus in Palestinian Jewry cf. Charles, *op. cit.*, I, 295.

[7] *Ibid.*, and Hastings' *Dictionary of the Bible*, IV, 550b.

[8] *Ibid.*

be slaughtered." M. Yoma 8:6 is also in general disagreement with the second of the Fragment sayings quoted, thus: "Wherever there is doubt whether life is in danger, this overrides the Sabbath." These Mishnaic sayings substantiate the gospel account of the rabbinical attitudes toward man and animal in the situations described. It is evident also that the Mishnah is more lenient toward animal and man than the priestly document, though more so toward the animal, which is to be rescued in any case, than toward man, who is to be given attention only if his life is in danger. Jesus in both L and M (Luke 14:5 and Matt. 12:11), while appealing to the popular Mishnaic leniency toward the animal as against the stricter priestly command, takes issue with both for their comparative inhumanity toward man. And the language of our Lord is so like that employed in the Zadokite Fragment as to suggest either that he was acquainted with its exact reading or that both his words and those of the Fragment reflect the popular mode of expression in such matters.

But it is in the matter of general *spiritual and ethical teaching* that Jesus more nearly approximates these extracanonical priestly writings, even as he quoted largely the prophetic elements of the canonical priestly literature. Thus it is a notable fact that in the well-known dispute between the Hillelites and the Shammaites relative to the grounds for divorce Jesus took the position also advanced in Zadok. Frag. 7:1-7, that divorce was not to be allowed on any grounds whatever; and it is if anything more striking that he even agreed with the latter in quoting Gen. 1:27 as the basis for his judgment against the Pharisaic use of Deut. 24:1 in this connection.[9]

Again, Jesus' opposition to the "fence" (M. Aboth 1:1) or "wall" (Zadok. Frag. 7:1; 9:21, 26) of tradition which the scribes had erected in the Oral Law about the divine Torah followed in the main the pattern found in the Zadokite Fragment.[10] As Canon

[9] Cf. M. Gittin 9:10 and Mark 10:6; Matt. 19:4.
[10] Cf. Mark 7:8-9; Matt. 15:6.

Charles remarks of the author of this work, "it is not to the principle of 'the fence' itself, but to its abnormal growth in the form of oral tradition that the Zadokite Fragment objected." [11] So our Lord quarreled with the oral tradition, not because he wished to oppose it as such, but because in striving to follow it the people of the book had deserted or actually infringed against "the commandment of God"—that is, they had allowed "their heart" to be "far from God," which is the point of his quotation from Isa. 29:13 at Mark 7:6-7.[12]

In their relatively equal stress upon "Law and Prophets" also, Jesus and the Zadokite Fragment approximate one another.[13] For both it is only as prophetic word and not as legal enactment that the Torah possesses interest and value, while like the prophets, by its teaching on "a perfect heart" (1:7), on the "longsuffering" of God and his "forgiveness" (2:3; 5:5), on the need of repentance on man's part for his "transgressions" (2:3), on a spiritual as well as national "Messiah" who shall make men know the "holy spirit" of God (2:10; cf. 9:10), on "the life of eternity" (5:6), on "atonement" and "salvation" as emanating from God rather than from man (6:6; 9:43), on the love of "brother as himself," the helping of "the poor and the needy and the stranger," and the seeking of "the peace of his brother" (8:17; cf. 9:16)—by these and other like emphases the Zadokite Fragment succeeds in creating an atmosphere which is nearer in spirit to the teaching of Jesus than either is to that of Mishnah or Talmud.

On the whole, however, the evidence that our Lord knew and was dependent upon the extracanonical priestly literature at first hand falls considerably short of demonstration. It seems more likely, in light of the above comparisons, that both had drunk deeply of the same prophetic well of spiritual and ethical truth and that

[11] Op. cit., II, 818.
[12] See also Q at Luke 11:42=Matt. 23:23, and cf. pp. 177-78 below; also T. W. Manson, The Mission and Message of Jesus, pp. 389 ff.
[13] Cf. Luke 16:16=Matt. 11:12-13 (Q); Luke 24:44 (L?); Matt. 5:17; 7:12; 22:40 (M); and Zadok. Frag. 9:4-9; 19:2, 11; 20:2-7; also Charles, op. cit., II, 789, 794.

this fact does not fail to shine through and illuminate their respective attitudes and teachings. In consequence Jesus is found to agree or disagree with these writings with entire freedom. For in actuality he and they belonged to different camps. Both had like interests, to an extent employed the same language even, and from time to time agreed to identical solutions to given problems, even as both alike valued the prophetic voice as the word of God. But in the end the priestly writer was limited by the considerations of his caste, whereas Jesus was bound by nothing save the demands of his own free spirit of truth.

Jesus and the Temple

Coming now to the subject of Jesus' relation to the temple and its ceremonial practices, we are here on ground of the greatest interest for the student of Christian origins. One could wish, however, that the evidence was more complete than it is. For while nothing in the Gospels precludes us from supposing that Jesus shared the interest common to all parties of the Judaism of his day in the temple and its feasts, actually only Luke (2:41-51) among the Synoptists refers to his attendance on them at any time previous to the Passover season which was the occasion of his death (Mark 14:1 ff.). John mentions a second Passover certainly (6:4), possibly a third (2:13), and less likely a fourth (5:1), also a Feast of Tabernacles (7:2) and a Feast of Dedication (10:22), all as having been attended by Jesus with the exception of the first named. But there is no measure of agreement among New Testament students as to the historicity of these visits of our Lord to Jerusalem.[14]

Such as it is, this evidence (with the single exception of the boyhood visit) points to the temple as being a scene of conflict for Jesus whenever he visited it. And it is a notable fact that on the occasion of the one peaceful visit, it was the rabbis with whom he was in

---

[14] Cf. J. H. Bernard, St. John (I.C.C. series), I, cii ff.; W. F. Howard, The Fourth Gospel in Recent Criticism and Interpretation, pp. 48, 51, et al.; and G. Ogg, The Chronology of the Public Ministry of Jesus, ch. iii, pp. 27 ff.

conversation rather than the priests (Luke 2:46). At Tabernacles John reports that "chief priests and Pharisees" conspired together "to take him" (7:32, 45), presumably with a view to doing away with him; at Dedication he was threatened with stoning at the hands of the "Jews" (10:31); and both of our major sources (John and Synoptic) agree that he cleansed the temple at a Passover season to the outspoken annoyance of the temple authorities (Mark 11: 27-33; John 2:18).

Nonetheless it is agreed among the sources that Jesus had no quarrel with the temple as such. Matthew's special source alone, it is true, contained an account of the incident of the temple tax (the "half-shekel"),[15] wherein Jesus is said to have committed himself to the maintenance of this historic Jewish worship center. This is a typical pronouncement story, as Vincent Taylor has pointed out,[16] and its authenticity cannot fail to be challenged, particularly in view of the patent interest of M in the life of the Palestinian Christian community as it stood related to the Judaism which preceded the destruction of Jerusalem.[17] The conciliatory tone of the saying, moreover, is quite in keeping with that of the early Jerusalem church (vs. 27).[18] Dibelius therefore holds that "its community reference is clear" and that its "original form cannot be recovered" as it was uttered by Jesus, for this "has been supplanted by concern for the life of the community." [19]

While it is difficult, therefore, if not impossible, to maintain the entire authenticity of Jesus' words in this incident, it should be noted that the final intent of the saying is in accord with the evidence of our other sources. In both Luke and John, Jesus speaks of the temple as "my Father's house," [20] while in Mark's source the point at issue in connection with the cleansing of the temple is that it is not being used for the purpose for which it was originally

---

[15] Matt. 17:24-27; cf. Exod. 30:11-13 (P).
[16] Op. cit., pp. 73-74.
[17] See T. W. Manson, op. cit., pp. 34 ff.
[18] Cf. Acts 15:21; 21:20 ff.; I Cor. 9:19-22.
[19] Message, p. 161; also see his From Tradition to Gospel, pp. 105-6.
[20] John 2:16; Luke 2:49.

intended, namely, as a "house of prayer" (Mark 11:17; cf. Isa. 56:
7). Presumably, then, Jesus had no quarrel with the right use of
the temple as a center of the worship of God, and he may very well
have been prepared to subscribe with all pious Jews to its maintenance, as Matthew avers was the case.

But did our Lord sanction the sacrifice of the temple or its
ritual generally, together with the laws of "clean and unclean" or
of ritual "holiness" which provided the motivation for the priestly
account of the sacrificial system? The answer to questions like this
depends upon the exegesis of several passages in the Gospels and
the fitting together of their respective intents into a likely pattern.

We begin with the one to which reference has just been made,
the cleansing of the temple (Mark 11:15-18). This, it has been
suggested with considerable plausibility, is an *acted parable* founded
on Mal. 3:1: "Behold, I send my messenger, and he shall prepare
my way before me: and *the Lord, whom ye seek, will suddenly come
to his temple; and the messenger of the covenant*, whom ye desire,
behold, *he cometh*, saith the Lord of hosts." [21] (Italics mine.) At
the cleansing Jesus takes the part of the Lord who comes to his
temple or of the messenger who cometh, if the two characters are
to be identified after the manner of Hebrew parallelism. But he is
to be preceded by another personality, the "my messenger" of the
first part of the verse. It is significant, therefore, that when challenged for his *authority* in connection with the cleansing, our Lord
immediately reverted to the problem of the Baptist's mission (Mark
11:30). This is as though he were saying, "Behold, you have here
the Lord come to his temple, preceded by his messenger, and the
fulfillment of the Old Testament symbolism ought to be clear to
you who know the Scriptures." It is difficult to resist the conclusion
that, had the religious leaders had the insight to give a satisfactory

[21] The exegesis of the verse is very difficult, and various interpretations of the
figures here have been given. Cf. Bewer on the passage in the commentary in the
I.C.C. series, pp. 62-63. A favorite identification of the "my messenger" was with
Elijah in 4:5-6. This latter passage, however, is considered an interpolation by a later
hand, so one cannot argue for the identification as intended by Malachi. During
Jesus' day, however, it may have been made.

answer about John, Jesus would have gone on to say that they could draw their own conclusion about his authority over the temple and the source of it, in line with the relation between the "my messenger" and the "Lord" coming to his temple of Malachi.[22]

It is true that this interpretation involves a double difficulty: (1) Malachi does not here speak of the "Messiah" but of the "Lord" as coming to his temple,[23] and (2) it commits Jesus to the identification, the Baptist=the "my messenger" of Mal. 3:1 and even "Elijah" of 4:5-6. But these difficulties are not insuperable. For though in Mal. 3:1 Yahweh is no doubt intended by the prophet when he writes "Lord," yet the word he uses is *hā-'Adhōn* (הָאָדוֹן) and not the Tetragrammaton (יהוה); and as I have said above, this figure appears to be identified with "the messenger of the covenant" by the parallelism of the Hebrew, Yahweh himself being the speaker throughout and not the subject of discourse.[24] This phenomenon might have appeared to our Lord to justify the interpretation of the "Lord" here in a messianic sense, as he undoubtedly so understood the term in Ps. 110:1 (cf. Mark 12:36-37). Moreover, that Jesus identified the Baptist in some sense with Elijah appears clear from Mark 9:13.[25]

It seems reasonably certain, therefore, that our Lord is assuming the role of the "Lord Messiah" in this acted parable of the temple's cleansing and that his purpose is to challenge the temple authorities by confronting them with the judgment of the divine sovereignty upon their stewardship of God's house. Malachi expresses this idea in the words:

But who can abide the day of his coming? and who shall stand when he appeareth? for he is like a refiner's fire, and like fuller's soap: and he

---

[22] Major calls the incident "a deliberate symbolic action by Jesus, setting forth an aspect of His Messianic office: the purging of contemporary Jewish religion from commercialism and materialism"; see *The Mission and Message of Jesus*, by Major, Manson, and Wright, *in loc.*

[23] *Ibid.*, pp. 359 ff.; a full discussion of the relevant passages will be found here.

[24] "Messenger of the covenant" appears nowhere else but in this passage; this might have rendered the identification of "the Lord" or "messenger" here with the "Messiah" more likely to our Lord's mind.

[25] Cf. also Matt. 11:14 (M).

will sit as a refiner and purifier of silver, and he will purify the sons of Levi, and refine them as gold and silver; and they shall offer unto the Lord offerings in righteousness. (3:2-3.)

It is instructive to note that in the sequel the "chief priests, and the scribes, and the elders" are said to have understood that this attack was made upon their position in the temple (Mark 11:27; cf. vs. 18). No doubt these "sons of Levi" were feeling the heat of the "refiner's fire" upon them.

The nature of this attack, then, becomes deeply significant for an understanding of our Lord's attitude toward the religion of the altar. Where lies the focal point of his interest and the object of his criticism? The dual quotation he makes from Scripture furnishes a key to the answer to this question (Isa. 57:7; Jer. 7:11). In Jeremiah's day the temple had become the center of a formal worship which gave expression to Judah's essentially materialistic view of religion. George Adam Smith observes that the Deuteronomic reforms under Josiah "had invested the one sanctuary" with a new sacredness as the old high places were given up. But this had resulted in the transference of the pollutions of these religious centers to the Jerusalem temple itself. It "was by this generation not only debased to a mere pledge of their political security but debauched into a shelter for sins as gross as ever polluted their worship upon the high places." [26] Our Lord conceived the materialism that reigned in the temple in his day to be of the same sort. Once again that edifice had become "a den of robbers." The Talmud, as is well known, says that the markets in the temple area were called "the bazaars of the sons of Annas," that is, of the high-priestly family.[27] In any case, the indictment would fall on those in authority in the temple.

But this was not all; for Deutero-Isaiah had devoted a short passage (56:1-8) to an unequivocal universalism in which "the sons of

---

[26] Jeremiah, p. 150.

[27] I am indebted to Edersheim for the reference to Jer. Peah 1:6 and Rosh ha Shan. 31a. (Life and Times of Jesus the Messiah, I, 371-72.)

the stranger, that join themselves to the Lord" (vs. 6) were promised a share in God's "holy mountain" and in his "house of prayer"; "for mine house shall be called a house of prayer for all people" (vs. 7; cf. vs. 8).[28] In Jesus' day the stalls for the selling of the sacrificial animals were found in the Court of the Gentiles.[29] The confusion, particularly at the time of the great feasts, can better be imagined than described. It is inconceivable, therefore, that in such turmoil the "sons of the stranger" (Gentiles) could have found the temple a fitting place for prayer or real worship of any sort.

Putting these two passages together we see that our Lord's attack on the temple at this point was directed against its materialism and provincialism. And with little wonder, for these were certainly its outstanding defects. They are faults, moreover, which lie close together in the realm of spiritual ineptitude. They are two phases of that egocentricity which neither honors God nor regards man, and their true antidote is that worship which is the expression at once of love to God and of love to man.

So low, then, had sunk the religion of the altar in our Lord's day. But in cleansing the temple with the "refiner's fire" did he mean to imply that its sacrifices and rituals were an actual detriment to the cause of true religion? that the priest in turning to the altar as a mode of religious response to the prophetic word had done mankind a distinct disservice? This way of stating (or re-stating) the problem with which we are dealing leads us to a consideration of other passages in the Gospels.

Jesus and the Temple Sacrifices

Matthew twice inserts into his Marcan source a quotation from Hos. 6:6 as on the lips of Jesus, namely, at the call of Levi (9:13; cf. Mark 2:13-17) and in connection with the plucking of grain on the Sabbath day (12:7; cf. Mark 2:23-28). The verse reads, "For

[28] Cf. Skinner, Isaiah, in loc.
[29] As were also "the tables of the money-changers," according to M. Shekalim 1:3, on the twenty-fifth of the month Adar.

I desire goodness, and not sacrifice; and the knowledge of God more than burnt-offerings." In both cases the fact that the verse from Hosea is thrust by Matthew into his Marcan source without apparent warrant casts grave doubt upon its authenticity, that is, upon its having been uttered by Jesus on these occasions. But even though it is conceded that Jesus may have said this, it would still remain unlikely that he meant by it wholeheartedly to condemn the priestly altar religion and its sacrifices.

We have already seen that the lines were by no means drawn as strictly between prophet and priest as has often been made out. Micah was typical of the prophetic attitude with regard to sacrifice, and in his sixth chapter at verses 6-8 he sharply contrasts "burnt-offerings" and the sacrifice of "calves a year old" with the doing of "justice" and the love of "kindness" and the walking "humbly with thy God." This passage, as J. M. P. Smith remarks,

lays hold of the essential elements in religion and, detaching them from all else, sets them in clear relief. It links ethics with piety, duty toward man with duty toward God, and makes them both coequal factors in religion. . . . This prophet makes religion an inner experience which determines [the] whole sphere of human activity. Religion becomes not merely the action, but also, and chiefly, character.[30]

And although Hosea had painted the priests in very dark colors indeed, it is doubtful whether even he intended to go beyond Micah in his condemnation of sacrifice as such.[31] Buchanan Gray has stated this prophetic view of sacrifice so well that I cannot do better than to quote his statement at length without comment:

They [the prophets] were prepared to tolerate, and even themselves to make use of, these ancient institutions of religion, if only the people would not abuse them, by giving them a place in life that Yahweh never intended them to have. Practically, however, their attitude toward sacrifice, even unabused sacrifice, is at best one of indifference; Yahweh is

[30] *Micah* (I.C.C. series), *in loc.*
[31] Cf. Albright, *op. cit.*, p. 239, and Wright, *op. cit.*, p. 44.

spirit and not flesh, and does not need man's fleshly gifts. . . . God desires not sacrifice but the knowledge of God, not sacrifice but justice and mercy which are the necessary outcome of knowledge of God.[32]

It is unlikely in the extreme that Jesus ever intended to go beyond this usual prophetic attitude in condemning the priestly sacrificial system. Furthermore the contexts of the two Matthaean quotations do not demand that he should have done so. In both the stress is upon the need of mercy and love in dealing with one's fellow men, whether these be publicans (9:13) or the disciples of a rival teaching (12:7). In any case it would have been quite out of character for Jesus to have made an unprovoked attack on the priestly religion of the altar for its own sake. His criticisms, even in the case of the Pharisees, were invariably leveled against the *abuses* or *false emphases* in the religious expressions with which he had to deal, not against their practices or institutions; and the principle which he annunciated was, "This ought ye to have done, and not to have left the other undone." If he ever scored the sacrificial system in Judaism, therefore, we may be sure that it had an immediately practical reference to the moral and spiritual needs of men and did not constitute a theoretical denunciation of the system as a whole. It is probably not without significance, I believe, that in no instance do our gospel sources ever put Jesus in conflict with the common priests of the time, as he no doubt would have been had he opposed their sacrificial system for its own sake. The nearest approach to such a conflict is found in the parable of the good Samaritan (Luke 10:31-32), wherein the "priest" and the "Levite" are made to be the *personae non gratae* of the tale. But even here it is not their religious observances that are in question but rather their ethical attitude.

The same result emerges from a study of our Lord's observations concerning the ritual laws and customs relating to "holiness" or to things "clean and unclean" and the "washings of cups, and pots,

[32] *Op. cit.*, pp. 43-44.

127

and brasen vessels," as well as of the hands (Mark 7:1-5; 14-23). There can be no doubt that Mark accurately transcribes our Lord's contrasting the "things which proceed out of a man" as those that "defile" with those "from without the man" that enter into him and cannot "defile him" (vss. 14-15). And the later interpretation of the church which Mark records—to the effect that Jesus meant by this saying to contrast qualities of ethical character with external matters, thereby declaring "all foods clean" (vs. 19b)—is certainly a correct insight into his meaning.

But the history of the Christian Church and its attitude toward this problem is the clearest witness that neither on this occasion nor on any other did Jesus make any sweeping condemnation of the practices associated with the laws of ritual cleanness. For the implications of such remarks as he is recorded to have made here were borne in upon the consciousness of the church only after the most bitter controversy had been waged in the early days, involving as our records show Stephen, Peter, James, and Paul, together with the Pharisaic party ("Judaizers") within the church.[33] As Principal Major has succinctly remarked, "St. Paul seems to have had no doubt that in ignoring the ceremonial distinction between clean and unclean foods he had the authority of Jesus behind him." [34] But it took insight on Paul's part to discover this fact which had not been discerned by the primitive community as a whole before his day. I cannot but feel, therefore, that the form critics are wrong in holding that the more intimate explanations which our Lord is supposed to have made to his band of disciples actually represent the later teaching of the church, as for example those just referred to in Mark 7:17-23. This explanation thrusts between Jesus and the later church a spiritual and intellectual barrier which in the end must mean robbing Jesus of his right to be called the founder of our Christian faith. It was not *knowledge* which the church lacked but *insight*; and when one of prophetic stature like

[33] Major, *op. cit.*, pp. 97 ff.   [34] *Ibid.*, p. 100.

Paul produced this insight, then the church brought out of its treasury of memory the nearly forgotten teaching of our Lord to his intimate disciples to match the apostle's rather marvelous understanding of the "mind of Christ." Such hindsight of the church also had its prophetic counterpart, as we have already seen, in the prophetic concept of "memory" which in the end gave the prophet his "philosophy of history." And as the prophet, looking backward, was able to see God's hand in history and so to face the future with serene faith, so the church, recalling her Lord's "words" and in their light reading the situation in which she found herself, was able to go forward with a conviction and a courage born thereof that has challenged every succeeding age to high faith and noble living.[35]

There are, however, three passages of a prophetic nature in which our Lord, while he does not condemn the customs of the religion of the altar, does at all events exhibit his insight into their transitory nature and eventual disuse. These are the bridegroom passage (Mark 2:18-20), the parables of the old garment and of the wineskins (Mark 2:21-22), and the eschatological discourse in Mark 13. The authenticity of the bridegroom passage has been challenged on insufficient grounds.[36] No one who accepts Jesus' insight into the nature of his own mission in terms of the great prophetic concepts with which we have already dealt in chapter 3 can doubt that Jesus uttered a saying in which he intimated to his auditors the possibil-

---

[35] Professor Manson's view that "as to matter and method the teaching of Jesus is conditioned by the nature of the audience" is in my judgment sound. It stands to reason that, as he says, it was only to his disciples that Jesus could give "his confidence" and speak "without reserve," and this was no doubt because he saw in them something of that "insight and understanding for which in the earlier part of the ministry Jesus is always seeking" (op. cit., p. 19). This would account for what I have called the church's "memory" of what Jesus taught. But there can also be no doubt that her early insight proved inadequate for her needs and that from time to time she required men of spiritual vision like Paul to bring her out of the doldrums of spiritual stagnation in which she recurrently seems to have found herself—even, indeed, as she does today.

[36] I have discussed this matter at some length in the Intention, pp. 196 ff. The metaphorical associations of fasting in Joel 2:12-14, M. Taanith 2:1, and like passages made the transition to a wholly parabolic use of the term easy. Cf. also Moore, Judaism, II, 258-59.

ity of his being taken away from his disciples. But such a saying as this was not meant by him to substantiate the type of "fasting" practiced under the religion of the altar. *Fasting* in the bridegroom passage was meant metaphorically and as a prophecy of the church's grief at his being taken away from it, in contrast with the joy at his immediate presence as indicated by the fact that his disciples were not then fasting. The later church's use of the passage, therefore, if its authenticity is conceded, to substantiate its own practice of fasting and its elevation of it to the status of a sacrament in a rejuvenated or Christianized form of the religion of the altar represents a curious lack of insight into the real intent of Christ for his church. And if it is argued that the church invented the saying in verses 19b-20 and placed it in our Lord's mouth with a view to underwriting its adoption of the practice, as C. H. Dodd following the form critics argues, then the case for the church's spiritual insight is no better, but if possible even worse.[37] Either way the church's practice of fasting in the literal sense appears to be a case of lacking anyone of prophetic stature who at the right moment could guide her in her search into the "treasury of memory" and interpret what she found there after the fashion mentioned above.

That the above metaphorical interpretation of fasting on our Lord's lips is correct appears to be guaranteed by the fact that Mark places our second passage in immediate juxtaposition with the former teaching. It is no doubt true, as the form critical school insists, that it cannot be certain whether our Lord spoke the parables of the old garment and of the old wineskins on this same occasion.[38] Mark, however, clearly sensed that an inner kinship of meaning and intent existed between the parables and the passage on fasting. This can only have been the case if the latter is interpreted metaphorically as the passage stands in its entirety, for the obvious teaching of the

[37] Cf. Dodd, *The Parables of the Kingdom*, p. 116, n. 2; and Dibelius, *From Tradition to Gospel*, p. 65. Whether one agrees with the form critics or not in holding that the church introduced the saying in vss. 19b-20 as a *vaticinium ex eventu*, there must be agreement with Dibelius that "a mode of life without fasting" (at any rate as a *necessary* religious "form") represents "the mind of Jesus."

[38] See Dibelius, *Message*, pp. 12, 139, 142.

parables is that the forms of the old religion—including, of course, fasting—are now outmoded. To quote Principal Major again, "Jesus indicates here His conviction that His Gospel cannot be contained within the limits of Jewish legalism. St. Paul saw this clearly; but Jesus saw it first." [39] Or at all events, so Mark understood him. The fact that Mark placed the two parables next to the fasting passage is proof, therefore, of an early tradition of the church which took the latter also in a parabolic sense and which antedated the contrary wish to support the practice of fasting within the church by a "word" of her Lord. In neither parables nor fasting passage, however, is our Lord's attitude one of condemnation of the old forms of the religion of the altar but rather an expression of his realistic approach to the problems of religion which are raised by differing needs and circumstances. With the old religion, he prophesies, will go the old forms.

We shall take up the third passage, Mark 13, in detail in chapter 12. For our present purpose it will be sufficient to note that, if it is granted—contrary to the opinion of many—that the contents of that chapter are on the whole from Jesus' lips, even so there is therein no condemnation of the religion of the altar as such. Jesus' enemies, it is true, accused him of saying that he would destroy the temple and its worship, but this statement failed to be confirmed at his trial and was evidently either a malicious misrepresentation of what he did say or else a misunderstanding of it.[40] To foretell the end of the temple worship as a result of keen prophetic insight was one thing; to have condemned its practices wholesale would have been something else; and as we have seen, there is no record of Jesus' having done this at any time. It is quite in accord with what we have seen to have been his teaching as a whole, then, that he should have prophesied as recorded in Mark 13:2: "Seest thou these great buildings? there shall not be left here one stone upon another, which shall not be thrown down."

[39] *Mission and Message*, pp. 55-56.
[40] Mark 14:57-59; 15:29; cf. John 2:19; Acts 6:14.

In bringing this discussion to a close, it should be noted that if our Lord did not condemn the practice of fasting and like customs of the Jewish religious culture, neither did he sanction them in the new age that was dawning. We have looked at the suggestion that the church inserted the clauses in Mark 2:19b-20 and wished thereby to substantiate by a "word" of Jesus its own practice of fasting. If it did not make such an insertion here, it certainly did so at other passages, as for example in Mark 9:29, where as is well known the "Western" text introduced the words "and fasting" into a genuine saying of our Lord.[41] The form critics would go further here and claim that the private conversation narrated from verse 28 forward is suspect, both on the general ground that what is taught in private by our Lord represents a late tradition or even fabrication of the church (cf. above, p. 128, on Mark 7:17-23) and again that here the three Synoptic writers fail to agree as to their reasons for the disciples' inability to cast out the demon to which reference is made in the discussion (vs. 28).[42] Matthew (17:20) says this was due to their "little faith"; Mark (9:29), to the lack of "prayer"—or such at all events is the implication; while Luke (9:43) deletes the private conversation in its entirety. While this critical procedure appears to me to be too drastic, it serves at all events to indicate how tenuous must be any endeavor to support such a Jewish practice as fasting from Jesus' teaching. The most that can be said for it is to be found in Matt. 6:16-18 (M), where our Lord appears to anticipate that his disciples will fast and is concerned merely to suggest that it be done with sincerity of motive rather than in a spirit of religious exhibitionism. Such teaching is in accord with his general attitude on the cultivation of a right religious spirit and more especially with his refusal to legislate against the

[41] The words are omitted by codices Vaticanus and Sinaiticus, as well as by the Old African Latin text k, by the Georgian version, and by Clement of Alexandria.

[42] Cf. Branscomb, Mark (Moffatt series), in loc.; though even Dibelius here appears to accept the private conversation as at least partly genuine. See his Message, pp. 100-101, 166.

customs of the Judaism of his day as though these were wrong or unworthy in themselves.

The Lord's Supper

It is a mistake to conceive of the Communion of the Lord's Supper in terms of Jesus' adoption of the priestly ritual of sacrifice. The Roman doctrine of transubstantiation explicitly subscribes to such a view, as does every other teaching, implicitly at any rate, which holds that the minister as he administers the sacrament is functioning as a priest.

If it could be proved that the Lord's Supper was merely the Passover rite taken over by our Lord and, so to speak, given a Christian baptism, then the theory that it is to be given a priestly interpretation would gain somewhat in credence. The inference, however, does not necessarily follow even in that contingency. But it is by no means certain that the Passover is the proper antecedent of the Christian Communion service. Oesterley's view that its precursor is rather the Qiddūsh ceremony appears to be gaining ground among biblical scholars.[43] And be it noted that ceremony has no priestly support whatever, either in Scripture or in doctrinal significance.

In either case there can be little doubt, if any, that our Lord's view of the Supper was *prophetic* in nature, and not priestly. As he initially observed it and in its essential meaning wherever it was repeated by the primitive church, it was a symbol or acted parable after the fashion of those we have seen the prophets employ.[44] "This is my body"; "this is my blood of the covenant"—these sayings cannot be other than metaphorical as originally employed by our Lord. His interest in adopting the rite, accordingly, must have been that it might serve as a vehicle for pointing to a spiritual reality transcending itself.

The only element of a priestly character which may be conceded

[43] *The Jewish Background of the Christian Liturgy*, pp. 172 ff.
[44] See above, pp. 68-69.

to attach to the sacrament is its *bare form as a rite*; and this conces-
sion, be it noted, depends upon the assumption that our Lord intended the perpetuation of the meal. If the view that he commanded his disciples to baptize and to observe the Communion supper is correct, then obviously he ordained two rites which, so far as
their *form as rites* only is concerned, were of priestly nature. In
view of the uncertain state of the evidence, New Testament scholars
generally are unprepared to pronounce judgment in favor of Jesus'
having so commanded his disciples. Obviously, therefore, a doctrine
of the nature of the Lord's Supper depending on a command which
cannot be certainly warranted is very precarious indeed. It is far
more likely, one imagines, that Professor Dillistone is correct in
writing:

The breaking of the bread was simply a continuation of the common
meals which the disciples had been accustomed to take in the presence
of their Master Who had blessed and broken the bread in a way which
none other had ever done and Whose Presence, therefore, they still
felt to be overwhelmingly real in their midst.[45]

That is to say, from the first the meal was conceived as one of real
fellowship enjoyed by those belonging to Jesus' *chabūrāh* or "fra-
ternity," whence it came to be called in the Greek κοινωνία, "fellowship" or "communion," the proper translation of the Hebrew
word. Our Lord on this view would have intended its perpetuation,
not for its own sake as an efficacious rite after the priestly pattern,
but because it served to remind the disciples of, and further to
cement, the fellowship whose visible expression it was. But its
value as a memorial would have more weight even than this, for
as Professor Dillistone goes on to point out:

Gradually, however, the breaking of the bread tended to become a
specially solemn repetition of what had happened on the night of the
Last Supper, and within the general meal, or following upon it, there

---

[45] *Continuing Stedfastly*, p. 56.

came to be an intense focussing of attention upon the actions with the bread and the wine which recalled all that Jesus had accomplished through His Suffering and Death and Resurrection.[46]

That is to say, to the original idea of fellowship of Christian brethren the Communion service took on the added thought of fellowship with the Lord in his passion. And thus the two teachings of the apostle Paul relative to the Lord's Supper would find in it clear expression: "The cup of blessing which we bless, is it not a communion of the blood of Christ? The bread which we break, is it not a communion of the body of Christ?" (I Cor. 10:16, where, as usual with Paul, "the body of Christ" means the Christian Church).

If this interpretation of its origin and significance is correct, then it would appear that our Lord in instituting the Lord's Supper did a unique thing: he took a rite—which in its mere form as rite, though not in its historical antecedents and certainly not in its teaching content, might deserve to be catalogued as priestly—and made of it the symbol of prophetic teaching, so that thereby it became the vehicle of the prophetic word to man. Luther was therefore right when he remarked of it that where the word fails to be heard in and through the Lord's Supper, it is no true sacrament. For its only *raison d'être* is that the prophetic word may be heard through and in it.[47]

It is not, then, as first officiant at his own table that our Lord deserves the title of "priest." As he reclines at that table and administers the bread and wine, he does so as the final and greatest of the prophets—as the Incarnate Word itself, which, having at the first been heard through them, is now present as prophet among his people. Nor are those who throughout the centuries administer the elements at the Lord's table thereby constituted priests. Their ministry at his table is, like his, a prophetic one, even as the rite

[46] *Ibid.*
[47] What is said here of the Lord's Supper may also in large part (and certainly in principle) be repeated relative to the sacrament of baptism.

which they perform points to a true and genuine sacrifice far transcending in spiritual efficacy any "value" residing in the elements which they administer.

Our Lord is, indeed, the great High Priest of his people, not because he instituted any rite similar to those at which the Old Testament priests officiated, but because quite unlike them and all their sacrifices he offered himself as a free personality for the sin of the world.[48] Similarly his people, and not alone the clergy of the church, constitute a "kingdom of priests" in so far as with him they share in his self-immolation for the salvation of the people of God.[49] But in choosing this way of self-sacrifice our Lord was following in the way, not of the Old Testament priesthood, but, as the church of the New Testament saw from the beginning, of the prophetic figure of the Suffering Servant of Deutero-Isaiah.[50] In fine, our Lord's sacrifice on Calvary—his one priestly act under the new covenant—found its exemplar and its motivation, not in the Priestly Code, but in the prophetic word of the old.

[48] Mark 9:30-32; Heb. 9:13-14.
[49] I Pet. 2:9; Rev. 1:6; Col. 1:19-23.
[50] This is the theme of W. Manson, *Jesus the Messiah*, and of my own *Intention of Jesus*.

JESUS and
THE RELIGION of the BOOK

Synopsis

Chapter 7:—The scribal religion of the book was the second religious response formulated in postexilic Judaism. The scribe's AUTHORITY for his sincere endeavor to take the divine Torah seriously and to implement it in life situations was TRADITION, which he held went back to Moses, the giver of both written and oral Torah. The METHOD of applying Torah to life involved the use of CASUISTRY, a system for resolving real and apparent conflicts within Torah itself. The obvious PRODUCT of such a method was a series of LAWS, and man's life in practice was reduced to the observance of ordinances held sacred, having the divine sanction. The scribe's characteristic INSTITUTION was the SYNAGOGUE, in which the Torah was expounded to the people.

Chapter 8:—The scribe's stress on Torah was carried out to its logical conclusion, namely, the near-deifying of the book. So OBEDIENCE to the book became the test of a man's SALVATION; and as the book was the possession of one people, incorporation into that people became the *sine qua non* of obedience to it. The characteristic doctrine of Pharisaism relating to salvation was that of the RESURRECTION of the dead.

Chapter 9:—Numerous points of similarity are observable between Jesus and the scribes. He, however, did not share their artificial view of Scripture, their adherence to a "conduct pattern," their interest in religious institutions for their own sake, their nationalistic particularism, their materialistic doctrine of the resurrection. His views on all these topics were prophetic in character.

CHAPTER

7

The Religion of the Book

LOUIS FINKELSTEIN has sug-
gested that the scribe should be reckoned as in direct line with and
heir of the prophet of Israel.[1] Indeed, he finds this line to pass suc-
cessively through Hebrew prophetism, Pharisaism, and modern
Judaism; and he sees moreover no great difference in principle between these three and what he describes as definitive Christianity, a
good example of which he finds in Puritanism. This would mean in
effect that the religion of the book was the normative outgrowth and
proper expression of the prophetic word. It would mean that of the
three popular religions which followed upon and endeavored to implement that word—those of altar, book, and throne—that of the
book should be given the preference as the one and only legitimate
effort at such implementation.

But this cannot be granted, not at any rate apart from thorough
investigation of the three religions in the light of the prophetic
word. For each of these religions made a sincere effort to realize in
human experience the claims of the divine word upon the life
of man. The scribe's major stress was upon the doctrine of the
sovereignty of God and the imperative necessity that man acknowledge this sovereignty.[2] And this was without doubt a proper pro-

[1] *The Pharisees*, I, xvi-xxi.　　　　　[2] M. Berakot 2:2, 5.

139

phetic emphasis. In this unilateral creed the scribe showed himself to be in the direct line of the Hebrew tradition, therefore, and scribism or rabbinism to be one possible direction in which the "faith of the fathers" could be developed. But this is far from saying that the scribal development was the only possible direction that religion could legitimately have taken or even that it was the direction which the prophets themselves would have wished it to take.

The scribe, alas, while no doubt sincerely attempting to put the prophetic word in its rightful place, somehow succeeded only in atomizing what had been one word into a thousand kaleidoscopic and essentially disrelated fragments. He changed the word religion of the prophets into a book religion, into a religion of laws rather than of Law, of words rather than the Word, of the "traditions of men" in place of the Torah of God.

Our sources for the history and teachings of the religion of the book are: (1) Ezra-Nehemiah, I and II Chronicles, and the Gospels and Paul within the canonical scriptures; (2) the apocryphal literature of the Old Testament, particularly I Maccabees, IV Esdras, and Ecclesiasticus; and (3) the Targums, the Mishnah, and the Jerusalem and Babylonian Talmuds.[3] These sources recount the beginnings of the scribal movement in several ways. There is, for example, a famous passage in the Mishnah which reads:

> Moses received the Law [i.e., "oral law," so Danby] from Sinai and committed it to Joshua, and Joshua to the elders, and the elders to the Prophets; and the Prophets committed it to the men of the Great Synagogue. (M. Aboth 1:1a.)

The purport of this statement is generally understood to be that the scribal movement goes back in origin to Moses and that its direct antecedents were, as Finkelstein holds, the prophets. And the implication not to be overlooked will be: the Mishnah, under

[3] This last group must be used with caution because of the late date of most of it. Josephus and Philo are also of some assistance in this field.

140

the garb of pseudonimity after the manner of the apocalyptists, would assure for its traditions the prestige which normally attaches to the names of the ancient fathers ('abōth).

It is, however, more in accord with the facts of history to date the beginnings of the scribal movement from the group which is here termed "the men of the Great Synagogue." [4] By this group the Mishnah intends the traditional "one hundred and twenty elders" who are supposed to have come back from exile along with Ezra.[5] During the exile the home of orthodox Judaism had been, of course, Babylonia; and when with the restoration of the walls of Jerusalem by Nehemiah (444 B.C.) it became possible for Jews to return to their native land, the first consideration of Babylonian Jewry was to transplant its interpretation of the Jewish religion and culture to the homeland. This was done under the leadership of Ezra (397 B.C.), the first worthy in the Hebrew tradition to be given the title of "scribe" (Ezra 7:6), if the apocryphal Enoch is excepted.[6] Ezra was priest as well as scribe, and he thus represented a striking, but by no means exceptional, combination of the religions of book and altar. His major interest is stated thus: "For Ezra had set his heart to seek the law of the Lord, and to do it, and to teach in Israel statutes and ordinances." (Ezra 7:10). There can be no doubt that here the central motivation of his life is recorded. The sequel indicates, however, that it was more especially with the ritual or ceremonial elements of the Law that Ezra concerned himself, and here his priestly connections assert themselves.[7]

With the arrival of Ezra and his associates in Jerusalem the scribal movement may be said to have become firmly established in the Jewish homeland. Thereafter its evolution proceeded apace, no doubt much after the manner outlined in the Pirke Aboth,

[4] Oesterley, History, II, 129.
[5] Danby, Mishnah, p. 446, n. 5.
[6] The apocryphal Baruch should also be excepted perhaps.
[7] Examples of Ezra's priestly interests are: the observance of the Sabbath (Neh. 9:14), the keeping of the set feasts (Neh. 8:13-18), abstinence from polluting contact with the surrounding pagan peoples in Palestine (Ezra 9–10), and the maintenance of the temple worship (Ezra 8:24-30).

where it is shown to have developed a variety of groups or schools with their varying emphases and interests. Eventually one of these, the Pharisees, attained the dignity of a sect or party in the days of the Maccabean struggle under the priest-king Jonathan.[8] This party in the end succeeded in capturing the scribal movement, and by the time of our Lord the terms "scribe," "scribe of the Pharisees," and to a limited extent "rabbi" were nearly, if not quite, identical.[9]

The Scribal Authority—Tradition

The endeavor of the Pharisaic rabbi was to apply the written Torah to the life situation of his day—an admirable attempt on the part of one who believed that Torah was God's last word to man for guidance in the minutest details of his life. As stated in the words of the "men of the Great Synagogue," this aim was the same as to "make a fence around the Law" (M. Aboth 1:1). That is to say, the true function of the scribe was to draft such a series of regulations in the spirit of one and another of the ordinances of the Law that would make it possible for the latter to function in the contemporary historical situation. These interpreters of the Law were therefore in a real sense legislators, and their product, the oral Torah as codified in Mishnah and Talmud, stood to the written Torah (Pentateuch) as statutory is related to constitutional law. In this way the rabbi succeeded in making the Torah livable in each succeeding age, if he did not actually alleviate its severity and lessen the burden of its "yoke." [10]

The authority which the scribe claimed for applying the written Torah as he did was the sanction of tradition. I have already alluded to the traditional account of the origin and transmission of the

[8] Cf. Josephus *Antiquities* XIII. x. 5; Oesterley, *op. cit.*, II, 282.
[9] Cf. Mark 2:6 and 16; Luke 5:17 and 30. Luke alone (vs. 17) speaks of them also as "doctors of the law" ($\nu o\mu o\delta\iota\delta\acute{a}\sigma\kappa\alpha\lambda o\iota$), a proper equivalent of the title "rabbi." A rabbi was one trained in the highest learning of the law and so considerably above the average "scribe"; the relation might well be expressed by our terms "professor" for "rabbi" and "teacher" for "scribe."
[10] Cf. M. Berakoth 2:2.

oral Torah (Mishnah) as found in the Pirke Aboth.[11] The intent of that tractate, as indeed of the entire Mishnah, was to trace the "traditions of the elders" back to Moses, their ultimate authority. The oral tradition was supposed to have been handed down from generation to generation along with the written Torah, and both were ascribed, therefore, in their entirety to Moses.

The ex-cathedra sayings of the rabbis who formed living links in this traditional chain were accorded equal reverence with the written Torah. Indeed, in one passage in the Mishnah the claim is made that "greater stringency applies to [the observance of] the words of the Scribes than to [the observance of] the words of the [written] Law." [12] This claim is quite intelligible on the assumption of the truth of the myth of tradition and when we note the relevant character of the Mishnaic ordinances to life situations. It is just another way of saying that statutory law sits nearer to the life of the average citizen of any state than that state's constitutional law. As Canon Danby remarks:

Inevitably the inference follows that the living tradition (the Oral Law) is more important than the Written Law, since the "traditions of the elders," besides claiming an authority and continuity equal to that of the Written Law, claim also to be its authentic and living interpretation and its essential complement.[13]

In the course of the transmission of the Mishnaic tradition resort was had to a sort of "case decision" or precedent like that which has a formative effect in the development of all statutory law. An interesting example of this occurred in the matter of the waving of the *lulab* or "bunch of palm-, myrtle-, and willow-branches" at the Feast of Tabernacles.[14] The Mishnah reads:

And when do they shake the *Lulab*? At the beginning and the end of the Psalm *O give thanks unto the Lord*, and at *Save now, we beseech*

[11] Above, pp. 140-41.
[12] M. Sanhedrin 11:3.
[13] *The Mishnah*, p. xvii.
[14] The definition is that of Canon Danby, *op. cit.*, p. 176, note 12.

thee, O Lord. So the School of Hillel. The School of Shammai say: Also at *O Lord, we beseech thee, send now prosperity.* R. Akiba said: "I once watched Rabban Gamaliel and R. Joshua, and while all the people were shaking their *Lulabs,* they shook them only at *Save now, we beseech thee O Lord.* (M. Sukkah 3:9.)

Practice in doubtful matters was often settled in this way by appeal to the decision of a well-known rabbi. Such a decision was called *halākhāh* (*hālakh,* to walk), that is, guidance for the way to conduct oneself in the situation involved. The Mishnah, then, is in reality the totality of the rabbinic *halākhōth* or decisions on how to act under the infinite variety of circumstances which had been considered by the rabbis.

A difficulty arose when different rabbis had made opposing pronouncements on a point. As time went on, such divergent opinions became common, and both Mishnah and Talmud are full of them. The most famous series of such differing judgments was that ascribed to Hillel and Shammai and their schools of disciples.[15] In the end the myth of tradition was unable to maintain itself in the face of so many conflicting *halākhōth,* and an end was put to such disputations, so far as the two major schools were concerned at any rate, by a *bat qōl* or echo of the divine voice which was said to have been heard at the Rabbinical College at Jamnia (or Jabneh) and which declared: "The teachings of both schools are words of the Living God, but in practice the Halakah of the school of Hillel is to be followed." [16]

The Scribal Technique—Casuistry

The method employed by the scribes in applying the written Torah to life situations—that is, in constructing the Mishnah or statutory law—is termed casuistry. This is a technique directed to the resolution of the tension created by conflicting, or apparently

---

[15] Cf. M. Berakot 1:3; 8:1-8 *et passim.*   [16] Cf. Moore, *op. cit.,* I, 85.

conflicting, duties, and the motive which prompts its use is the laudable one of the maintenance and workability of law. It is an undoubted necessity in a legalistic system like Pharisaism which takes the commands of Deity seriously and endeavors to obey them literally.

An example will serve to make this plain. The fourth commandment of the Decalogue forbade "work" on the Sabbath day. "Six days shalt thou labor, and do all thy work; but the seventh day is a sabbath unto the Lord thy God: in it thou shalt not do any work." (Exod. 20:9-10.) It is obvious that this commandment can be interpreted so literally as to preclude the possibility of every sort of human activity on the Sabbath. Even the exertion required for a man to quit his bed might be interpreted as "work," and in consequence he would be forced to remain abed the entire day. Or, inasmuch as the Jewish Sabbath began at dusk, he could be made to stop in his tracks wherever he was and under whatever circumstance. The word "work" therefore required definition that life on the Sabbath might not be reduced to the monotony of mere existence.

Accordingly two books of the Mishnah, Shabbath and Erubin, were devoted to a minute definition of what constitutes work. This was said to embrace thirty-nine categories, such as sowing, threshing, baking, shearing wool, weaving, writing two letters (characters of the alphabet), hunting a gazelle, lighting a fire, and the like—employments reflecting the agricultural and pastoral pursuits and village trades in practice at the time the Mishnah was committed to writing (A.D. 200).[17]

A general rule which was applied in numerous cases was: any man who should *completely* perform an act involving physical effort of any sort should be adjudged a transgressor of the Sabbath law. If, however, in conjunction with another he performed *a part*

[17] M. Shabbath 7:2.

only of such act, then neither he nor his confederate should be considered a transgressor.[18] Another rule intended to serve in cases of illness or accident read: "Whenever there is doubt whether life is in danger this overrides the Sabbath" (M. Yoma 8:6). Still a third dictum of a general character was credited to Rabbi Akiba (d. A.D. 135) to the effect that "any act of work that can be done on the eve of Sabbath does not override the Sabbath, but what cannot be done on the eve of Sabbath overrides the Sabbath" (M. Shabbath 19:1b).

The application of these rules and many others of like nature made it possible to carry on to a degree a normal life on the Sabbath day; and this, be it noted, was the rabbinic intent in the elaboration of the Law. Thus circumcision (M. Shab. 19:2), the duties of the midwife at childbirth (18:3), the anointing of the dead (23:5), the moving about of furniture within the house (17:1-2), and the maintenance of cooked food warm for eating on the Sabbath (3:1 ff.)—these and like services were all permissible. The completion of an act, however, which could well enough await the morrow after the Sabbath was adjudged a transgression. Such acts included even the lighting of a lamp (2:7), the placing of an egg "beside a kettle" with a view to its being cooked (3:3), the removal of food or other stored materials from a granary or warehouse (7:3), and the use of "wine or vinegar" to heal a wound (14:4). One famous passage reads:

They may not go down to Kordima[19] [i.e., on the Sabbath], and they may not use artificial emetics; they may not straighten a [deformed] child's back or set a broken limb. If a man's hand or foot is dislocated, he may not pour cold water over it, but he may wash it after his usual fashion, and if he is healed, he is healed." (M. Shab. 22:6.)

---

[18] M. Shabbath 1:1. The example of the "poor man" or beggar is employed here. In putting his hand in the door of his benefactor he must be careful not to take the alms from the other's hand, who in turn in reaching out to him must not place it in the hand of the beggar, thus in either case performing a complete act.

[19] Of doubtful meaning, but the prohibition was "because of the danger of persons falling into the water and afterwards squeezing out their clothes" on the Sabbath. So Danby, *op. cit.*, p. 119, n. 12.

Locomotion on the Sabbath presented a series of problems to the rabbi for two reasons. In the first place, there was the command of Exod. 16:29: "Let no man go out of his place on the seventh day." " 'To go out' " was interpreted by the rabbis "to imply also 'carrying a burden' (Jer. 17:22) from one domain (e.g., a private house) into another (e.g., a public thoroughfare or another private house)." [20] In a country like Palestine accustomed to hot nights in the summer months in some districts, it could constitute a real hardship not to be able to carry one's cot out of the stuffy, generally windowless house into the common court or lane upon which the house faced. In the second place, the Law stipulated that a man should not travel farther than two thousand cubits on the Sabbath day.[21] But suppose a man had two duties to perform, both legitimate on the Sabbath day and in two cities or towns separated by more than the legal two thousand cubits (or three thousand feet). This could readily happen in the case of the rabbi himself or in that of the priest performing his "course" in the temple at Jerusalem.[22]

To cover both these sets of problems a system known as erub (fusion, i.e., of certain limits) was evolved. On Friday afternoon one was permitted to deposit a cache of food amounting to two ordinary meals per individual concerned, within a radius of two thousand cubits in the latter case, or within the coveted courtyard or alley in the former. By this means a man could establish his residence or better "fuse" the limits of the new area with those of the old, so on the Sabbath day he was allowed access to the extended domain thus brought under his purview.

These examples will serve to illustrate the application of the rabbinical technique of casuistry to the Pentateuchal laws. It had been worked out with a meticulous care for details over a period of

[20] So Danby, op. cit., p. 100, n. 2.
[21] Cf. Num. 35:5.
[22] Various contingencies are discussed in M. Erubin 4.

several hundred years before its final codification in the Mishnah by Yahudah ha Nasi in A.D. 200.[23]

The Scribal Product—Law

The rabbi believed the whole of the Law to be "from Heaven" (M. Sanh. 10:1) and the entire volume of scripture to be inspired.[24] All, therefore, must be obeyed with equal zeal. This belief produced an unmistakably legalistic attitude toward all matters pertaining to God (religion), human relations (ethics), and the conduct of human life generally. The whole of life, and not simply the portion to which we are accustomed to attach the name of "religion," therefore was to be regulated by the Mishnaic laws, which as we have seen were merely so many attempts to interpret and apply the written Torah to the demands of daily living.

To this end the Mishnah was divided into six parts, each of which was devoted to the application of some phase of the Law to the requirements of pious living. In the first of these (Zeraim) were given regulations for private and family devotions, and for the proper tithing of one's substance and the method of giving alms to the poor—i.e., for prayer, alms, and fasting, the three major duties of the pious Jew according to Pharisaic teaching.[25] Each of these duties had its appropriate halākhāh or rule of guidance provided by the rabbis. The Shema', the nearest approach to a creedal statement in Judaism, was to be recited twice daily—in the morning "so soon as one can distinguish between blue and white . . . , and it should be finished before sunrise" (M. Ber. 1:2), in the evening from sunset "until the end of the first watch" (9 or 10 P.M.; M. Ber. 1:1). The Tefillah or daily prayer was to be said three times—in the

[23] C. C. McCown has a discerning statement regarding modern Jewish sensibilities on the subject of criticism of the Pharisees. "But all religions," he writes, "including modern Christianity, sooner or later develop people of exactly the character ascribed to the Pharisees in the Gospels." (Search, p. 139.)

[24] The scribal statement was that the Scriptures "render the hands unclean," a phrase of doubtful origin but certainly referring to divine inspiration as employed in Mishnah and Talmud; cf. M. Yadaim 4:5-6.

[25] Cf. Matt. 6:1-18.

morning "any time until midday," in the afternoon "until sunset," and in the evening at any time (M. Ber. 4:1). Moreover, the posture, attention, and general manner to be followed in saying both Shema' and Tefillah were closely described (M. Ber. 2:1-8; 4:1-5: 5). M. Ber. 5:1 is typical:

None may stand up to say the Tefillah save in sober mood. The pious men of old used to wait an hour before they said the Tefillah, that they might direct their heart toward God. Even if the king salutes a man he may not return the greeting; and even if a snake was twisted around his heel he may not interrupt his prayer.

Alms and tithes were discussed together, and relevant halakhoth given in M. Peah 8:1 ff., Demai 3:1, and elsewhere. Regulations for both the private and public observance of the great feasts and fasts were minutely set forth in M. Moed, the second of the six general sections into which the work was divided.

The third section of the Mishnah (Nashim) was devoted to matters in any way related to women—thus, the law of the Ketubah or marriage deed with its dowry (M. Ket. 1 ff.), the manner of drafting a bill of divorce (M. Gittin), the rules governing betrothal (M. Kiddushin) and intermarriage (M. Kidd. 4). One entire book in this section (M. Nedarim) is given over to a discussion of vows in general—the manner of assuming them, their validity, their binding character, and the way of securing release from them; a second book here gives detailed information regarding the vow of the Nazarite in elaboration of Num. 6:1-21 (M. Nazir).

In section four the laws pertaining to the trial of civil and criminal cases are elaborated with considerable attention to detail (M. Nezikin). Here are to be found ordinances regarding man's duty to his neighbor in matters of restitution of stolen or destroyed property (M. Baba Kamma 7:1–10:10), of injury caused by either man or beast (M. Baba Kamma 1:1–6:6), of hired service (M. Baba Metzia 7:1-11), of loans and usury (M. Baba Metzia 3:1–5:11), and of bequests and inheritance (M. Baba Bathra 8:1–10:8). The great

149

tractate M. Sanhedrin also includes the proper procedure for the trial of all cases coming under the jurisdiction of the three "sanhedrins," severally of three, of twenty-three, and of seventy (-one) members.[26]

The last two sections of the Mishnah (M. Kodashim and Tohoroth) dealt respectively with the manner of presenting the various offerings required in the service of the temple and the laws of "clean and unclean." From these examples it will be seen that no single aspect of the life of a Jew was overlooked in the regulations to be found in the Pharisaic traditions. It would be fallacious, of course, to deny that the rabbis experienced occasional flashes of moral or spiritual insight which transcended the generally legalistic view of life entailed in this code. One of these occurs in M. Ber. 2:2, where in the midst of a discussion relating to the proper method of repeating the Shema', R. Joshua ben Karha (A.D. 140-65) suggests that the norm for the order of the recitation of the first two of its three sections is ordained, "so that a man may first take upon him the yoke of the kingdom of heaven and afterward take upon him the yoke of the commandments." That is to say, it is useless to suggest that a man should obey certain specific commands of the legal code until he has first made a genuine commitment of himself to God as the sole Lord of his life.

Another such flash of insight occurs in the delightful story of Rabban Gamaliel II (ca. A.D. 100), who was in all probability the grandson of the teacher of the apostle Paul. I quote it as it appears in M. Ber. 2:5:

Once when Rabban Gamaliel married he recited the Shema' on the first night. His disciples said to him, "Master, didst thou not teach us that a bridegroom is exempt from reciting the Shema' on the first night?" He said to them, "I will not hearken to you to cast off the yoke of the kingdom of heaven even for a moment!"

[26] It is, of course, difficult to determine how much of this legislation antedates the first destruction of Jerusalem in A.D. 70; cf. Moore, op. cit., I, 130-31; also Danby, op. cit., pp. xxi-xxii.

But such insights were rare. Claude G. Montefiore was undoubtedly right in remarking that the scribes lacked the "capacity to distinguish between the great and the little, between the solemn and the trivial" and that "their teaching seems so childish and so absurd" on the whole.[27]

The more common attitude on the part of the rabbis toward moral and spiritual problems alike was the thoroughly legalistic one exemplified in the dispute between the followers of Hillel and those of Shammai over the question of divorce. I quote:

The School of Shammai say: A man may not divorce his wife unless he has found unchastity in her, for it is written, *Because he hath found in her indecency in anything*. And the school of Hillel say: [He may divorce her] even if she spoiled a dish for him, for it is written, *Because he hath found in her indecency* in anything." (M. Gittin 9:10.)

It will be seen that both schools appealed in the course of this discussion to the same passage of scripture (Deut. 24:1); both used the same literal method of interpretation of this passage; and both were concerned in the last analysis to find a way of applying the written Torah as the basis of current Jewish practice.

The Scribal Institution—The Synagogue

The center of scribal influence from Ezra forward was the synagogue with its worship and educational programs. This typical institution of the later Jewish cultural life was probably developed in Babylonia during the exile and at a time when the Jews were severed from the homeland and its temple services.[28] It was admirably adapted to the promotion of the scribe's central thesis that life was to be lived by the dicta of a book. The ark in which the Scriptures were kept and the bema from which they were read constituted the center of interest and attraction in the building, even as the reading of the book and the address based on the lesson

---

[27] *Old Testament and After*, p. 298.   [28] See Oesterley, *op. cit.*, II, 137-38.

for the day were the focal points round which the worship service revolved.[29]

Rabbi Jacob Mann has shown that from the earliest times—certainly, he thinks, before the destruction of Jerusalem in A.D. 70—the lesson read from the Prophets and the address given by the preacher for the day were both required to take their cue in some fashion from the reading appointed from the Torah (Pentateuch).[30] Thus the Torah under scribal influence became the focal point for the Jewish worship service during the period of the second temple. This unique reverence for the Law was also manifest in the custom, dating no doubt from the time of Ezra (Neh. 8:4-5), for both the reader and the people to stand as it was read. The Mishnah is witness to this custom as regards the high priest on the day of Atonement (M. Yoma 7:1), the king on the "first festival day of the Feast (of Tabernacles)" (M. Sotah 7:8), and the reader in the usual synagogue service (M. Meg. 4:1). Agrippa I was particularly commended for his reverence as displayed in his standing as he read the Torah.[31] The same peculiar reverence for the Law was also intended in the rubric at M. Meg. 4:4 which refers to the reading of the Law in the synagogue: "He that reads in the Law may . . . not read to the interpreter more than one verse"—that is, at a time, lest the latter forget to translate exactly as it was read. And again with the same intent: "They may leave out verses in the Prophets, but not in the Law."

When the elementary school appeared in Jewish circles (at an indeterminate date[32]), it was attached to the synagogue and became known as the Beth ha Sefer, or House of the Book, from the fact that the Scriptures in Hebrew and more especially the Law were made the textbook. The secondary school equally took its name from its association with the Scriptures, being termed the

---

[29] Cf. M. Meg. 4:1 ff.; Luke 4:16-20.
[30] The Bible as Read and Preached in the Old Synagogue, Vol. I; the thesis of the book as a whole and all the Seders illustrate the point.
[31] M. Sotah 7:8.
[32] See Moore, op. cit., I, 316.

Beth ha Midrash (House of Interpretation), and it likewise was attached to the local synagogue wherever it existed.[33]

The whole life of the synagogue, therefore, was organized about the book. Both its worship services and its educational program were so fashioned as to be focused upon the latter's teachings. And so far as the scribe was able to accomplish his purpose, the divine Torah was made the center of the people's communal life.

[33] *Ibid.* p. 314.

CHAPTER

8

The Scribes Sit on Moses' Seat

THE history of religion shows that the tendency is almost, if not quite, universal for man to make his own "god." This may be done by fashioning a god after man's "own image" or "in the likeness" of any creature. It may also be done by separating one attribute of the true and living God from the rest of his being as a whole and molding that one characteristic into a new "god."

This latter was the scribe's peculiar fault. He accepted wholeheartedly and built his entire religious teaching upon the prophetic doctrine of the sovereignty of God. Taking his start with this teaching, the Pharisee or his rabbinic mentor made the divine lordship, or the divine will or law—or even the book containing that law, which he identified with it in the most thoroughgoing manner —his "god." Unconsciously no doubt, but the more truly therefore, he deified the book. Men's words in which the word of God was written down became identical with that word in every particular. The former were as they stood in their every "jot and tittle," every phrase and syllable, the inspired word of God.[1] In consequence it becomes intelligible that the scribe felt impelled to develop a literalistic method of exegesis and a meticulous sort of casuistry to deal

[1] M. Sanh. 10:1; cf. Moore, op. cit., I, 239 and his well-considered references.

154

with scripture.[2] This was the only possible recourse of one who took seriously the identification to which reference has been made.

The Pharisaic Doctrine of the Law

The rabbis made their rigid doctrine of inspiration and its acceptance the test of a man's salvation. Whoever should say "that the Law is not from Heaven" has "no share in the world to come" (M. Sanh. 10:1)—such was their teaching. This doctrine and this test, be it remarked, were applied to both oral and written Torah (Mishnah and Pentateuch) alike in accordance with the dictum already cited: "Greater stringency applies to [the observance of] the words of the Scribes than to [the observance of] the words of the [written] Law" (M. Sanh. 11:3).

After the Council of Jamnia (A.D. 90), which finally pronounced the Old Testament canon closed and declared its contents, it became possible to apply this test in a quite rigid manner. Even the reading of the books excluded from the canon became a mark of heresy, as Rabbi Akiba's saying suggests, "He that reads the heretical books [has] no share in the world to come." (M. Sanh. 10:1.) The forbidden books to which Akiba refers probably included both the New Testament literature and the apocalyptic writings produced within both Christian and Jewish circles, the latter by Akiba's day (d. A.D. 135) having become taboo among the rabbis. In the same spirit and to much the same intent a contemporary of Akiba, R. Eleazar of Modiim by name, declared: "If a man . . . discloses meanings in the Law which are not according to the *Halakah*, even though a knowledge of the Law and good works are his, he has no share in the world to come" (M. Aboth 3:12). This pronouncement was intended to stultify all independent exegesis of the Torah which did not follow the lines already laid down in the Mishnah.

It would be easy to multiply quotations from the Mishnah in proof of the high regard paid the divine Torah by the rabbis. Thus R. Yohannan ben Zakkai, who lived through the first destruction of

[2] M. Aboth 3:12 and Danby's notes.

Jerusalem in A.D. 70 and reformed the Sanhedrin at Jamnia after that event, is reported to have said: "If thou hast wrought much in the Law claim not merit for thyself, for to this end wast thou created" (M. Aboth 2:8). Two generations later R. Hananiah ben Teradion remarked: "If two sit together and words of the Law [are spoken] between them, the Divine Presence rests between them"— that is, they become so to speak the cherubim on the Ark of the Covenant supporting the Shekinah (M. Aboth 3:2). His contemporary, R. Simeon ben Yohai, in like fashion taught: "If three have eaten at one table and have not spoken over it words of the Law, it is as though they had eaten of the sacrifices of the dead" (M. Aboth 3:3).

In the end the rabbinism of Mishnah and Talmud—i.e., of the third to fifth centuries A.D.—completely identified the Law with the word of God and so accomplished its apotheosis. Rabbi Akiba, for example, is reported to have taught: "Beloved are Israel . . . , for to them was given the precious instrument . . . by which the world was created, as it is written, *For I give you good doctrine; forsake ye not my Law*" (M. Aboth 3:15). The same thought is implicit in the teaching of R. Hananiah ben Teradion quoted above and can be duplicated in the words of others.[3] The damaging nature of such a deification of the Law, whether written or oral, for the cause of true religion can hardly be overestimated. In the last analysis such teaching resulted in the Law's having an independent and universal authority and reference apart from God himself and his immediate relation to man in particular historic situations. Its ultimate effect, therefore, was to divorce God from human life after the fashion of deism generally, to make the Law a sort of mediator between God and man, and to leave no room for the contact of human spirit with divine Spirit.

This doctrine of the hypostatized Law was the exact opposite of the Johannine teaching on the Word made flesh, as it was also contrary to the spirit of the prophetic stress upon the constancy

[3] See below, p. 159.

of the word's contact with God's person in the events of creation and revelation.[4] For the point of both these teachings was: the Word of God never became dissociated from the personality of God, whether in eternity, where it was "with God" and "was God"; or in time, where it was one with the incarnate Son, in whom resided the "grace and truth" and the "glory of the Father." [5] This thought will receive further development in chapter 14. For the moment it will be sufficient to note that in the end the religion of the book developed into what was in effect the worship of an impersonal God, namely, the divine law, identified point for point with the divine book.

Legal Righteousness—Salvation by the Book

As the Pharisees kept alive the prophetic doctrine of the sovereignty of God, so to them must be given the credit for an earnest and sincere endeavor, like that of the prophets before them, to see God's will fulfilled among men. R. Judah ben Tema (ca. A.D. 175), for instance, is said to have taught: "Be strong as the leopard and swift as the eagle, fleet as the gazelle and brave as the lion to do the will of thy Father which is in heaven" (M. Aboth 5:20). This is the intent also of R. Joshua ben Karha's truly great saying: "A man may first take upon him the yoke of the kingdom of heaven and afterward take upon him the yoke of the commandments" (M. Ber. 2.2; cf. p. 150). With the author of Deutero-Isaiah the rabbis interpreted salvation in terms of a "righteousness" which God demands of man, though they differed from that writer regarding the source of that righteousness in man and the method of its attainment. When, therefore, they quoted Isa. 58:8, "And thy righteousness shall go before thee; the glory of the Lord shall gather thee [in death]," it was of *particular meritorious works* that they were thinking and not of a *character of goodness* like to God's own and implanted by his Spirit in man (M. Sotah 1:9). And when

[4] Cf. above, pp. 32-33.　　　　[5] Cf. John 1:14.

they uttered the aphorism, "With what measure a man metes it shall be measured to him again" (M. Sotah 1:7; cf. Matt. 7:2), they meant it, as the immediate context and the whole Mishnah make clear, in the sense of a *quid pro quo* ("tit for tat")—i.e., so much goodness, so much reward; or contrariwise, so much infringement of God's law, so much punishment.

There can be no question that, just as the sovereignty of God degenerated in time with the rabbis into the sovereignty of a book, so the thorough "righteousness" God demands of man was displaced by a righteousness made up of the meticulous observance of a series of laws and ordinances. The Pharisee became, so to speak, a sort of ethical behaviorist who interested himself in endeavoring to conform to a peculiar pattern of conduct, in things trivial as well as in the more "weighty matters of the law," and in trying to persuade his fellows to do likewise. A contemporary of the apostles, R. Eleazar ben Azariah (A.D. 50-120), is credited with voicing the usual rabbinical point of view in this matter when he said, "If there is no study of the Law there is no seemly behavior; if there is no seemly behavior there is no study of the Law" (M. Aboth 3:18). And Yahudah ha Nasi, the compiler of the Mishnah, credits himself with the teaching:

Which is the straight way that a man should choose? That which is an honor to him and gets him honor from men. And be heedful of a light precept as of a weighty one, for thou knowest not the recompense of reward of each precept; and reckon the loss through [the fulfilling of] a precept against its reward, and the reward [that comes] from transgression against its loss. Consider three things and thou wilt not fall into the hands of transgression: know what is above thee—a seeing eye and a hearing ear and all thy deeds written in a book. (M. Aboth 2:1.)

As Canon Danby has remarked:

Granted the acceptance of the Written Law as God's will for Israel, Israel's teachers had not the right to determine the relative importance of this or that injunction. Therefore the Oral Law preserves with equal piety customs and decisions arising out of the lightest as out of the "weightiest" precepts of the Law revealed to Israel at Sinai.[6]

It is for this same reason also that the Mishnah and Talmud are concerned with the laws relating to the service of the temple, its offerings and sacrifices, long after it had ceased to exist. From the point of view of the rabbi the relevance of a given law was of no importance, but rather whether God had uttered it or not: this was the direct converse of the prophetic view that God, when he spoke, spoke always to the situation and that it was his speaking to the situation that made his word important for man.

"Righteousness" was thus converted by the rabbi into the doing of particular specific acts, and conversely "sin" became for him the failure to perform those acts.[7] Judah ben Tema taught, for example, that "at thirteen" years of age the Jewish boy was to be thought of as having attained his majority, and he characteristically described that stage in the child's development as his being now ready for "[the fulfilling of] the commandments" (M. Aboth 5:21). Accordingly the two categories of the "righteous" and the "sinners" with which we are familiar from the Gospels stood for those who did and those who did not observe the Pharisaic code as laid down in the "traditions of the elders"—i.e., the as yet unwritten Mishnah. In the Judaism of the Mishnaic period the rabbis and their "associates" (chāberīm)—the Pharisees or others attempting to follow the teachings of the Mishnah—alone were accounted to be "righteous," while the 'ammē hā 'āretz—"ignorant men" who knew not the law (Acts 4:13; cf. M. Aboth 2:6)—were identified with the group called "sinners." The great Hillel in a famous passage in the Mishnah is credited with saying that "an 'am hā 'āretz cannot be saintly" (i.e., righteous), his meaning being that "righteousness" is to be obtained only by following the laws of Torah, both written

---

[6] *Mishnah*, p. xvii.
[7] Cf. Charles, *op. cit.*, II, 496, note on II Bar. 24:1; also Moore, *op. cit.*, I, 498-99.

and oral, which the common man did not know or follow.[8] For such a teacher knowledge was necessary to goodness in the most literal sense of the word.

In this connection it is notable that Paul's remark at Rom. 2:13, "For not the hearers of the law are just before God, but the doers of the law shall be justified," is good Pharisaic doctrine and can be duplicated more than once from sayings in the Mishnah. Thus Simeon ben Gamaliel, a contemporary of Paul and son of his great teacher, R. Gamaliel I, in one of the two teachings recorded in the Mishnah as by him says, "Not the expounding [of the Law] is the chief thing but the doing [of it]" (M. Aboth 1:17).

The reward for this bookish righteousness enjoined by the scribe was "salvation." Such is the intent of the Mishnah throughout, and its achievement constituted the motivation for the latter's production. Rabbi Tarfon (ca. A.D. 130) said in this connection: "If thou hast studied much in the Law much reward will be given thee, and faithful is thy taskmaster who shall pay thee the reward of thy labor. And know that the recompense of the reward of the righteous is for the time to come" (M. Aboth 2:16). There is early evidence for a "treasury of merit" stored up from the superior righteousness of the fathers and upon which their successors could draw if need be. R. Gamaliel III (after A.D. 200) taught: "And let all them that labor with the congregation labor with them for the sake of Heaven, for the merit of their fathers supports them and their righteousness endures for ever. And as for you [will God say], I count you worthy of great reward as though ye [yourselves] had wrought" (M. Aboth 2:2).[9]

The issue of such teaching was bound to be a self-righteousness which considered itself independent of the divine grace. This is not to say, however, that there was consistence at this point in the rabbinic teaching any more than elsewhere. Rabbi Akiba, in a passage in which he is discussing the paradox of predestination and

[8] See M. Aboth 2:6.   [9] Cf. Moore, op. cit., I, 494 ff.

free will, adds that there is another, which he sets forth thus: "And the world is judged by grace, yet all is according to the excess of works [that be good or evil]" (M. Aboth 3:16). This paradox the rabbis were never able to resolve: its final resolution awaited the coming of the gospel with its Redeemer. In the meantime, though they taught that man could not only fulfill the Torah but store up merit quite beyond the strict demands of God, yet there was within their ranks a laudable spirit of self-criticism which is evidence of deep sincerity and genuine piety. There is in the Jerusalem Talmud an admittedly late passage, but one which no doubt reflects the attitude of a much earlier Pharisaism as well, and which divides Pharisees into seven categories. I shall give it with Moore's interpretation. The seven categories are:

The "shoulder Pharisee," who packs his good works on his shoulder (to be seen of men); the "wait-a-bit" Pharisee, who (when someone has business with him) says, Wait a little; I must do a good work; the "reckoning" Pharisee, who when he commits a fault and does a good work crosses off one with the other; the "economizing" Pharisee, who asks, What economy can I practice to spare a little to do a good work? the "show me my fault" Pharisee, who says, Show me what sin I have committed, and I will do an equivalent good work (implying that he had no fault); the Pharisee of fear, like Job; the Pharisee of love, like Abraham.[10]

Of these, the Talmud goes on to say, only the last is acceptable to God.

Corporate Nature of Salvation Under the Torah

Side by side with the doctrine that "righteousness" consisted in the strict observance of the divine Torah as interpreted in the Mishnaic traditions and that its fulfillment would bring merit from God, the Pharisees held as well to the old preprophetic teaching that Israel as such had a unique position of privilege as the "chosen

[10] Op. cit., II, 193.

people" of Yahweh.[11] This paradoxical way of viewing salvation as, on the one hand, an individual experience and, on the other, a national one was never resolved within Pharisaism, any more than the others pertaining to predestination and free will and to grace and good works, to which we have just referred. Typical expression is given to it in M. Sanhedrin 10:1: "All Israelites have a share in the world to come, for it is written, *Thy people also shall be all righteous, they shall inherit the land forever; the branch of my planting, the work of my hands that I may be glorified*" (cf. Isa. 60:21). In the apocalyptic literature of Pharisaic origin, too, it finds a large place. Thus in IV Esdras the nations appear against the Messiah in war (13:34), but he will destroy them with the Law and without resort to battle (vs. 38). Israel alone, therefore, will be saved "when He shall destroy the multitude of the nations that are gathered together" (vs. 49). Ecclesiasticus predicts the eternal duration of the kingdom of God in Israel under David's line (47: 11), while the heathen will be judged (33:1 ff. [Greek text]).

Support for this view could be found, of course, in the Old Testament, and it was one way of interpreting and applying the prophetic teaching of the corporate nature of God's dealings with men.[12] As we have seen, the sense of community was strong in Judaism as a result of the prophetic teaching, and it was obvious that one of the groups into which men were divided was the nation or people. It was equally obvious that God had dealt with Israel in a peculiar way throughout her history from Abraham forward. What was more certain, then, than that the salvation he had to offer should come through attachment to the people of his special choice?

Such particularism had two normal corollaries, both of which the rabbis accepted and stressed: first, to be saved the Gentile must accept the rites of baptism and circumcision and assume the obligations of the Jew which pertained to the worship of the temple and

---

[11] The prophets strenuously objected to this thought. Cf. Amos 3:2; 5:14, 18-19.
[12] See A. G. Hebert, *The Throne of David*, pp. 74 ff.

the laws of "clean and unclean." [13] It is a notable fact that, though circumcision had been practiced in Israel from the earliest times on the testimony of our oldest documentary evidence,[14] yet it was only during the exile that the rite "became the mark of differentiation between Jew and Gentile" and "received a new meaning," accordingly, as a "symbol of purification" and so of entrance into the holy people.[15]

In other words, it was the scribal movement from the time of Ezra onward which, by reason of its doctrine of the peculiarly privileged position of Israel, found it necessary to give the old Semitic rite a new significance relative to the Gentile and his salvation. There is a famous passage in M. Nedarim in which circumcision is praised beyond measure, and there the following lines among others occur: "Rabbi Eleazar ben Aazariah [ca. A.D. 100] says: Hateful is the uncircumcision, whereby the wicked are held up to shame, as it is written, *For all the nations are uncircumcised*" (3:11; cf. II Sam. 1:20). In the same passage R. Yahudah ha Nasi writes in direct opposition to Paul at Rom. 4:11-12: "Great is circumcision for, despite all the religious duties which Abraham our father fulfilled, he was not called 'perfect' until he was circumcised, as it is written, *Walk before me and be thou perfect*" (cf. Gen. 17:1). The Pharisaic Christians generally termed "Judaizers," who gave Paul so much trouble during the course of his labors, are first-rate examples of normative Pharisaism at this point, even as they are both anti-prophetic and anti-Christian in spirit.[16]

Again, the Messiah and the messianic kingdom were conceived wholly along national lines within Pharisaic circles. They took their start for messianic doctrine from Hos. 3:5: "Afterward shall the children of Israel return, and seek the Lord their God, and David their king, and shall come with fear unto the Lord and to his

[13] Jewish *Encyclopedia*, "Proselyte."
[14] Exod. 4:25-26 (J); Josh. 5:2-9 (E?); Gen. 17:9-14.
[15] Exod. 31:12-17; cf. Oesterley, *History*, II, 135-36.
[16] See Gal. 2:14 for the word "Judaize."

goodness in the latter days." [17] This and related passages were interpreted by the scribes to mean that God would bring in the kingdom for his people without man's help. Belief in the doctrine of predestination, which the Pharisees took with utter seriousness, had its effect here also. In open opposition to the Zealots, who from the days of the Maccabees to those of the two wars against Rome in A.D. 70 and 135 were characterized by their fervid nationalism and opposition to the foreign rule in Palestine, they held that God himself would raise up his Messiah and through him would accomplish the salvation of his people from the hand of the oppressor. This did not mean that the Pharisees were unprepared to fight when their religious liberties were jeopardized. They had learned by bitter experience that, if Israel were not to be annihilated wholly, she must be ready to contend at times for the maintenance of her ancestral faith.[18] But to bring in the messianic kingdom was God's sole prerogative, and in his own time he would do it by raising up his Messiah. In the meantime, as the prophets had declared, Israel was being punished for all her sins; let her, therefore, repent and return to Yahweh and keep his Sabbaths, for this alone would avail so far as man was concerned.[19]

The Resurrection of the Dead

The distinctive eschatological doctrine of Pharisaism was the teaching of the resurrection of the dead. Aside from the sporadic interest in apocalyptic which was early developed and as suddenly dropped among the Pharisees, the scribes produced nothing else original in this sphere. Josephus is our authority for the existence of a difference between the Pharisees and Sadducees at this point. The former, he said, held "that all souls are incorruptible," while the latter "[took] away the belief of the immortal duration of the soul." [20] It seems, however, that it is quite impossible for this

---

[17] Cf. also Ezek. 24:23; 37:24-25.
[18] Cf. I Macc. 2.
[19] See Moore, op. cit., II, 350-51 for references.
[20] Antiquities XVIII. i. 3; Jewish War II. viii. 14.

statement to be correct as it stands. It is well known that the Greeks, along with all primitive peoples, accepted the idea of immortality in some guise, and the Sadducees were the Hellenizers among the Jews of the late pre-Christian centuries. It is likely, therefore, that Josephus, writing for Romans as he was, was endeavoring to represent the disputes between the two Jewish parties in terms which he judged would prove intelligible to his readers.

The real dispute between the two sects had to do, as both Gospels and Mishnah bear witness, not with the immortality of the soul, but with the doctrine of the resurrection of the dead, a subject which would have proved quite unintelligible to Josephus' Roman readers.[21] The dictum in M. Sanhedrin 10:1, "And these are they that have no share in the world to come: he that says that there is no resurrection of the dead prescribed in the Law," is evidently a covert criticism of the Sadducaic party and is couched in more accurate terms than those by Josephus. There is in the Mishnah, besides this passage, but one other dealing with the subject. This is found in the "saints' progress" incorporated in M. Sotah 9:15 and attributed to R. Phineas ben Jair (A.D. 165-200) which reads in part, "The Holy Spirit leads to the resurrection of the dead." [22]

George Foot Moore in several illuminating passages has shown that the doctrine of the resurrection of the body was the normal Hebraic teaching, in view of the Semitic doctrine of the integral part the body occupies in the constitution of the personality, just as for the opposite reason the immortality of the soul was the normative pagan teaching.[23] For as is well known, the person in the Semitic view was distributed throughout the body, the "spirit" ($r\bar{u}^a ch$) being the animating principle which gave "life" to every part of the body.[24] Moore therefore comments:

---

[21] M. Sanh. 10:1; Mark 12:18-27; cf. Moore, op. cit., II, 317.

[22] For a like progression, cf. Rom. 5:1 ff.

[23] Op. cit., II, 295, 314, 379, 382-83.

[24] Cf. I Cor. 15:45 for a statement of the Hebrew idea; also Rom. 8:11; also Burrows, op. cit., pp. 134 ff.

The resurrection seems, indeed, so necessarily the consequence of the whole teaching of Scripture concerning the salvation of the righteous and their great reward that it is not strange that the Pharisees found it explicit or by intimation in all parts of the Bible.[25]

Taken together the two passages from the Mishnah above quoted limit the resurrection to Israelites and even within Israel to those revivified by the power of the Holy Spirit. This revivification would await the coming of Elijah, who, according to the Pharisaic hope, was destined to "restore all things" previous to the Messiah's advent.[26] This restoration by Elijah would include the resurrection of those who were to share in the messianic kingdom.[27] Paul, upon his conversion from the Pharisaic viewpoint, significantly displaced both Elijah and Spirit with the risen Christ as the power at work in the resurrection of believers. He, the "last Adam," would be in effect a "life-giving Spirit" and "the first fruits of them that are asleep," so that "in Christ shall all be made alive." [28]

The Pharisaic doctrine of the resurrection was one of the most extreme literalness. It would be a resurrection of the body of the flesh exactly as the latter had lived in this world. Even the garments of the righteous would be renewed and raised along with them, for as Rabbi Meir is quoted as saying, "as a grain of wheat which is buried naked comes forth clad in many garments, how much more the righteous who are buried in their garments!" [29]

Acts 23:8 suggests that the Pharisees and Sadducees disputed over not only the resurrection but the existence of angels and spirits as well. On this point we have very little evidence from early sources.[30] The authentic literature of the Pharisaic movement as distinguished from the works of that wing which went over to the apocalyptic school contains indeed slight evidence of a belief in spirits good and bad (angels and demons). No mention whatever

[25] Op. cit., II, 314.
[26] M. Sotah 9:15.
[27] See Moore, op. cit., II, 384, n. 2, 3, 5.
[28] Cf. I Cor. 15:22, 45.
[29] See Moore, op. cit., II, 381-82.
[30] Ibid., I, 404.

of angels occurs in the Mishnah, either by name or otherwise,[31] and the three references to evil spirits in that book merely cite the popular belief on the subject without comment.[32] The most extended apocryphal reference is found throughout the book of Tobit, where the entire tale hangs on the leading of the angel Rafael provided Tobit for his journey from Babylonia into Medea.[33] With the intrusion of the Iranian influence the apocalyptic literature becomes replete with references to both angels and demons, and extended mention of both occurs in the later rabbinical literature as well.[34] Satan was identified by the later rabbis with the Yētzer hā-Raʿ or "evil impulse" within man.[35] Accordingly it is quite likely that as early as the first Christian century the Pharisees rather generally had accepted more of this apocalyptic doctrine than either Apocrypha or Mishnah bears testimony, whereas the Sadducees undoubtedly resisted such influence as an intrusion without sanction in the written Torah, including the Prophets, both Former and Latter.

[31] *Ibid.*, I, 411, n. 1.
[32] M. Shab 2:5; M. Erub 4:1; M. Aboth 5:6.
[33] See Moore, *op. cit.*, I, 404, n. 7.
[34] See Strack-Billerbeck, *Kommentar zum Neuen Testament aus Talmud und Midrasch*, on Matt. 12:27.
[35] See Moore, *op. cit.*, I, 492.

CHAPTER

9

Jesus and the Scribes

N<small>O ACCOUNT</small> of Jesus' relation to the rabbinical movement within the Judaism of his day would be adequate that did not begin with the observation that there was much common ground between them. How, indeed, could it have been otherwise? Both were the spiritual heirs of the Jewish cultural tradition, of the "religion of the fathers," and particularly of the prophetic revelation from which in the end, as we have seen, every religious movement in Jewish circles stemmed.

Moreover it was possibly in the beth ha sefer attached to the synagogue in Nazareth that Jesus as a lad had learned to read the Hebrew scriptures,[1] and it had been "his custom" from childhood also to attend the corporate worship service in the synagogue on the Sabbath day.[2] Accordingly it was natural for him to begin his ministry in the same center of the religious life of his people.[3] The importance of these facts in the present context lies in this: both the synagogue and the school attached to it had traditionally been under the dominance of the Pharisees and their scribes. Canon Herford therefore is probably correct in suggesting:

The most natural and obvious source for the common teaching [between Jesus and the Rabbis] is the Synagogue. . . . It would be remarkable

[1] Cf. Moore, op. cit., I, 316, and II, 104, n. 92.
[2] Cf. Luke 4:16; Matt. 4:23; Mark 1:39.
[3] Cf. Luke 4:16-20 and Mark 6:1-6.

168

if Jesus and the Jewish teachers, on lines of study pursued quite independently of each other, arrived at results not merely similar but sometimes identical. The teaching which forms the "common ground" has to be accounted for, and also the fact that it was common, taught alike by Jesus and the Pharisees. To assign the Synagogue as the source of it, is a simple and natural explanation, and one that really explains.[4]

The traditional Christian desire to stress the points of opposition between Jesus and the Pharisees is such a prominent feature of the Gospels and later apologists that it will be worth our while to pause a moment and mention some of the items in which they are alike. Among these should be noted the following:

a) Jesus and the scribes often employed the *same religious and ethical terminology*. They spoke, for example, of God as both "King" and "Father," ideas derived from the prophetic literature of their common heritage.[5] Both expressed their devotion to the divine will and plan in terms of the "Kingdom of God (Heaven)," that is, by acknowledging the divine lordship.[6] This term also, of course, goes back originally to the prophets.[7] But the scribal movement of Ezra and his successors had at once enriched and implemented the conception by giving the people a symbol (the Shema') of their acknowledgment of the sovereignty of Yahweh. To pronounce the Shema' morning and evening was to "take up the yoke of the kingdom of heaven." [8] It cannot be accidental, then, that our Lord spoke of the necessity for his disciples to "receive [take up] the kingdom of God [heaven] as a little child." [9]

In addition to numerous other terms common alike to all branches of the Jewish cultural life—such as "repentance," "forgiveness of sins," "salvation," and the like[10]—our Lord also shared

---

[4] *Judaism in the New Testament Period*, pp. 192-93.
[5] See Strack and Billerbeck, *op. cit.*, on Matt. 6:4; M. Sotah 9:15, *et al.*
[6] Cf. *ibid.*, I, 172 ff.; M. Berakot 2:2; M. Yoma 3:8, *et al.*
[7] Cf. Pss. 22:28; 45:6; 103:19; 145:11-13; Obad. 21; Zech. 14:9.
[8] Cf. M. Ber. 2:2.
[9] Mark 10:15.
[10] Cf. Mark 1:15; 2:5 ff.; Luke 19:9 (L); M. Yoma 8:8, 9; and for the origin of these terms such passages as Ps. 106; Joel 2:12-14, *et al.*

with the Pharisees numerous characteristic phrases and modes of expression descriptive of one or another phase of religious experience. These include: "all thy deeds written in a book," [11] "the evil eye," [12] sinning "in secret" and being "requited openly," [13] "lowly in spirit," [14] the hallowing of God's name,[15] "woe to the world," [16] "woe to that man," [17] and "occasions of stumbling," [18] together with many others of like nature.

b) Again, Jesus' aphoristic and parabolic methods of teaching were those not only made familiar by the Hebrew prophets but further elaborated as well by the scribes. Rabbi Meir indeed was so far noted for this method of teaching that it was said, "When Rabbi Meir died, there were no more makers of parables." [19] From the day of Jesus ben Sirah (200 B.C.) the ideal scholar or scribe had been one "well versed in the elusive turns of parables and in making out enigmatical utterances." [20] Many of the rabbis qualified according to this standard; and as Moore remarks, such "epigrammatic sayings" as those composing the Pirke Aboth were "among the most highly appreciated features of homiletic discourse in the synagogue and the school house." [21]

It would be possible here to multiply illustrations almost indefinitely on a wide variety of subjects covering nearly every sort of human interest and all phases of religion and ethics. We shall content ourselves with several examples of singular merit. Thus Rabbi Simeon ben Yohai (A.D. 140-65), when the remark was made in his presence that only "King's children" might "anoint their wounds with rose-oil" on the Sabbath day, coined the aphor-

---

[11] Cf. Luke 10:20 (Q or L?); M. Aboth 2:1.
[12] Cf. Matt. 6:23 (Q); M. Aboth 2:11.
[13] Cf. Matt. 5:4-12 (M); M. Aboth 4:4.
[14] Cf. Luke 6:20 (Q); M. Aboth 4:10.
[15] Cf. Matt. 6:9 (Q); M. Yoma 3:8.
[16] Cf. Strack and Billerbeck, op. cit., I, 778.
[17] Cf. Luke 6:24; M. Aboth 6:2.
[18] Cf. Luke 17:1 (Q); Strack and Billerbeck, op. cit., p. 779.
[19] M. Sotah 9:15; his date was ca. A.D. 140-65.
[20] Ecclus. 39:6; cf. Moore, op. cit., I, 309, n. 5, 310-11.
[21] Ibid., I, 311.

ism, "All Israelites are kings' children!" [22] The great Hillel is reputed to have said on one occasion, "Where there are no men, strive to be a man." [23] Simeon the Just (ca. 280 or 200 B.C.?) taught: "By three things is the world sustained: by the Law, by the [temple] service, and by deeds of lovingkindness," that is, by revelation, by religion, and by social ethics.[24] Rabbi Eleazar ben Shammua (A.D. 140-65) said, "Let the honor of thy disciples be as dear to thee [as thine own and] as the honor of thy companion, and the honor of thy companion as the fear of thy teacher, and the fear of thy teacher as the fear of Heaven." [25] Rabbi Jacob (ca. A.D. 140-65?), who may have been the teacher of the great Yahudah ha Nasi, is said to have taught, "This world is like a vestibule before the world to come: prepare thyself in the vestibule that thou mayest enter into the banqueting hall." [26]

c) It is even more to the point to remark that *the subject matter* of many of Jesus' aphoristic sayings and parables can be nearly, if not quite, duplicated from rabbinic sources. Herford estimates that "parallels can be found in the Rabbinical literature for perhaps as much as 90 per cent of the recorded sayings of Jesus." [27] This appears to me, however, to be an overstatement, or at any rate to convey a wrong impression of the facts. No student of the literature referred to has amassed such a volume of evidence on this subject as Hermann L. Strack and Paul Billerbeck, and one gains the impression from a study of their vast collection of materials that the similarity between Jesus' teaching and that of the rabbis extends in a majority of cases only to the use of the same chance word or phrase or half-sentence, and not to the complete teaching or conception.[28] It is very easy here to be governed by one's prejudices, and I wish merely to sound a word of caution against the overhasty assumption that the similarity generally goes beyond a very striking use of the same terminology to serve diverse ends.

[22] M. Shab. 14:4.
[23] M. Aboth 2:6.
[24] M. Aboth 1:2.
[25] M. Aboth 4:12.

[26] M. Aboth 4:16.
[27] Op. cit., p. 187.
[28] See op. cit.

However, it may be said with candor that since the publication of the monumental work of Strack and Billerbeck the existence of a certain similarity between the *substance* of Jesus' teaching and that of the rabbis has been a commonplace among students in the New Testament field.

Again a few examples of this phenomenon must suffice. These are some of the more striking whole sentences that occur amidst a great mass of relevant materials.

With what measure a man metes it shall be measured to him again. (M. Sotah 1:7; cf. Mark 4:24 and Matt. 7:2=Luke 6:38 [Q?].)

What thou hatest, do to no man. (Tobit 4:15.)

As thou desirest that evils should not befall thee, but to partake of all that is good, thou shouldest act in this spirit to thy subjects and to offenders, and shouldest very gently admonish such as are virtuous. (Letter of Aristeas, para. 207; cf. Hillel in Shab. 31a and Luke 6:31= Matt. 7:12 [Q].)

If thou hast wrought much in the Law, claim not merit for thyself, for to this end wast thou created. (M. Aboth 2:8; cf. Luke 17:10 [L] and M. Aboth 1:3.)

The day is short and the task is great and the laborers are idle and the wage is abundant and the master of the house is urgent. (M. Aboth 2:15; cf. Matt. 9:37-38=Luke 10:2 [Q], and John 4:35-36.)

But if two sit together and words of the Law [are spoken] between them, the divine presence rests between them. (M. Aboth 3:2; cf. Matt. 18:20 [M]. It is certainly difficult to resist the impression that there is a more than casual connection between these two sayings.)

As regards these and like similarities between Jesus and the scribes, I should like to associate myself with Canon Herford's well-considered remark that ofttimes when Jesus uttered a saying like that of the rabbis, this was "not because it was what was taught in the Synagogue but because it was what he meant to say—none the worse for being hallowed by old associations." [29] This is well said; Jesus never followed the rabbis slavishly, nor could he possibly have done so. For when all is said, there still remains an unbridge-

[29] Op. cit., p. 197.

172

able gulf between him and them. It was, therefore, not without reason that the multitude discovered quite readily that Jesus "taught them as having authority, and not as the scribes" (Mark 1:22; cf. Matt. 7:28-29 [M?]). The difference was one that set Jesus quite apart from the scribes and made the coincidences between their teachings and his—however numerous and striking—purely incidental. For the difference was of a character that transcends particulars and renders them irrelevant. It was a fundamental difference in spirit and, therefore, in the whole approach to the subjects of religion and ethics. Claude G. Montefiore has stated this difference in these words:

However fine and noble their [the rabbis'] teaching may have been or was, it cannot properly be called prophetic. They were not called prophets, and they could not properly have been called so. . . . Hillel was ever the servant of the Law, and never its judge. . . . That is why, or that is one "why," the production of parallels from the teaching of Hillel with the teaching of Jesus is mostly futile. The spirit is different. The prophetic touch is present in the one case and absent in the other, and it is the prophetic touch which makes the difference.[30]

[30] *The Synoptic Gospels*, I, cxx. This is perhaps the place to remark that "Matthew" or his special source (M) appears to have a strong rabbinical interest. He or his source interprets Jesus' teaching as more nearly in accord with that of the scribes than we should be lead to believe it to be from the other gospel sources. There appears to be a disposition here to make Jesus uphold, not only the Law of the Old Testament, but the prestige of the Pharisees as well (Matt. 23:1-2). In one famous pronouncement M seeks to ally Jesus with the party of Shammai against that of Hillel. This is in the matter of divorce and its proper ground. The school of Hillel claimed that this could be granted even if a wife merely "spoiled a dish" for her husband in cooking; that of Shammai, only on the ground of adultery (M. Gittin 9:10; cf. above, p. 151). In narrating the incident wherein Jesus was asked to render a decision in the case, Mark had made it clear that Jesus differed from both schools by justifying divorce on no grounds whatever (10:2-12), but Matthew added "except for fornication" (19:9), an addition which if made by Jesus would obviously have placed him on the side of the Shammaites. There is also an M account of Jesus' teaching on the subject of divorce (5:32) which has suffered from ecclesiastical handling, as Dibelius suggests (*Tradition*, p. 249), and the same may be said for Matthew's treatment of Mark here. For the Marcan teaching bears the mark of authenticity on its face. The idea of equality of privilege and responsibility on the part of husband and wife in the matter of marriage and divorce which is indicated here was quite unknown in Pharisaic circles, where the sin of adultery was defined technically as an infringement of the rights of a married man performed by the man who had

This is well said, and its significance for us here will perhaps be best indicated by setting over against it another contention of Canon Herford. He makes much of the fact that Jesus, as he claims, was largely ignorant of the Pharisaic system which he spent some time in rebuking. Jesus had never been trained in the rabbinical college, and such knowledge as he possessed of Pharisaic teaching was the hearsay of the provincial town. The Pharisees on their part had little opportunity of knowing what Jesus' teaching was, Herford contends. Accordingly Jesus and his opponents never really came to grips with the differences between them.

Perhaps Herford's contention is very near the truth, but if so it is irrelevant. For both Jesus and the Pharisees, however little or much they may have known of each other's teachings as a whole, give substantial evidence of knowing that at all events there was a great spiritual and moral gulf between them. This gulf appears clearly in the course of their reported disputes on a variety of topics and must be allowed to stand despite what I have already said regarding the chance similarities in their teachings. We now look at some of the features of this spiritual hiatus between the two.

Jesus' Appeal to the Scriptures

The scribes, as we have seen, were concerned above all else to "make a hedge about the Law" (M. Aboth 1:1). This is just another way of saying that their interest first and last was in a book. They were concerned at all costs to maintain it inviolate, to copy and transmit it with verbal accuracy, to interpret it literally, and to obey it implicitly. They made a "hedge" about it with their traditions in order that men might be kept far off from even unwitting infraction of its commands. To say, "It is written," therefore, was for them the final argument on any subject; and the

---

attacked the former's wife (cf. M. Sotah 2:6; 4:1, and M. Ketuboth). To grant a divorce was also the prerogative only of the man, though the woman could sue her husband for a divorce for certain specified reasons (cf. M. Ketuboth 7:10; also T. W. Manson's suggestion relative to Matt. 5:32, *Teaching*, p. 200 and n. 5).

only problem that remained was the mode of applying this written word to the life situation.[31]

It would be wholly misleading to interpret Jesus' attitude toward Scripture along these lines. He, too, it is true, could use the common formula "It is written"; and the gospel sources report nineteen occasions on which he is said to have done so. The schema which follows shows the distribution of these among both gospel sources and the Old Testament writings.

Quotations	Mk.	Q	L	M	Jn.
Isa. 29:13	7:6				
56:7	11:17				
Zech. 13:7	14:27				
Deut. 8:3		Lk. 4:4			
6:13-14		Lk. 4:8			
Ps. 91:11-12		Lk. 4:10			
Deut. 6:16		Lk. 4:12			
Mal. 3:1		Lk. 7:27			
Ps. 118:22			20:17		
Isa. 53:12			22:37		
Isa. 54:13					6:45
Ps. 82:6					10:34

Citations	Mk.	Q	L	M	Jn.
	9:12				
	9:13				
	14:21				
			18:31		
			21:22		
			24:46		
					8:17
Totals	6	5	5	nil	3

An analysis of these data shows that our Lord used Scripture: to substantiate an argument (John 8:17; 10:34), in stating a prin-

[31] See M. Gittin 9:10 *et passim*.

ciple of the divine rule (Mark 11:17; Luke 4:4, 8, 10, 12[32]), in describing the nature of man (Mark 7:6), and as prophetic of the circumstances of his own ministry and that of the Baptist (Mark 9:12-13; 14:21, 27; Luke 7:27; 18:31; 20:17; 22:37; 21:22; 24:46; John 6:45). In none of these passages, however, is Jesus represented as appealing to Scripture as a final authority to whose dictates he must conform or subscribe. Some of the references are obviously of an *ad hominem* type. In a variety of ways he made it appear that he was the Lord of Scripture and sat in judgment upon it, his person, teaching, and work being the standard of its moral and religious values. One or two examples will serve to make this fact clear.

Reference has already been made to the scribe's perennial debates on the subject of divorce. The one concern of the schools of both Hillel and Shammai on such occasions was to create an impression of rigid adherence to the letter of the Torah. Jesus on the contrary pointedly asked for the "law" on the subject and then swept it aside as entirely out of accord with God's high demand in the matter of married life. "For your hardness of heart he [Moses] wrote you this commandment. But from the beginning of the creation, Male and female made he them," he said, quoting Gen. 1:27, and then followed that quotation with the pronouncement toward which the argument had been purposely directed, "What therefore God has joined together, let not man put asunder" (Mark 10:9).

This is a flat contradiction, not only of the rabbinical opinion on the subject, but of the Torah as well. It takes high ethical ground of an absolute character not found in the purview of either. Jesus rather allies himself with the prophetic view of family life and its inviolable nature as found in the creation narrative. One gains the impression, therefore, that the appeal to Scripture here is

---

[32] I am assuming here that the devil's quotation at the temptation is actually a reflection in the mind of Jesus and that, therefore, the quotation from Ps. 91:11-12 is his own.

not for any authority it possesses for Jesus but purely for the reason that there was an inner accord between its spirit and his own. Accordingly he could have quoted any passage that would have exhibited such accord and have discarded any that did not. Nor was he conscious of being bound by the letter or limitations of such passages as he chose to quote; first and last his own word was capable of supplementing, nullifying, and wholly supplanting them. A saying like Matt. 5:17 (M), "Think not that I came to destroy the law or the prophets: I came not to destroy, but to fulfill" (A.S.V.), if it is taken as authentic, must be matched with another from the same source, "Ye have heard that it was said . . . , but I say unto you" (Matt. 5:21, A.S.V., et al.), if it is to be rightly understood and interpreted. Jesus knew himself to be morally and spiritually atune with the prophetic scriptures; and in consequence he could employ them with the utmost freedom rather than be impelled to follow them slavishly, as was done by the scribes.

The rather general impression, therefore, that Jesus set the written scriptures (Torah and prophets) over against the rabbinical traditions and supported the one while rejecting the other, much after the fashion of the Sadducees, does not adequately represent his point of view. The passage generally cited in proof of this contention is Mark 7:9-13. The law relating to qorbān was a famous source of dispute among the rabbis themselves. The general rule was that if a man repeated some such formula as " 'May what I eat of thine be the Korban,' or 'as a Korban,' or 'a Korban,' it is forbidden to him" (M. Nedarim 1:4)—i.e., he was forbidden by the rabbis to retract his vow. It was recognized, however, that a man might make such a vow in a fit of anger or ill temper and later wish to retract it. Such a case might well reflect on the honor due the man's parents, in that they had given birth to such a foolish son. The Mishnah records a discussion on the point among the rabbis which reads:

R. Eliezer says: They may open for men the way [to repentance] by reason of the honor due to father and mother. But the Sages forbid it.

177

R. Zadok said: Rather than open the way for a man by reason of the honor due to father and mother, they should open the way for him by reason of the honor due to God; but if so, there could be no vows. But the Sages agree with R. Eliezer that in a matter between a man and his father and mother, the way may be opened to him by reason of the honor due to his father and his mother. (M. Nedarim 9:1.)

This statement is confused, if not contradictory; and one wonders whether Jesus' criticism of the rabbinical decision on the point may not have had its effect here.

But in any case it would be quite unfair to both Jesus and the Pharisees to interpret the Marcan incident as indicative that Jesus was here upholding the written Torah and the Pharisees their traditions. The Pharisees were above everything else zealous for the Torah, and their traditions were the product of an earnest wish to put it into practice in daily living. That Jesus knew this is certain; the Sabbath controversies make it plain. Probably a right understanding of our Lord's attitude here will be arrived at if we assume that he is presenting an ad hominem argument to his enemies along the lines of their attack on his disciples. They had accused them of disobeying the Law by not washing their hands before meals (vs. 2). He replies in like kind, therefore, and shows that in obeying their traditions they too are actually— though to be sure, unwittingly—disobeying the very Law which they were attempting earnestly to uphold and to implement.

His own view, then, will not be found in his staunch support of the Law, as appears on the surface, but rather in the quotation which he makes from Isa. 29:13, wherein the prophet's concern is that the "heart" of God's people shall cease to be "far from" him, and in the conclusion which he is said to have drawn from the incident: "There is nothing from without the man, that going into him can defile him; but the things which proceed out of the man are those that defile the man" (vs. 15). Literal obedience to the Law, lip service, emphasis on externals of religious piety—to obey God is not this, however conformable it may be to either Law or traditions, but rather the inner intent and motivation of mind and heart.

There is a Q saying in Luke 11:42=Matt. 23:23 [33] which looks in the same direction. As usual Luke probably presents the Q form of the saying in its purer state.[34] Luke speaks of "rue," which was not tithed, and of "mint," which was unlikely so; Matthew has "dil" and "cummin," both of which were subject to tithe.[35] Whichever reading we accept, our Lord's eventual meaning will be the same—namely, that internal attitudes, as represented by the terms "justice," "mercy," "truth," and the "love of God," are the important matters. If we possess these attitudes, it matters not whether we obey the traditions, as Matthew suggests, or even go beyond them and tithe what neither traditions nor Law requires, as Luke seems to mean. But contrariwise, if we do not exhibit such a right character, our meticulous observance of the Pharisaical super-religiosity will avail us nothing in God's sight.

Jesus therefore was concerned with obedience to neither written nor oral law as such, but with the cultivation of the attitude which enthrones God as the sole Lord of one's life. And there can be no doubt that this was something new in the Judaism of his day; for a like attitude we must go back to the prophets.[36]

Jesus' Interest in Character

We have already noted that the rabbis were "ethical behaviorists" who interested themselves primarily in conduct and demanded that their disciples exemplify a prescribed "conduct pattern." By the use of several different devices it could be shown that the laws of the written Torah numbered 613 in all. One method was to take the sum of the numerical equivalents of the Hebrew characters in the word "Torah" and then to add to these the two com-

[33] The Matthaean form probably represents a combination of like sayings from M and Q.
[34] See Streeter, op. cit., p. 291.
[35] See T. W. Manson, Mission, p. 390.
[36] Cf. Hos. 6:6 and its use by M at Matt. 9:13; 12:7.

mandments found in Exod. 20:2-3.[37] But these 613 were only a beginning, for Mishnah and Talmud multiplied these many times over in the endeavor to apply them to life and so to make the written Torah livable. The living up to the requirements of the thousands of Mishnaic ordinances or "traditions of the elders" which this system eventually developed furnished a pattern of conduct as nicely schematized as that ever produced by the "rule" of a monastic order. The only significant difference was that the Pharisaic rule was open to all without their undergoing the necessity of abandoning their ordinary occupations or ways of livelihood.

Jesus' controversies with the Pharisees had in a number of cases to do with this "conduct pattern." This was true of the Sabbath disputes, those having to do with eating—whether with unwashed hands or in the homes of "publicans and sinners"—and the whole matter of prayer, almsgiving, and tithing. The pattern included abstention from thirty-nine kinds of work on the Sabbath (M. Shab. 7:2), as well as from the healing of the sick on that day except in those cases where "there is doubt whether life is in danger" (M. Yoma 8:6; cf. M. Sanh. 19:1). This explains why Jesus' healing of the withered hand (Mark 3:1-6), of the case of dropsy (Luke 14:1-6), and of the woman bent double (Luke 13:10-17)—all on the Sabbath day—aroused such opposition among the Pharisees.[38] Similarly the rubbing of grain in the hands was interpreted as "threshing" and therefore forbidden.[39]

Our Lord's relations with the Pharisees cannot be adequately understood apart from a recognition of his complete rejection of this rabbinical pattern of conduct. His attitudes on the occasions above mentioned constituted a direct challenge to that pattern. Moreover he made it clear that the division of men into "righteous" and "sinners" on the basis of such a pattern did not conform to the divine will for men's lives. "Judge not that ye be

---

[37] Thus ת=400, ו=6, ר=200, and ה=5, or 611 in all; add to these 2 more as above indicated, and the number 613 is found. Cf. Moore, op. cit., II, 83, n. 3.

[38] See, however, below, p. 186.

[39] M. Shabbath 7:2.

not judged" was a maxim which he commended to his auditors; and, as the context makes clear, he meant by it that every man had either the "mote" or the "beam" in his eye and therefore could not call himself "righteous" and the other "sinner" by reason of any man-made pattern of conduct to which he conformed while the other failed to do so.[40] In this connection it is highly significant that Jesus took the sinner's part wherever he found the Pharisee leveling criticism at him. This fact stands out clearly, for example, in the incident of the anointing in the house of Simon the Pharisee, in the case of the adulteress brought to Jesus in the temple, and in parables like those of the Pharisee and the publican and of the prodigal son.[41]

In numerous ways our Lord indicated that a man's duty consists in the acquisition of character, in getting the heart right toward God and toward one's fellows, and in the securing of a proper motivation of the entire personality. He called all men, accordingly, to repentance that they should thereby come to accept God's sovereignty over their lives (Mark 1:14-15). With him it was the making of the tree good and the sweetening of the waters of the spring that mattered, for then the fruit of the one would be good and the water flowing from the other, sweet (Luke 6:43-45=Matt. 7:17-19 [Q]; cf. Matt. 12:33 [M?]).

It is in the light of such teaching of our Lord that his acceptance of the two commandments already joined in the Testaments of the Twelve Patriarchs is to be understood.[42] His meaning was not that in the formation of a conduct pattern these two should come first but rather that love alone was essential to at once a true religion and a right ethic.[43] Jesus therefore accepted the conjunction of the two commandments in a far more drastic fashion than either the apocalyptists or the rabbis were in a position to understand. He meant that with the acquisition of the

---

[40] See Matt. 7:1-5.
[41] Cf. Luke 7:36-50; John 7:53–8:11; Luke 18:9-14; 15:11-32.
[42] See p. 231.
[43] See Rom. 13:8-10.

181

spirit enshrined in this conjunction the Law as law came to an end. This meant also the abolition of the casuistical system which determined that one or other of opposing duties should be followed. *There could be no conflict of duties when the only law men must obey was to love God by loving God in the neighbor.* For Jesus, at pains to point out that even these two commands were really one in essence, said, "So if you are offering your gift at the altar, and there remember that your brother has something against you, leave your gift there before the altar and go; first be reconciled to your brother, and then come and offer your gift" (Matt. 5:23-24 R.S.V.). This saying is from Special Matthew; but there can be little doubt regarding its genuineness, both because in placing the ethical motif above the religious it displays an originality over against the Pharisaical attitude of the Judaism of Jesus' day which is unmistakable, and also in view of the logical necessity of the case. All that I have thus far said about Jesus' distrust in "conduct patterns" is proof positive that he would have nothing to do with a system of casuistry whose purpose was to resolve conflicting duties; further, by teaching and example he made it clear that for him no conflict *could* exist between a duty to God and a duty to fellowman. Obviously, however, it does not require 613 commands to create such a conflict; two are enough. Had our Lord therefore foreseen any possible conflict between duties to love God and to love man, his repugnance for "patterns of conduct" and casuistical systems would have proved itself irrational.[44]

Once again, Jesus' approach to the problem of divine obedience takes us back to the prophets for its counterpart. For they like him were interested in conduct, not for its own sake, but as the fruitage of character or as the evidence of the "imago Dei" within man. It was the "new heart" or the "new spirit" of which Yahweh spoke by the mouth of Ezekiel (36:26-28), and "my law in their inward parts, and . . . in their hearts" in which he was

---

[44] T. W. Manson has an illuminating discussion of Jesus' reflections on the two great commandments (*op. cit.*, pp. 302 ff.).

interested above all else, according to Jeremiah (31:33-34). And it must be said at this point with the utmost candor that it was the Pharisees, and not Jesus, who misunderstood, perverted, and distorted the prophetic revelation of the Old Testament relative to divine obedience, to ethical conduct generally, and to the place of character and its relation to conduct. For that prophetic revelation was in no sense legalistic in its attitude toward these problems.[45] For both Jesus and his apostles, as for the prophets before them, the power and motivation to achieve, and the pattern for, character in man were found in the Spirit of God alone. It was this character, moreover, which all of these were concerned to see produced in man, not that thereby man might vaunt himself in opposition to God or claim any merit before the Holy One, but merely that man might appear as the reflection or "likeness" or "image" of what God is and at every stage acknowledge in full his dependence upon God, even as the moon shines by reflected light and is dependent at every moment on the sun for her light.

Jesus' Interest in Men

In the realm of religion, institutions have a curious habit of inhibiting in the end the very thing which they are intended to serve, namely, man's approach to and fellowship with God. We have already seen how this phenomenon appeared in the religion of the altar. It is exemplified also in the religion of the book. For in spite of attempts like the one of Israel Abrahams to deny as much,[46] and the probability which I would concede that an aphorism like "The sabbath was made for man, not

[45] It would of course go beyond the limits of our present study to discuss Paul's relation to this problem of the connection between conduct and character. I may perhaps be permitted the luxury of pointing out, however, that Paul's definition of what he terms the "fruit of the Spirit," his discussion of the relation between the Divine Spirit and the human, and his stress on the "imago Dei" in man (cf. Rom. 8:1-11; II Cor. 3:18; Gal. 5:22-24), are all perfectly in line with the attitude of prophets and Jesus. His difficulties with the Judaizers were simply a repetition of our Lord's disputes with the Pharisees about a "conduct pattern."

[46] See above, p. 116; cf. his Studies, I, 129-35.

man for the sabbath" (Mark 2:27b R.S.V.) was current in Jesus'
time and merely quoted by him, there can be no doubt nonetheless that for the rabbi, the Sabbath, circumcision, the Jewish feasts
and fasts, the techniques of worship (Shema', Tefillah, phylac-
teries, and the rest), the ritual of almsgiving—in short, the entire
paraphernalia of religion—had attained value for their own sake.
As the Torah in time was objectified and given a value for itself
quite apart from, and out of character with its purely dynamic
functional relation to, the God who gave it, so the institutions of
Judaism by Jesus' day had attained with the Pharisees a worth for
their own sake out of all proportion to the original intent.

Thus it had become more important to keep the Sabbath than
to "straighten a child's back" (M. Shab. 22:6) or to "set a dislocated limb" (ibid.) or to attend to the healing of the sick
generally (M. Shab. 14:3-4). The general rule as stated in this
last passage is instructive.

He may eat any foodstuffs that serve for healing or drink any liquids
except purgative water or a cup of root-water, since these serve to cure
jaundice; but he may drink purgative water to quench his thirst, and he
may anoint himself with root-oil if it is not used for healing. If his teeth
pain him, he may not suck vinegar through them, but he may take
vinegar after his usual fashion; and if he is healed, he is healed. If his
loins pain him, he may not rub thereon wine or vinegar, yet he may
anoint them with oil but not with rose-oil. Kings' children may anoint
their wounds with rose-oil since it is their custom so to do on ordinary
days.

The whole of the Mishnah may be quoted in proof of the thesis
with which we are here dealing. The Sabbath and the other institutions of religion must be preserved at all costs; as for man,
however, "if he is healed, he is healed." The occasional flashes of
insight on the part of one or another of the rabbis which point
away from this institutionalization of religion only serve to throw
into relief the fact that generally the maintenance of the religious
institutions had become for them more important than the hu-

man personalities for whom these institutions were originally created.

Our Lord on the contrary spared no pains to assert that men are of more value than the institutions which serve them, even though these be of a religious nature. The words "Of how much more value is a man" than a "sheep" (Matt. 12:12 [M]), than "the birds" (Luke 12:24=Matt. 6:26 [Q]), than "many sparrows" (Luke 12:7=Matt. 10:31 [Q]), than "the grass [or lilies] of the field" (Luke 12:28=Matt. 6:30 [Q]), or some other equivalent (Luke 13:15; 14:5 [L]), which ring like a refrain throughout the gospel sources, are brought into direct contact with the Sabbath controversies in at least two of these (L and M). In Mark, Jesus sets the problem in absolute fashion with the alternative "Is it lawful on the sabbath day to do good or to do harm, to save life or to kill?" (3:4), where the immediate context shows the contrast to be between our Lord's efforts to help human beings and the Pharisees' determination to do away with him (cf. vss. 2 and 6). In like fashion he taught, as we have already seen, that fasting may be considered of religious value only if it serves the immediate needs of human personalities but not for its own sake.[47] The indiscriminate healings of our Lord on the Sabbath day were the practical fruitage of such conviction on his part in the field of action.

This leads us to observe that, just as Jesus' love of men in the end proves him worthy of being their Lord,[48] so by the same token he is also Lord of the institutions which are intended to serve their best interests. He is the Lord of the Sabbath, for example, because he acted consistently on the principle "The sabbath is made for man, and not man for the sabbath" in a way that the Pharisee did not and could not. He implemented, so to speak, the saying with appropriate action which made it clear that it was the only law of the Sabbath that he observed. No

[47] Cf. Mark 2:18-20; Matt. 6:16-18 (M).
[48] See The Intention of Jesus, pp. 145-53.

Pharisee could have done that and remained a Pharisee overnight. It was this sublimation of all the institutions of religion to the good of mankind that made Jesus Lord of them as he was also Lord of men, and hence the sequence becomes intelligible: "The sabbath was made for man, not man for the sabbath; so the Son of man is lord even of the sabbath" (Mark 2:27-28 R.S.V.).[49]

The dilemma has been proposed: either the gospel accounts of Jesus' controversies with the Pharisees are unhistorical, or else there was a deep-seated reason for the controversies which does not appear on the surface of the narratives.[50] May I suggest that if the Pharisees sensed in Jesus' sabbath healings a claim to be Lord of both men and Judaism's religious institutions, then they might well enough have found reason in these things for opposing one who in their judgment and from their point of view was making a blasphemous claim while he was breaking down the very institutions of which he claimed to be Lord.

Jesus' Mind on the Extent of the Kingdom of God and on the Future Life

It was Adolf Harnack who popularized the idea that Jesus failed to see any further than the Pharisees into the universal implications of the prophets' teaching about Israel's mission.[51] According to the German scholar our Lord never looked beyond the confines of his own people or anticipated that the salvation he had to offer men would affect those outside Israel. The universal mission of Christianity was only gradually sensed by the church as persecution and the open door of the Greek world with its roads, language, Pax Romana, and like "universal" factors led her out into new and uncharted areas. It is astonishing how congenial this view has proved to be in New Testament circles. Many

[49] On this passage and the difficulty of maintaining its authenticity, cf. pp. 83, 134-35.

[50] See Jewish Encyclopedia, "Sabbath," and cf. Mysterium Christi, pp. 75-77.

[51] The Mission and Expansion of Christianity in the First Three Centuries, Vol. I, ch. iv.

would be found today quite prepared to subscribe to Rabbi Joseph Klausner's contention that, inasmuch as within the Jewish tradition no other view of the Messiah and the kingdom was ever entertained than the particularistic one which associated both as a matter of course with Israel or, at any rate, with the Jewish cultural ethos, therefore no competing view was available for Jesus to have adopted.[52]

And yet not only does this contention sweep aside the universalistic elements in the prophetic teaching to which reference has already been made (pp. 38, 55), but it ignores with almost inconceivable hardihood the implications of Jesus' interest in men as men. Harnack himself was one of the first to call attention to this undoubted phenomenon to which we have been adverting (pp. 185-86). This interest carried our Lord in imagination far beyond the confines of the Judaism in which he had been reared, as his saying that "men will come from east and west, and from north and south, and sit at the table in the kingdom of God," [53] and the parable of the good Samaritan,[54] and the like bear testimony. As Father Hebert has pointed out, such facts as these can be given but one valid interpretation, namely, that for both prophets and Jesus the "particularism" of the old covenant of God with Israel had in view the "universalism" of the new, so that the maintenance of the one was necessitated that the other might be achieved, and the realization of the latter was conditioned by the temporary adherence to the former.[55]

But even Father Hebert's thesis does not carry us far enough, nor is it upon such considerations as those which we have been advancing alone that a final judgment can be made. Even the Pharisees and with them certainly their successors, rabbinic and modern Judaism, deserve better from our hands than Rabbi Klausner's thesis would suggest. There is a real sense in which all of

---

[52] *Jesus of Nazareth*, pp. 199 ff.
[53] Luke 13:28-29; cf. Matt. 8:11-12.
[54] Luke 10:29-37 (L).
[55] *Op. cit.*, p. 74.

these cannot fairly be said to have been "particularists" at all. For it is a well-known fact that the Pharisees through the synagogue had established a *universal mission* long before Paul's day. It represents, therefore, an oversimplification to state the problem which confronted the Pharisees and Pharisaic Christian party (the "Judaizers"), on the one hand, and Paul and the early Christian Church which followed his lead, on the other, in terms such as "particularism versus universalism." The question at issue was never this—neither within Judaism as such nor between Judaism and Christianity, as many biblical students appear to assume. The question was rather, On what terms shall pagans be brought into the orbit of the covenant privileges? The Pharisaic answer traditionally was: On condition that they adhere to the Law and Jewish customs. The church's answer was equally clear and unequivocal: On condition that they accept Christ as their Lord and Redeemer. It was Paul, of course, who waged—nearly if not quite singlehanded—the fight that brought to the church this insight into the right answer to give.

The problem relative to Jesus' consciousness, then, is not to be stated as Harnack did: Did Jesus' view reach out beyond the confines of his little Jewish world and take into its concern the spiritual needs of all men, or was that view restricted to the interest of his own people? Surely it will not be seriously argued that Jesus' outlook was narrower than that of the Pharisaism of his day! Moreover it is striking to observe that Harnack's proposal was capable of proof even by himself only on condition that one adopted the critical method then in vogue of deleting from the gospel record that portion of the evidence that failed to support, and of leaning heavily or exclusively upon that which gave credence to, one's thesis. And it is if possible even more striking that the bulk of that which supported his view was drawn from Matthew's special source, an ecclesiastical document or series of passages with a distinctly Jewish bias.[56]

[56] See his *Mission*, pp. 38ff.

We are not to seek the solution of the problem, however, by making the opposite—though in principle the same—mistake that Harnack made, namely, by eliminating the Special Matthew evidence from the record of our inquiry. Doubtless this evidence will be sufficiently taken care of if we assume that it falls under the head of that "particularistic interest" which we have seen to be necessary to the "universalistic" in the prophetic stream of thought and teaching. The solution so far as Jesus is concerned rather would seem to lie in the restating of the problem to read: Did our Lord foresee and accept the eventual Pauline-churchwise solution in preference to the Pharisaic one? Better still perhaps: Did that Pauline-churchwise solution stem from his own teaching and find its ultimate ground in that teaching and in Jesus' unique consciousness of mission?

The answer to this question in my judgment should take the following direction. Jesus *agreed* with the Pharisees in rejecting "particularism" in the absolute or ultimate sense of total exclusion of pagans on all terms from the privileges of the "covenant people." Indeed, no such teaching has ever been acceptable to any reputable group within Judaism. But at the same time our Lord as certainly *disagreed* with Pharisaism in holding to a "universalism" which accepted pagans only on condition they subscribe to Jewish customs and to the Mosaic law. Otherwise, what I have been saying above (pp. 179-82) relative to Jesus' disputes with the Pharisees and their scribes on the subject of a "conduct pattern" has no meaning. Mark's observation at 7:19 relative to our Lord's ruling on the subject of defilement—"Thus he declared all foods clean"—represents surely a true insight of the church into the conscious significance of Jesus' teaching. Further, he taught that to be acceptable to God men were required to "come unto" and to "follow" him,[57] to take his "yoke" upon them,[58] to assume the "cross" which his obedience would lay

[57] Mark 8:34.   [58] Matt. 11:29 (M).

189

upon them,[59] to become his "disciples" [60]—in short, to attach themselves wholly to his allegiance, believing in him as their leader, teacher, and Lord.[61] And there can be no doubt that he attached to his ministry, work, and death a redemptive significance which rendered him worthy of being man's Redeemer and Lord.[62]

All this is merely to say, of course, that Jesus' entire world view was in accord with that of the prophets before him and not like that of the Pharisaism of his day. Instead of being particularistic (in the modified sense provided by a legalism whose demands were literal, materialistic in the main, and wholly inflexible), it represented a spiritual and highly ethical interpretation of the phenomena of revelation and religion which by virtue of its essential nature was forced to include men of all races and peoples without distinction—that is, men as men—the only genuine universalism.

In closing this chapter, a word about our Lord's attitude toward the future life and the resurrection. His reticence with regard to the subject is one of the most marked features of his teaching. In this once again he stands with the prophets and their primary, all-absorbing interest in the life of man on the historical plane. And our sources here are united in their testimony to this striking phenomenon.

According to the Synoptic account our Lord never made the resurrection the subject of his teaching save after Caesarea Philippi and then only to his intimate disciples on three occasions.[63] These all referred to his own resurrection and are sufficient proof that he believed in the doctrine, as did the Pharisees, though in some sense not sharply defined. In John two passages give us a deeply mystical doctrine of the resurrection which in one passage is sharply contrasted with that "in the last day" (11:24), and in

---

[59] Luke 14:27=Matt. 10:38 (Q).
[60] Mark 3:13-19.
[61] Luke 6:40=Matt. 10:24 (Q).
[62] See below, pp. 280-81.
[63] Mark 8:31; 9:9-10, 31-34.

the other is as clearly identified with it (6:39 ff.). It is a spiritual experience resulting from belief in Jesus (6:40) and associated with the acquisition of "eternal life" through eating the flesh and drinking the blood of Christ. There is here, however, no clear definition of the nature of the resurrection any more than in the Synoptic accounts. In two further passages (Luke 14:14 [L]; John 5:29) the resurrection is associated with judgment.

This leaves us but one instance—that in which the Passion Week discussion between our Lord and the Sadducees occurs—in which the nature of the resurrection is somewhat defined (Mark 12:18-27). Here the point under discussion is *the materialistic view of the resurrection as taught by the Pharisees.* Our Lord's rejoinder, therefore, it should be noted, is as much a reply to the latters' crass views on the subject as to his immediate interlocutors. His point is that, whatever the nature of the final resurrection, it introduces those who experience it into a spiritual kind of life where men "are as angels in heaven" (vs. 25), even as the patriarchs are at the present moment (vss. 26-27). There is no evidence, therefore, that, though Jesus was prepared to subscribe to the *fact* of the resurrection, he ever held to the crude views on the subject embraced by the Pharisees. In this he was certainly the precursor, and possibly the mentor, of Paul.[64]

---

[64] In I Cor. 15:35-58 the apostle appears to be steering a perilous but true course between the Greek doctrine of the immortality of the soul, on the one hand, and the Pharisaic crudities referred to, on the other. Charles holds that Jesus' teaching here is nearly identical with that in I Enoch 104:4, 6 (*op. cit.*, II, 184).

IV

And one that was ancient of days did sit: . . . his throne was fiery flames.

—Dan. 7:9

He that overcometh, I will give to him to sit down with me in my throne, as I also overcame, and sat down with my Father in his throne.—Rev. 3:21

JESUS and
THE RELIGION of the THRONE

Synopsis

Chapter 10:—The raison d'être of apocalypticism was the obvious sufferings of that "people of God" which the scribe had termed "righteous." Ignoring the prophets who roundly condemned that people for its failures to do God's will, the apocalypticist appealed for his AUTHORITY to ancient worthies who had walked with God or to more modern scribes who endeavored to apply his Torah to life. His METHOD of presenting their supposed teachings was the "vision"—a purely literary technique akin to the parable, the poem, and other literary devices. By means of the vision, the apocalyptist claimed to be able to disclose the divine mystery of the ages, i.e., to set forth God's ways with men. The religion of the throne arose within orthodox Judaism and produced no institution comparable to those of the other religions studied. But its characteristic PRODUCT whenever it has been cultivated is the SECT.

Chapter 11:—The pivot about which this teaching revolved was the transcendent THRONE OF GOD in heaven. From this idea arose the doctrine of the TWO KINGDOMS, those of God and Satan. It also resulted in the transcendent MESSIAH, the transcendent ORDER, and the transcendent ETHIC.

Chapter 12:—Jesus was acquainted with this teaching but not necessarily with the literature. His "visions" were prophetic in type, as were also his messianic consciousness and his world view. The theory that he believed the end of the age to be near is rejected on exegetical grounds.

CHAPTER

10

The Religion of the Throne

THE apocalyptist followed the scribe, the religion of the throne that of the book. This was natural. The book had no authority indigenous to itself to enforce its precepts. The existence of such authority had in consequence to be declared, and this was done from the throne of the apocalypse. The law of the book was intended in the divine economy to "become our tutor to bring us unto Christ" (Gal. 3:24), but its first result was to make all men as sinners "stand before the judgment-seat of God" (Rom. 14:10). It was the object of the religion of the throne to make this clear, and in the religious milieu of post-exilic Judaism it was this function which the apocalyptist as the creator of the third of the "people's religions" served.

The scribe's outstanding *merit* had been that he took the Torah seriously. He out-Barthed Barth in his insistence that God had spoken and that his word placed man in the "crisis" of decision, for or against God. With the prophet before him he succeeded in portraying vividly for the common man the fact of sin as disobedience to the revealed will of God. The scribe's chief *defect* had been that he divided men into two categories, the "righteous" who kept God's law and the "sinners" who failed to do so.[1] The grouping

---

[1] See Moore, *Judaism*, I, 494 ff.

was absolute and allowed for no grays between the black and white. At times it was made to follow *national* lines, the "covenant people" over against all pagan peoples; at others, *sectarian* or *party* lines, Pharisees versus *'ammē hā 'āretz* or versus Sadducees; at still others, lines drawn within Pharisaism itself. Thus the Talmud distinguished the seven types of Pharisees to which allusion has already been made,[2] of whom only one was acceptable to God and like Abraham his "friend."

But, though the grouping of all men in the two categories of "righteous" and "sinners" on the scribe's part was absolute, the definition which he gave to "righteousness" was not. This term carried with it for him "no suggestion of sinless perfection" on man's part, for "God was too good, too reasonable, to demand a perfection of which he had created man incapable."[3] It was this paradox of an absolute division of men into two groups respectively acceptable and condemned in the sight of God, combined with adherence to a relative righteousness, that gave the apocalyptist his opportunity in view of contemporary events which seemed to negate the Pharisaic notion that God would always vindicate the "righteous." It was no mere accident of history that the apocalyptist appeared a scant two hundred years after the scribe.

No religious book of any people has ever taken man's life in time as seriously as the Hebrew prophetic literature. Not only did the prophet ascribe to historical events—and so to man's religious and ethical motivations and attitudes within history—a character of "actuality"[4] quite opposed to the *maya* of Hindu philosophy for example,[5] but he was generally content to find in the satisfaction of knowing God in this life sufficient reward for the man who chose

---

[2] See p. 161. The schools of Hillel and Shammai recognized a "gray" in the sense that there were some persons who were now of one group, now of the other. Cf. Moore, *op. cit.*

[3] *Ibid.*

[4] The category is Wheeler Robinson's; cf. above, p. 52.

[5] To be sure the prophet's thought was not conceived in the context of Hindu metaphysics, nor did it remotely deserve the descriptive adjective "metaphysical." The prophet was a religious realist who showed no concern for problems of philosophy, if indeed he had ever heard of such.

to follow God's will. Not so the apocalyptist. He came on the scene so long after the collective sins of the twin peoples of Israel and Judah, about which the prophets had thundered their warnings, had received in the land of the Captivity the judgment they merited that these lingered only in the memory of such prophetic souls as chose to turn over the darker pages of the history of the chosen people. And the apocalyptist, in spite of the endeavor of modern scholarship to make him out the direct successor of the prophet,[6] was not one of these.

Indeed it is a striking fact that the prophets receive as scant reference in the noncanonical apocalypses as they do in rabbinical works like the Mishnah and Talmud. Such paucity of interest in the prophets is intelligible in the latter works, as they are what the scribes termed Halākhāh, whereas from their viewpoint much in the prophets was capable only of haggadic treatment.[7] The same excuse, however, cannot be made for the apocalypses—or at any rate for those written by Pharisees—for these were generally Haggādāh and might well have been expected to deal with the prophetic writings if, as the modern theory holds, they were written in the prophetic spirit and with the prophetic motivation. Actually Isaiah and the twelve minor prophets are never so much as mentioned in the noncanonical apocalypses. Jeremiah comes off little better with several references in II Baruch.[8] Moses alone receives much attention at the hand of the apocalyptists generally.[9] One has to turn to the fragment of the Book of Noah in I Enoch (108:6) to find anything like the following:

[6] See, for instance, Charles, Apocrypha and Pseudepigrapha, II, viii. Some Christian scholars appear to be as vitally concerned to demonstrate that the apocalyptist is the direct spiritual descendant of the prophet as those of Jewish faith are to show that the scribe is such. Cf. above, p. 139.

[7] Canon Danby's distinction between these terms is the one I have in mind here. Haggādāh he defines as "the type of rabbinical interpretation and exposition of Scripture which aims at edification (as opposed to Halākhāh, which aims at defining or supporting legal usage)" (The Mishnah, p. 793).

[8] II Bar. 2:1; 5:5; 9:1; 10:2, 4; 33:1.

[9] I Bar. 1:20; 2:2, 28; I En. 89:16-18, 29-38; Test. Sim. 9:2; Test. Zeb. 3:4; Sib. Or. 3:253; Assump. Mos. 1:1, 4, 5; IV Esd. 7:106, 129 et al.

And he said unto me: "This place which thou seest—here are cast the spirits of sinners and blasphemers, and of those who work wickedness, and of those who pervert everything that the Lord hath spoken through the mouth of the prophets—[even] the things that shall be."

This appears indeed to be the only reference to the "prophets" in the extant noncanonical apocalyptic literature with a single unimportant exception in the Sibylline Oracles (3:781).[10]

This comparative slighting of the prophetic literature on the part of the apocalyptist was because, while profiting by the prophet's emphasis upon the requirements of true religion and a pure ethic, he found the latter's excoriation of the sins of the "people of God" peculiarly distasteful to him. *The scribe's identification of the people of Israel with the "righteous" group acceptable in God's sight had had its effect.* The apocalyptist accordingly found it far more agreeable to his purpose to return to the patriarchs and to draw warnings against moral and religious obliquity from examples taken from the lives of the twelve sons of Jacob or even of such antediluvian figures as Cain, Seth, Enoch, Noah, and Methuselah.[11] These after all were mere individuals, and their sins could be held up to criticism without wounding the sensibilities of those who would have taken offense at upbraiding the chosen people as a whole for the same transgressions. As the "righteous" of God Israel was now to be treated as sacrosanct.

Historically, if not morally or religiously, a certain justification could be found for the view of the apocalyptist in this regard. In his day the tables seemed to be turned from what they had been in that of the prophets. With the latter the children of God had been the sinners and the heathen nations God's instruments for the punishment of their sins. By the time of the apocalyptists (200 B.C. to A.D. 100 roughly) it had begun to appear that these roles were due to be reversed. As Rowley has observed:

---

[10] It reads: "And the prophets of the Mighty God shall take away the sword."
[11] Cf. I En. 22:7; 85:9; Test. Dan. 5:6; Test. Benj. 10:6; II En. 68:5.

In the Maccabean age men were suffering because they refused to disobey what they and the author of Daniel believed to be the law of God. It was because of their very loyalty that they were being martyred, and the revolt began in the uprising of persecuted saints. The position was therefore wholly different from that of the days of the great pre-exilic prophets.[12]

It now seemed that, except for all-too-brief intervals, right was on the scaffold and wrong upon the throne! When it is recalled that the period of the apocalyptic literary output extended roughly from the end of the Seleucid regime through the times of the Maccabees and the Romans to the end of the Jewish state, it becomes intelligible that a good case could be made out for the rabbinical view of the relative righteousness of God's people or at any rate of the Pharisaic or Hasidic element therein.

And yet it could no longer be said with the psalmist, "I have been young, and now am old; yet have I not seen the righteous forsaken, nor his seed begging bread." (Ps. 37:25.) Nor yet was it possible to say with the "wise man," "For the upright shall dwell in the land, and the perfect shall remain in it. But the wicked shall be cut off from the land, and the treacherous shall be rooted out of it." (Prov. 2:21-22.) Unfortunately for the oppressed saint, God's judgment on evil and his vindication of his own did not take such clear and unmistakable forms in the apocalyptist's day.[13]

Accordingly the problem to which the apocalyptist addressed himself was that of *the paradox of an all-righteous God and the coexistent undoubted sufferings which he permitted his people to experience.* This doctrine of God he had inherited from his prophetic forebears, and his acknowledgment of the plight of God's people was the product of his own realistic observations. In general the solution at which he arrived was quite different from that of the prophet. For the latter this lay in repentance of their sins on the part of God's people, their return to God for forgive-

[12] *The Relevance of Apocalyptic*, p. 20.
[13] See T. W. Manson's discussion in his *Teaching*, pp. 149-160; also H. H. Rowley, op. cit., pp. 8, 13-14, 34, 160-61, et al.

ness and vindication, and the assurance of the re-establishment of God's "covenant" of peace with them and through them with all peoples (Jer. 31:31-34; Isa. 57:14-21). The apocalyptist was by no means so optimistic that this desired fruition would occur on the temporal plane. Despairing generally of the possibility of a final solution under historical conditions, the apocalyptist looked for an eventual divine intervention in the affairs of men that would mean at once the end of history and the vindication of the saints of God.[14] This would come on the "day of the Great Assize" when God's throne would be set up and all men would appear before him to give account of their deeds done in the flesh.

It is not easy to bring under a few general headings the multifarious phenomena which confront the reader of the Jewish apocalyptic literature. The danger of oversimplification here is great, and it is peculiarly easy to pass hasty judgment to the detriment of eminently sincere men. Probably no single example of this literature exhibits all the characteristics usually assigned to the whole, and it is to be borne in mind that the absence of one or two such characteristics may radically alter the nature of a given book. The fact that both Jewish and Christian Churches chose to incorporate into their respective canons of scripture but two examples of apocalyptic is sufficient proof that in their judgment these two differed materially from the bulk of this class of writing.

The Authority of Apocalyptic—"The Book of the Dead"

Apocalyptic introduces the "dead hand" into the realm and problems of religion. It is pseudonymous, being written long after his day in the name of some Old Testament worthy preferably of the patriarchal period. Enoch was at first a great favorite because of his reputed close fellowship with God (Gen. 5:22), and an extensive literature arose about his name. Two books written under his nom de plume are at present extant, namely,

[14] On the element of "despair" or of pessimism in apocalyptic, see below, p. 269, n. 7. For the contrary view, see Rowley, *ibid.*, pp. 34, 153.

I Enoch or The Book of Enoch, written by a variety of authors between 175 and 1 B.C.; and II Enoch or The Book of the Secrets of Enoch of ca. A.D. 1. When Judaism rejected the Enochic literature and with it even the name of Enoch for purposes of pseudonymous writing, the name of "Baruch, the scribe" suggested itself as a proper substitute for the presentation of an apologetic to the religious world of the first century A.D., perhaps as a counterfoil to the original function of Baruch, which had been to write down Jeremiah's judgment of doom on the Judaism of his day.[15] Three works are extant under this new nom de plume: I Baruch (A.D. 70-78), II Baruch or Syriac Apocalypse of Baruch (A.D. 50-90), and III Baruch or Greek Apocalypse of Baruch (second century A.D.). Other popular names were those of Moses (e.g. Assumption of Moses, A.D. 7-29) and the twelve sons of Jacob (e.g. Testaments of the Twelve Patriarchs, 109-106 B.C.).[16]

Charles has advanced the view that it was because of "the evil character of the period" in which he lived that the apocalyptist was forced to take a pseudonym and under its aegis to do his work.

The Law which claimed to be the highest and final word from God could tolerate no fresh message from God, and so, when men were moved by the Spirit of God to make known their visions relating to the past, the present, and the future, and to proclaim the higher ethical truths they had won, they could not do so openly, but were forced to resort to pseudonymous publication.[17]

There is no doubt a certain amount of truth in this statement, and one hesitates to "cross swords" with a scholar of the undoubted erudition of Canon Charles. But his theory does not explain why these particular names should have been chosen rather than the names, let us say, of the great prophets. This remark is the more relevant in view of the fact that Charles is one of those who con-

---

[15] See Charles, op. cit., on II Baruch 13:3; also Jer. 36.

[16] For a different set of dates for these and the other apocalyptic writings, see T. F. Glasson, The Second Advent, ch. v, et al.

[17] Op. cit., II, 163.

tend that the apocalyptists exhibited "on occasion the inspiration of the Old Testament prophets." [18]

If this is the case, why then did the apocalyptists not choose to write in the name(s) of those prophets whose inspiration their writings are said to share? All parties within the Jewish cultural ethos during the Greek, Maccabean, and Roman periods—with the single exception of the Samaritans—accepted the prophets as inspired and placed them beside the Pentateuch as equally divine Torah.[19] It would seem, therefore, that with the exception of Moses himself the names of the "writing prophets" would have had a more likely claim of commending the apocalyptic literature to its readers than any others, and certainly more so than those of the patriarchs. Further, certainly works under the names of prophets would have stood a better chance of being taken as authentic than those purporting to have been written by men so long since dead that the memory of whether they had ever written anything had faded from the annals of history.

More likely than Charles' theory, then, would seem to be the suggestion that in selecting a nom de plume the apocalyptist had no thought of being taken seriously. The choice of names was due to the fact that the writers of this class of literature felt themselves to a degree in harmony with the patriarchs whose names they adopted and that they wished, so to speak, to write "in character" as they imagined those worthies might have felt and thought. They did not feel themselves alike in sympathy with the writings of the prophets, whose views they knew far better than they could possibly have known those of the patriarchs, for the reasons indicated above; hence they did not choose to write under prophetic names. The fact that no such impediment as Charles suggests hindered the choice of the names of two scribes —Baruch and Ezra (cf. IV Esdras) ca. A.D. 120— and of a figure from the exile like Daniel, though all three of these lived long

[18] Ibid.

[19] See Pfeiffer, op. cit., p. 61: "Before the beginning of our era . . . the Bible was called 'The Law and the Prophets' (Matt. 5:17, etc.)."

after the date accepted by the Judaism of the day for the writing of the Law, would seem finally to disprove Charles' theory. In point of fact the general viewpoint of the religion of the throne is nearer to that of the book than it is to the revelation of the prophetic word, as some of the apocalyptic writers were undoubtedly Pharisees.[20] The appropriateness of the names of the two scribes as pseudonyms is, then, apparent.

In any case it is safe to say that the pseudonymous nature of the apocalypses deceived no one—neither Jews nor Christians— nor were they intended to do so.[21] Moreover such books never really stood a chance of inclusion in the canon of Scripture; the fiction was entirely too transparent. It is surely significant that the only two examples of this type of literature to secure a place in the canon were done in the names of individuals, Daniel and John, who stood some chance of having actually written the books which go by their names. There can be no doubt, in fact, that from the time of the canonization of these books the Jewish and Christian Churches respectively believed that they had been written by those whose names they bear, while in the other cases neither community was taken in by the pseudonymous character they wore.[22]

The Method of Apocalyptic—The Vision

The means whereby the apocalyptist represented himself to have acquired the divine truth contained in his apocalypse was the *vision*, occasionally the *dream*. Nominally this was the same method as that used centuries before by the ancient seer (*chōzeh, rō'eh*) in Israel, as well as by his contemporary pagan confreres.[23]

[20] It seems clear, for example, that the authors of II Baruch, The Psalms of Solomon, Testaments of the Twelve Patriarchs, and IV Esdras were either themselves Pharisees or else very close to the sect in their views.

[21] See Rowley, *op. cit.*, pp. 35-36, who like myself finds it impossible to accept Charles' theory, though his account of the origin of the apocalyptist's pseudonymity differs from mine.

[22] For Daniel, cf. Matt. 24:15; for Revelation, Justin Martyr, *Dial.* 81.

[23] See above, pp. 26-27.

There was, however, a marked difference between the techniques employed in the two cases: both seer and prophet accepted the vision as a medium of genuine mystical or revelational experience, whereas the apocalyptist adopted it as a mere *literary device* comparable to others employed by him and his associates in the Hebrew literary tradition, such as the parable, the poem, the chronicle, the wisdom saying or aphorism, the psalm, and the like. That this is the case appears to follow from two considerations.

In the first place, as we have seen, the *authorship* of this literature is pseudonymous, which seems at once to preclude the possibility of our taking its vision motif seriously. Many a prophet staked his life on the word which he claimed to have heard from God. The courage with which he declared this goes far to commend the genuineness of his prophetic utterances. The same can hardly be said for the deliverances of a man who for reasons of "tact" refuses to divulge his name. Modern scholars have tried with limited success to evade the moral problem involved here; but whatever may be thought of the ultimate truth or falsity of the pseudonymous writings of the apocalyptist judged purely on their merits as teachings, the fact remains that the moral judgment balks at the suggestion that a book be accepted as a genuine revelation, the product of a divine vision, whose author for any reason whatever is unwilling to underwrite it with his own name.

In the second place, the *content* of the apocalyptic vision appears to render quite improbable any suggestion other than that it was a mere literary device. The mar'āh of the ancient seer and prophet had been a simple vision of God himself accompanied by a divine "call." [24] The experiences of Isaiah (Isa. 6) and of Saul of Tarsus (Acts 9:1-9) are typical. The apocalyptist on the contrary, in a detailed series of visions whose like is to be found in ancient literature only in materials from Iran and Babylonia,[25]

[24] Cf. Gen. 15:1; I Sam. 3:15; II Sam. 7:4.
[25] Cf. R. Otto, *The Kingdom of God and the Son of Man*, pp. 176-200; Albright, *op. cit.*, pp. 275 ff. C. C. McCown in "Hebrew and Egyptian Apocalyptic Litera-

gives us on a grand scale a picture of heaven and hell; and in the light of what he sees there he casts his glance back over human history to the beginning and so succeeds in interpreting it in the light of the eternal purpose for the "ages of the ages." Virgil's *Aeneid* and in later times Dante's *Inferno* and Milton's *Paradise Lost* are parallel in both purpose and plan to these Jewish apocalypses, and it is impossible to escape the impression that the one is a literary device on an exact par with the other. Such a "vision" technique certainly had no kinship with the prophet's method of audition of the word, and it had little more with the limited visions and dreams of the seer who preceded him on the Hebrew stage. It was indeed a phenomenon utterly unique so far as Israel's religious tradition was concerned.

But if this is so, it seems then to follow that the view which is dominant at the moment—that the apocalyptist was the legitimate successor of the prophet and partook of his spirit—is proved untenable. The apocalyptist, of course, like the priest, the king, the scribe, or the commoner, could become a prophet on the same terms as they. This was so in view at once of the democratic character of the prophetic office and of its dependence upon the divine *charisma*.[26] But to suggest that there is any real similarity between the two figures by reason of the use of the metaphor of "audition" to the divine word, on the one hand, and of the literary fiction of "vision," on the other, is to compare incommensurate concepts and results in the end in debasing the prophetic belief in genuine revelation to the level of pure naturalism.

Far from the apocalyptist's having been the normal successor of the prophet, it is noteworthy that, with the single exception of II Baruch (10:1), no noncanonical apocalypse ever speaks of the "Word of God" as having come to its author; and in the one instance cited the writer uses the common prophetic expression

---

ture," *Harvard Theological Review*, Oct., 1925, argues for a relation between these two types of apocalyptic.

[26] See above, pp. 18-21.

in connection with an actual violation of the "historic tradition." [27] It has been averred that Judaism rejected the apocalyptic literature because it proved acceptable to the Christian Church and was widely used by it. There is no doubt some measure of truth here, but it is by no means the whole truth. It seems rather to lie on the surface of this matter that both Judaism and the Christian Church adopted as Scripture such portions of the apocalyptic literature as proved acceptable to each for the same reason, namely, that these appealed as containing prophetic elements and the prophetic spirit, whereas those rejected did not. This will account for the large amount of apocalyptic which was incorporated into the already-existing prophetic literature of the Old Testament. It accords also with the remarkable disparity between the Revelation of John and the noncanonical apocalypses, first, as regards the use of the prophetic phrase "Word of God" as the medium of the divine revelation (once in all the noncanonical apocalypses together! and eight times in Revelation alone: 1:2, 9; 3:8, 10; 6:9; 12:11; 19:13; 20:4); second, in the matter of their respective references to the prophetic writings. Like the noncanonical apocalyptists, John does not refer to the prophets by name (p. 197); but whereas all of them combined have but two references to "the prophets" generally (pp. 197-98), he alone has seven such references: 10:7; 11:18; 16:6; 18:20, 24; 22:6, 9. Moreover his thought is so saturated with their teachings that Nestle is able to list 149 direct quotations from the prophets, exclusive of Ezekiel and Daniel, and the major apocalyptic interpolations into the prophetic writings. Daniel had to be placed among the Hagiographa because the canon of the Prophets was closed, but the church considered him a prophet (Matt. 24:15) as it did also John, the author of Revelation, and so accepted this apocalypse on that ground (Rev. 22:7).

The distinctive mark of the canonical apocalyptic writings,

[27] Here Jeremiah is told by God to accompany the captives to Babylon, whereas in Jer. 39:11-14; 40:1-6 he remains in Judah of his own volition; see also Charles, in loc.

therefore, as opposed to those which were not adopted into Scripture, will be the same as that which served to distinguish the post-prophetic priestly literature.[28] In both cases it will be the large prophetic element which gives these two types of canonical literature their true tone and which justifies their presence in the canon of Scripture. This is not to say that either priest or apocalyptist as such was the normal successor to the prophet. It is rather to say that, in spite of what each was otherwise, there were some apocalyptists and some priests who—like some kings, some shepherds, some artisans, and what not—were also in the providence of God prophets.

The Product of Apocalyptic—Unveiling of the Mystery

The product, the "apocalypse," which resulted from the apocalyptist's literary fiction of the detailed vision was essentially a philosophy of history written from the standpoint of certain leading ideas entertained by him. Of these the most important was without doubt the conviction that God is the Moral Governor of the universe and that history is throughout the expression of his will. This idea he derived from the prophet before him.[29] Amos had taken God's righteous ruling of the nations as the major theme of his prophetic symphony. Yahweh was the God of all peoples, equally interested in the welfare of all and not of Israel and Judah alone. "Are ye not as the children of the Ethiopians unto me, O children of Israel? saith Yahweh. Have not I brought up Israel out of the land of Egypt, and the Philistines from Caphtor, and the Syrians from Kir?" Pfeiffer remarks:

In fact, God was no more concerned with Israel than with the Negroes of Africa (9:7); and if he selected Israel as his peculiar people it was only

---

[28] See above, pp. 106-7.

[29] And it was continued by the apostle after him; cf., for example, Rom. 9:24-26; I Cor. 12:13; Gal. 4:28; Eph. 2:11-22, et al. The Amos passage herewith, however, was never used in the New Testament in proof of the universal application of the gospel message. This was taken rather from such passages as Isa. 57:19 (Eph. 2:13, 17; cf. Acts 2:39), Hos. 2:1, 23 (Rom. 9:25-26), and even Isa. 56:7 (Mark 11:17).

to enforce a more rigid standard of conduct and penalty (3:2). Thus
Amos, without discrimination of race or nation, planted the roots of a
universal religion, from which were to grow the great monotheistic religions of salvation, Judaism, Christianity, and Islam.[30]

Following Amos other prophets developed the concept of the
universal God into its only possible logical corollary—that of a
universally proffered salvation for man, the logic that was later to
grip the apostle Paul profoundly (Rom. 3:29-30). Such universalism is found with varying clarity in Isa. 2:1-4 (Mic. 4:1-5);
18:7; 19:23-25; Zeph. 2:11; 3:9.[31]

This prophetic concept of the one universal God who dealt
with righteousness in all his relations with the peoples of the
earth was the basic assumption of all apocalyptic, though for historical reasons there was a lack of uniformity regarding acceptance
of the corollary regarding a universal salvation for man.[32] Like the
apostle Paul, the apocalyptist would have us believe that the
"mystery" of the divine will had been made known to him (cf.
Eph. 3:2 ff.) and that he possessed a peculiar "understanding"
(vs. 4) or "knowledge" (vs. 14) of the significance of history as
a whole. This understanding embraced not only the past but the
present and future as well.

It is here that the choice of a nom de plume by the apocalyptist
gains point. A patriarch or scribe of sufficiently distant date from
the author's own day was chosen in order to give a view of a large
and typical segment of history through which the meaning of the
whole might be observed.[33] The individual chosen was, then,
represented as prophesying the intervening events between his day
and that of the writer of the apocalypse, as pointing out the eth-

[30] Op. cit., p. 580.
[31] "Monotheism," as Millar Burrows observes, "logically implies universalism. . . .
According to the most probable interpretation of ch. 53" of Isaiah "even the suffering of Israel is a means to the salvation of other nations" (op. cit., p. 279; see
also Gen. 12:3 [J]).
[32] See below, pp. 228-29.
[33] As has been said above (p. 202), however, a prophet's name and distant
date would have served the same purpose.

ical lessons and theological ideas to be observed from these events (*Haggādāh*, in the scribe's nomenclature), and as stating that in the day of the author of the work history would come to an end in some catastrophic event associated with phenomena on a grand scale in heaven and on earth.[34]

Thus, under the aegis of an honored name the apocalyptist succeeded in assuring the persecuted saints of his own day of their final vindication in the soon-to-be-realized judgment of God. To those who cried out to God for such vindication the answer was always the same; they were to wait patiently till the role of God's witnesses ($\mu\acute{\alpha}\rho\tau\upsilon\rho\epsilon\varsigma$) was made up (Rev. 6:11; I Enoch 47:1-4; IV Esdras 4:35; II Baruch 30:2)[35] in the assurance that "yet a little while, and the coming one shall come and shall not tarry" (Heb. 10:37) but shall bring to them the promised salvation.

Fundamentally the differences between prophet and apocalyptist as to their understanding of the "divine mystery" were three: first, the final vindication envisaged by the prophet was that of God's own righteous rule, whereas the apocalyptist returned to the preprophetic standpoint of primitive Hebrew thought and longed rather for the vindication of God's "righteous people";[36] second, the prophet looked for the justification of the righteous and sovereign rule of God to be accomplished on the plane of history, whereas the apocalyptist contrariwise did not anticipate that this could be in "this present evil age" and so threw it forward into the eternal order beyond history; third, the prophet, as we have seen, set no date for the end of history, nor was he greatly concerned about such matters, whereas the apocalyptist always foresaw the immediate coming of this event in his own time and that of his associates.[37]

---

[34] T. W. Manson has presented this matter with great force and clarity (*Teaching*, pp. 254 ff.).
[35] See R. H. Charles, *The Revelation of St. John*, I, 178-79.
[36] See above, pp. 53-54.
[37] See above, pp. 58-62.

The Institution of Apocalyptic—The Sect

It is generally agreed that the apocalyptic writings arose within orthodox circles of postexilic Judaism and the later, but still contemporary, Christian Church.[38] This means that "there is no recognizable sectarian peculiarity in them," such as would have been the case if the view were to be accepted that they emanated from a group like the Essenes.[39] It means also that, although as we have seen some of these books were written by Pharisees, they did not depart sufficiently from the straight path of the prophetic revelation to be pronounced heretical or sectarian by the great body of Jews previous to the inception of the Christian movement in the first century. The volume of these writings as well as their relevance for an age of suffering and persecution combine to suggest that they must at first have been very popular with the masses, though the extent of their actual usage is difficult to determine.[40]

At the same time orthodox Jewry was not prepared to admit the great bulk of this literature into the canon of Scripture, for the reason already assigned (p. 206). It was felt, apparently, that however helpful it might appear in time of stress and though it did not give evidence of any actual heretical teaching, nonetheless it was essentially "outside the main current of thought and life," [41] which within orthodox Judaism as within Christianity was always *the prophetic current.* Accordingly there is little or no evidence that the Pharisaic leaders of Jewish thought were influenced by apocalyptic previous to A.D. 70, whereas at the Council of Jamnia (A.D. 90), which drew up the canon of the Old Testament scriptures in their final form for continuing Judaism, it was definitely excluded

[38] Cf. Charles, op. cit., II, vii ff. and Moore, op. cit., II, 280, 344.
[39] So Moore, ibid.
[40] Moore, op. cit., II, 281.
[41] Ibid., I, 132. Moore suggests that "the authorities" never "felt it necessary even to repudiate" the apocalypses (p. 127), though on this point M. Sanh. 10:1 may be relevant. It reads, "R. Akiba says: Also he that reads the heretical books"—or as Canon Danby says, "Lit. 'external books,' books excluded from the canon of Hebrew Scriptures"—has "no share in the world to come."

with the single exception of Daniel, the apocalyptic intrusions into the prophetic literature also being allowed to remain intact. Both Mishnah and Talmud are evidence that after that date the influence of this class of literature upon the development of rabbinical Judaism was nil.

For this reason the history of medieval and modern Judaism has been a far happier one than that of Christianity so far as the growth of a spirit of sectarianism is concerned. The esoteric nature of the knowledge imparted in the apocalypses, like other esoteric knowledge, was well calculated to produce division within any religious group which should take it too seriously. This is not to say, of course, that such was the inevitable effect of the apocalypses. We shall see in the next chapter that the details of apocalyptic were always secondary to the mind of the author himself and were intended by him as so many "props" for the support of his main thesis. That this is so appears from the fact that these props can be moved about and altered or even discarded according to the will of the writer. In some cases perhaps the significance of the props was known to the author's contemporaries, though this has in the meanwhile become lost for us. This fact, if true, is however of small importance, as it is the over-all prophetic teaching of the divine rule in the affairs of men and the assurance of his abiding righteousness and grace that constitute the unveiled mystery which is the theme of the apocalyptist and which must be held to have abiding meaning for us.

Nonetheless the bare fact that there was in these apocalypses an esoteric knowledge and a "mystery" to be solved has through the centuries attracted to them those who would search out and resolve riddles. " 'Students of prophecy,' as they are often called, are firmly persuaded that by the exercise of their ingenuity they can break the seal which is on these books, and lay bare their secrets." Yet "on their view they are compelled to believe that God Himself decreed that the Book of Daniel should be sealed till the time of the end (Dan. xii. 9). The belief that they can break the seals is therefore a belief that they can defeat the purpose of God!" [42]

The Christian Church, unlike Judaism, acclaimed apocalyptic from the first and, along with the Ebionites (the relic of the sect of Pharisaical or Judaizing Christians of Jerusalem) and Cerinthian Gnostics, for long read even the noncanonical apocalypses and looked on them with favor.[43] The result has been the emergence of a number of chiliastic sects and groups within the church whose history exemplifies the judging, divisive influence of the religion of the throne.[44] It should say something to those who are interested in apocalyptic for its own sake and quite apart from the prophetic spirit it enshrines that in the end the Christian Church followed the Jewish in discrediting the great bulk of this literature for the reason that its tendency was nonprophetic. And those who seek out the apocalyptic portions of the Scriptures for the riddles they are supposed to contain and elucidate are failing to follow the Spirit of the Lord who is thus guiding his church. If it is the nonprophetic elements of the apocalyptic literature that they wish to search out, they will find much more material to their liking in the noncanonical apocalypses which were rejected by the church under the Spirit's direction than is available to them in Scripture. But if contrariwise the Spirit's choice of certain apocalypses only as containing the prophetic word is to be accepted, then it is only reasonable to inquire into the cause of such choice being made and to follow the Spirit's guidance in laying stress upon that reason. That there are far more riddles in the noncanonical apocalypses than in those that are scriptural is itself proof that the Spirit's interest does not lie in this direction.

That the religion of the throne, when left to her own devices, has never been able to produce an institution other than the "sect"

[42] Rowley, op. cit., p. 12.
[43] Cf. the use of the Assump. Mosei by Jude (vs. 9) and of I Enoch by I Pet. (3:19-22).
[44] See below, p. 270.

is abundant proof of her essential sterility. Both of the other religions within postexilic Judaism were able to do better than that; for the one gave Judaism the temple and the other, the synagogue. Where the religion of the throne has been true to her prophetic heritage, she has glorified the church and the church's Lord; in this context her sterility has been her chief ground for praise. Because, however, of her proved sterility, her greatest danger has always lain in the direction of the "besetting sin" of divisiveness, a religious vice whose moral counterpart is to be found in those unnatural aberrations that occur from time to time in the realm of physical begetting (cf. I Cor. 12:25). It ought not require the wisdom of a Solomon to decide that she who would divide the church for the sake of her own whims is not that church's true mother (cf. I Kings 3:23-28).

11

Understanding in All Visions

IT has become popular to say that "apocalyptic is the most direct continuation of prophecy." [1] This, it might almost be said, is the dominant contemporary Christian reply to modern Judaism's identical claim for Pharisaism. [2] And yet when we pass from Hebrew prophetism to Jewish apocalypticism, we become conscious of a great change in ethos.

The subject is one of extraordinary difficulty for a variety of reasons, of which four are worthy of mention here. In the first place, as we have already noted there was a paucity of canonized apocalyptic literature among the Jews—nothing in comparison with the canonized prophetic, priestly, and even rabbinic writings (Mishnah). In consequence apocalyptic teaching failed to attain anything like a standardized pattern comparable to the patterns to be found in the remaining literature. The only bounds set for the apocalyptist were those accorded by his religious insights, his fertile imagination, and his general acceptance of the somewhat elusive tenets of Jewish orthodoxy.

Again, there is the uncertainty as to how apocalyptic is to be understood and interpreted. The crucial question is, of course, how the Jewish and Christian apocalyptists themselves wished to be

[1] See H. Wheeler Robinson's illuminating essay, "The Religion of Israel," *A Companion to the Bible*, edit. by T. W. Manson, p. 307.

[2] See above, p. 139.

taken—whether literally, or allegorically, or prophetically, or symbolically, or in some other way. In all probability we should not look for entire uniformity in this area. The lack of pattern in the teaching of the religion of the throne would lead us to expect the like lack of pattern in its authors' intentions regarding how their writings should be construed. Moreover apocalyptic in the wide sense belongs with theosophy, astrology, mysticism, and other like systems to a type of mental activity which requires for its elucidation not one but a thousand keys with which to unlock its devious chambers, subterranean vaults, and supraterrestrial treasuries.

The third major difficulty in this field arises out of the fact that scholars have thus far failed to agree as to the source(s) from which the Jewish and Christian apocalyptists drew their materials. As suggested above on page 204, Babylonia, Iran, and Egypt have proved favorites among the possibilities at hand. Final agreement in detail is hardly to be expected here, and yet some degree of unanimity would appear essential, as apocalyptic terminology to be understood requires a knowledge of (a) the matrix of ideas out of which it arose, and (b) the use made of it in the new context. It is reasonable to suppose that, in some cases at least, (b) would be influenced by (a); hence some sort of settlement regarding the origin of biblical, as well as of noncanonical, apocalyptic would lead to illuminating results.

A final complication arises from the fact that some of the apocalypses in their present form have been worked over by both Jewish and Christian hands. For example, the claim has long been made by some New Testament scholars that the so-called Little Apocalypse of Mark 13 and the Revelation of John came originally in large part from Jewish hands. The Sibylline Oracles is likewise generally recognized to be the work of various Hellenistic Jewish and Christian writers "who lived at various times between c. 160 B.C. and the fifth century, or even later, A.D." [3] A curious variation on

[3] H. C. O. Lanchester in *The Apocrypha and Pseudepigrapha of the Old Testament in English*, R. H. Charles, ed., II, 368.

this theme concerns the possibility that the later Jewish apocalypses were directly or indirectly influenced by Christian doctrinal teachings. Thus Charles has written, "No Jewish book except 2 Esdras teaches undubitably the doctrine of a general resurrection; and this may be due to Christian influence, as 2 Esdras cannot be earlier than A.D. 80." [4]

In spite of these facts, however, apocalyptic presents us with a sufficiently clear "pattern" of doctrine for us to estimate its general character and worth, provided always that we are prepared to resign from the start all claim to omniscience regarding the infinite variety of confusing and often admittedly conflicting details which it comprises in its literature. It is at once with this diffidence and yet with a sense of real, if limited, comprehension that the following schema of apocalyptic teaching is presented.

The Transcendent Throne

The center and focal point of all genuine apocalyptic, around which everything else revolves, is the throne of God. "And lo, a throne stood in heaven, with one seated on the throne!" (Rev. 4:2 R.S.V.) In this passage John is employing a motif to be found in the apocalyptic literature generally, previous to, as well as contemporary with, his own day. The same motif occurs, for example, in I Enoch in its various sections written by different authors, in the Assumption of Moses, in the Testaments of the Twelve Patriarchs, in II Enoch, in the Sibylline Oracles, and in IV Esdras, as well as in the canonical Ezekiel, Zechariah, and Daniel.[5]

The throne represents, of course, merely a dramatization of the prophetic idea of the sovereignty of God over his world; and its origin may be ascribed perhaps to the vision of one of the greatest of the prophets, Isaiah (see 6:1 ff.). The throne appears as well in the prophet-inspired Psalms (11:4; 45:6; 47:8). There is, however,

---

[4] I am indebted to T. Francis Glasson for the quotation (*The Second Advent*, p. 216, n. 2).
[5] For references see the schema below, p. 217. Assum. Mosei 4:2; Sibyll. Or. 3:1; Zech. 6:13 might be added to the schema.

the striking difference between the prophetic and apocalyptic dramatizations: whereas in the former the throne is set up on earth, in the latter it appears in heaven.

This is surely symptomatic. The prophet conceived God's rule as realizable within history and on earth as presently constituted. The apocalyptist, on the contrary, characteristically transferred it to the heavenly sphere; and with its transference the throne of God also was withdrawn farther and farther from its prophetic abode in the temple at Jerusalem. It is illuminating to observe the several stages of the throne's upward progression in the apocalyptic literature. In the table which follows the relevant passages from the prophetic literature are added for purposes of comparison.

Stage I: 600 to 165 B.C.—the throne on earth and specifically in the temple at Jerusalem (I Kings 22:19; Isa. 6:1; II Chr. 18:18; Ezek. 1:26; 10:1; 43:7; I Enoch 25:3; 90:20; cf. Jer. 3:17)

Stage II: 550 B.C. to A.D. 100—the throne in heaven (Pss. 11:4; 103:19; Isa. 66:1; Dan. 7:9; Rev. 4:2; I Enoch 14:18; 71:7; IV Esdras 8:21; cf. I Kings 8:27; Matt. 5:34; 23:22)

Stage III: ca. 109 B.C.—the throne in the third heaven (Test. of Levi 3:4; 5:1; cf. II Cor. 12:2)

Stage IV: ca. A.D. 1— the throne in the seventh heaven (II Enoch 20:1 ff.; 21:1; 22:1)

This upward progress of the throne is in line with "the increasing sense of the transcendence of God after the exile," [6] a sense so strong "that a gap seemed to be left between Him and the world." [7] The point cannot of course be pressed too far. There is no doubt some overlapping between Stages I and II above, for example; and probably one of prophetic spirit could speak of God's throne as being in both heaven and earth at once in the sense that he is sovereign in both spheres (see Matt. 6:10). Moore's caution regarding "names or epithets of God significant of his abode in the height of heaven"—such as 'El 'Elyōn (Most High God),

[6] Burrows, op. cit., pp. 120-21.   [7] Ibid., p. 62.

'Elōhē Mārōm (God of High Heaven), and 'Elōhē ha-shāmaim (God of the Heavens)—that they "are no novelty in later Jewish writings; they go back at least as far as the age of the kingdoms," needs to be observed here also.[8] The prophet, as well as the apocalyptist, believed in God's transcendence. Nonetheless, as we have seen, the apocalypses were written at a time when it was not easy to see that God was in his world and governing it with equity and righteousness. It is better at such a time, it is true, as Moore remarks, for men to "cling with all their souls to the inscrutable sovereignty of God,"[9]—though to do so means shoving him off into the highest heaven—than to give up faith in him altogether. But this cannot be allowed to obscure the fact that such indefinitely prolonged stress on God's other-worldliness—his wholly "otherness" or unapproachable holiness—and the consequent or concomitant inability to observe his historic vindication of his sovereign rule among men in the end are bound to result in an attitude of despair such as was without doubt the typical apocalyptic weakness.

The Two Kingdoms

Animistic beliefs among most primitive peoples, including the Semites, peopled the universe with "spirits" good and bad.[10] But as Burrows remarks, "The Old Testament is remarkably free from such ideas, perhaps because the records were edited by advanced theologians (sic) who allowed only occasional fragments of early conceptions to slip through their fingers as parts of stories that were preserved for the sake of higher spiritual values."[11] The prophets, for example, had no doctrine of evil spirits. Satan appears in the Old Testament but rarely, and the few references show signs of only a rudimentary teaching regarding him.[12] As we have seen,

[8] Judaism, I, 430.
[9] Ibid., Vol. I, 433.
[10] See W. O. E. Oesterley's discussion in the chapter on "Worship and Ritual" in The People and the Book, A. S. Peake, ed., pp. 323 ff.
[11] Op. cit., p. 124.
[12] See Burrows, op. cit., pp. 124-25, for a good statement of the Old Testament evidence.

for the prophets of Israel our world was under God's dominion, and his sovereign sway was felt throughout his creation; this left little room, if any, for irresponsible or even immoral creatures roaming at will through his universe and converting its cosmos into the chaos of irrational animism. Islam with its elaborate jinn folklore is an example of a prophetic faith vitiated by primitive animistic beliefs.

There is also but limited reference to angels, seraphim, and cherubim in the Old Testament scriptures. So far as they occur, they are all beings—whether animate or inanimate—which serve the will of God and do his bidding. With the exceptions about to be noted, none are ever mentioned by name. The "angel of God" or "of Yahweh," however, attains particular eminence and is so spoken of as to merge into the person of God himself.[13] Reference to these benign beings in the writings of the prophets is of such a character as to indicate assumption of its intelligibility to the general reader, and no doctrine of angels is ever elaborated therein.[14]

With the apocalyptists Jewish thought took over highly developed systems of both angels and demons from Iranian, as well as perhaps from other Eastern, circles. These influences first made themselves felt in Daniel (cf. 3:28; 6:22), where the names of two angels are given, Gabriel (8:16; 9:21) and Michael (10:13, 21; 12:1). Of these, Michael is the "prince" or angelic guardian of Persia and apparently also of Israel,[15] while Gabriel is represented as Daniel's heavenly interpreter. These two with five others made up a special order of archangels with duties as follows: Uriel was "over the world and over Tartarus"; Raphael, "over the spirits of men"; Raguel, over "the luminaries"; Michael, over "the best part of mankind and over chaos"; Saraqael, "over the spirits, who sin in the spirit"; Gabriel, "over Paradise and the serpents and the

[13] Cf. Gen. 32:30; Judg. 13:22.
[14] Cf. I Sam. 29:9; II Sam. 14:17, 20; 19:27; 24:16-17; I Kings 13:18; 19:5, 7; II Kings 1:3, 15; 19:35; Pss. 34:7; 35:5-6; Isa. 37:36; 63:9.
[15] Such Michael is also in Jude 9; Rev. 12:7; cf. Charles, op. cit., I, 376, note on Sirach 17:17.

219

Cherubim"; and Remiel, "over those who rise" (I Enoch 20). In addition to these high beings, the apocalyptic literature knew many others whom it divided into various orders or ranks, including the "angels of the Presence," who stand before the throne of God;[16] the angels of sanctification,[17] of natural phenomena,[18] of punishment,[19] of mediation or intercession, especially for Israel[20] (three orders); and the guardian angels of men and Israel.[21] Three further orders—cherubim, seraphim, and ophanim—are created of fire.[22]

This apocalyptic development of orders of benign beings whose function was to serve God was necessitated by the doctrine of the transcendent throne. Intermediaries or mediators in the manner of the Gnostic systems and for a like reason became absolutely essential in order that God's will might be accomplished in his universe and he might remain at the same time uncontaminated with its evil. Medieval rabbinic Judaism carried this series of ideas further, developing it into the complicated system known as the Kabbalah, a sort of medieval counterpart of the Hellenistic Gnosticism of a much earlier period (from the second century A.D.).

In addition to the good angels the apocalyptists also supply us with an abundance of materials for the portrayal of a "counterkingdom" of evil. Taking their start from the "watchers" of Gen. 6:1-4—that is, the angels sent "to instruct the children of men to do judgment and uprightness"[23]—the apocalyptic writers account for the demons in the world as being children begotten by the unnatural union of these high beings with the "daughters of men" through "lust."[24] From this evil beginning these beings grew in

[16] Cf. Isa. 63:9; I Enoch 40:2; Test. Levi 3:5, 7; Test. Jud. 25.
[17] See Jub. 2:2, 18.
[18] Cf. Jub. 2:2; IV Esdras 8:21.
[19] Cf. I Enoch 40:7; 53:3; 56:1; 62:11; 63:1; II Enoch 10:3.
[20] Cf. Test. Levi 3:5; II Enoch 20:1, 3; Adam and Eve 48:5; also I Enoch 89: 59; 86:1, 3; 87:2 for three orders.
[21] Cf. I Enoch 20:5; II Enoch 22:6; Jub. 35:17; Adam and Eve 33:1.
[22] Cf. II Enoch 29:1, 3.
[23] Cf. Jub. 4–5; Test. Reub. 5:6; I Enoch 6:1–16:4; for an alternative explanation, see Burrows, op. cit., pp. 121, 123, and Jude 6, II Pet. 2:4, also perhaps Matt. 25:41.
[24] Cf. I Enoch 16:1; 69:2, 3; Jub. 4:15, 22; 5:1 ff.; II Enoch 7:18.

numbers—presumably by self-propagation like other animate creatures—until they came to represent a sizable kingdom of evil in the
world. For the time being they represent the dominant force in the
world, though their continuance is entirely due to the sufferance
of God. This apocalyptic teaching of the two kingdoms is therefore
never more than a limited dualism.[25]

The names of twenty-one of the leaders of this rebellious movement against God—for such it proved to be, as they are represented
as binding themselves with an oath (I Enoch 6:4-5)—are given in
I Enoch, though the two lists do not agree (cf. 6:7-8; 69:2-15).
Their overlord is Satan or Mastema (I Enoch 54:6; Jub. 10:8-9).
Their work consists in tempting men to sin,[26] in accusing men,[27]
even in ruling over men,[28] and in punishing those who fall into
sin.[29] They are to continue their nefarious activities until their own
judgment or that of their leader,[30] or alternately until the setting
up of the kingdom of the Messiah.[31.]

The Transcendent Messiah

As the prophetic view of the messianic kingdom looked for its
setting up on earth, so its conception of the Messiah was of one
who should arise from among men, of the stem of Jesse, of the tribe
of Judah, of the house of David.[32] Here was a regal figure, indeed,
but nonetheless one that should come from among his own people.

Apocalyptic at this point divides along two lines, the one
prophetic, the other nonprophetic. The former view, stemming
from the prophetic tradition, anticipated the rising up of a Messiah
from the tribe of Judah (cf. Test. Jud. 24:5-6; Test. Levi 8:14a).
A variation from this usual prophetic theme occurs in the Testaments, to the effect that the Messiah would be of the tribe of Levi

---

[25] See Burrows, op. cit., p. 130. On this whole subject of Iranian influence in the
biblical demonology, see Albright, Stone Age, pp. 279 ff.

[26] Cf. Jub. 10:8; I Enoch 69:4, 6.

[27] See I Enoch 40:7.

[28] See Jub. 10:3, 6.

[29] Cf. I Enoch 53:3; 56:1.

[30] See Jub. 10:8.

[31] See Jub. 23:29.

[32] Cf. Isa. 9:6, 7; 11:1-5.

and therefore in the first instance a priest. This is to be explained from the contemporary situation at the time of the writing of the book. As Canon Charles remarks, "it was the priestly character of the Maccabean priest-kings that gave rise to the expectation that the Messiah was also to be a priest as well as a king." [33] This hope, however, proved short-lived; for within thirty or forty years the older view reappeared.[34]

In addition to the above prophetic view there appeared for the first time in apocalyptic another nonprophetic view which resulted generally from the characteristic pessimism of its philosophy of history. With a view to clarification of this point it will be necessary to indicate in parallel columns certain materials for which the evidence will be presented in the next section, "The Transcendent Order." In the present context our interest concerns the fact that, in addition to the prophetic conception of a kingdom of God to be set up on earth, apocalyptic contained a pessimistic strand of thought which issued in the idea that no kingdom would be set up on earth, but that such a kingdom could be looked for only after the final judgment of mankind and, therefore, in the heavenly order. These two doctrines—one prophetic, the other nonprophetic —lie side by side in the extant apocalyptic literature. They may be illustrated as follows:

PROPHETIC STRAND	NONPROPHETIC STRAND
1. *Kingdom of God* for a limited period—human Messiah	World too evil for appearance of the kingdom on earth
2. Gentiles brought into kingdom	
3. *Final Judgment*	*Final Judgment* accompanied by cosmic catastrophe
4. *Kingdom of God* in heavenly order	*Kingdom of God* in heavenly order —no Messiah, or superhuman one; Gentiles become Jews and so enter the kingdom [35]

[33] *Op. cit.*, II, 294.
[34] *Ibid.*
[35] I am indebted in large part for this summary to Dr. Thomas Walker, *The Teaching of Jesus and the Jewish Teaching of His Day*, ch. ii, particularly pp. 99-100.

The above-outlined nonprophetic strand of thought in apocalyptic gave birth to two new views regarding the Messiah. According to one of these, there would be no Messiah at all for the reason that it envisaged no messianic kingdom—i.e., a kingdom of God realized within history. So far as our evidence goes, this extreme pessimism appears to have been limited to the period 65 B.C. to A.D. 30 and is found only in I Enoch 91–104, the Assumption of Moses, and II Enoch.[36] As these portions of the literature appear to have been written by members of the better element (Hasidic) within Pharisaism, or at any rate from the ranks of the orthodox Jewry of the day, it is quite likely, as Canon Charles contends, that this extreme pessimism is due to the unwillingness of these authors to accept the "growing secularization of Pharisaism" which conceived of the messianic kingdom along political or nationalistic lines almost exclusively.[37] If this view is sound, then the nonprophetic abandonment of the doctrine of an earthly Messiah represents a reaction against an equally nonprophetic Pharisaic Messiah. The like necessity of making a choice between "unholy opposites" has been illustrated many times in the history of revealed religion.

But nonprophetic apocalyptic had another solution for the difficulty; and it is important to point out, as Dr. T. Francis Glasson has done with much force, that this solution occurs only in I Enoch 37–71 (the Similitudes), whose date may be as early as 105-64 B.C. (Charles) or as late as the "middle of the first Christian century" (Bousset, Dalman, N. Schmidt).[38] In this view the Messiah would be a supramundane "Son of Man" (also called the "Anointed One," Messiah, the "Righteous One," or the "Elect One"), who should come to *judge* the world rather than to *save* it.[39]

The origin of the term in the Similitudes is in dispute. Thus Otto thinks that it "points back in some way to influences of the Aryan east," though he refuses to identify it with any "concrete

---

[36] *Ibid.*, pp. 87-88.
[37] *Op. cit.*, II, 412.
[38] See Glasson, *op. cit.*, pp. 20 ff., 60 ff.
[39] Cf. e.g., ch. 38; also R. Otto, *The Kingdom of God and the Son of Man*, p. 187.

figure." [40] Others more specifically suggest Iranian, Babylonian, Hindu, Egyptian, or Hellenistic connections.[41] Without wishing to pronounce final judgment for myself on these theories, I would like to make an observation regarding all of them at once which appears relevant. It comes from no less an authority than George Foot Moore and was made with reference to a related theme. "Borrowings in religion," wrote Professor Moore, "are usually in the nature of the appropriation of things in the possession of another which the borrower recognizes in all good faith as belonging to himself, ideas which, when once they become known to him, are seen to be the necessary implications or complements of his own." [42]

In the present instance this will mean that I Enoch, while he may, it is true, have added to the "Son of Man" motif certain attributes which he found far afield and there attached to a figure or to figures other than the one with which he was more immediately concerned, yet knew that he had nearer at hand the basic conception which he could use for his purpose. This was, of course, the corporate figure of Daniel 7:13. Though it is true that the Danielic figure stood for the "saints of the Most High," whereas in the Similitudes it is an individual that is in mind, yet there are a number of items suggestive of borrowing from the former by the latter. Thus in Daniel the "Son of Man" comes to the "Ancient of Days" (7:9); in Enoch he is associated with the "Head of Days" (46:1 ff.). In both he appears as an eternal figure or related to eternal rule and "glory" (Dan. 7:14; I Enoch 39:6b; 39:9; 45:3). In both "ten thousand times ten thousand" stand for judgment before the throne of God (Dan. 7:10; I Enoch 40:1).[48] In both

---

[40] Ibid.

[41] Cf. Albright, op. cit., pp. 290 ff.; H. H. Rowley, The Relevance of Apocalyptic, pp. 28-29; C. C. McCown, The Search for the Real Jesus, pp. 248-49; A. Schweitzer, The Quest of the Historical Jesus, pp. 269 ff.; C. J. Cadoux, The Historic Mission of Jesus, ch. viii, pp. 90 ff., et al.

[42] Op. cit., II, 394-95.

[48] It is notable, too, that in I Enoch the stress is on the judgment and wisdom in ruling exercised by the "Son of Man" in conjunction with or in the name of God. As Dr. Glasson has recently pointed out, this motif and even the phraseology may

the pre-existence of the "Son of Man" is asserted or assumed (Dan. 7:13; I Enoch 43:2; 48:6).[44]

It seems unnecessary, therefore, to go farther afield than Daniel, chapter 7, to account for the "Son of Man" of I Enoch 37–71, though elements from other sources may have been drawn into the picture. In my judgment Glasson has also made out his case for the suggestion that the immediate progenitor of the "Son of Man" motif in Dan. 7:13 is I Enoch, chapters 6–36 (especially 14:8).[45] But I would further suggest that I Enoch, chapters 6–36, may very well have drawn in turn upon the "Son of Man" of Ezekiel (1:4; 2:1 ff., et al.), as in each book the person referred to is the seer himself; in both, therefore, the reference constitutes a sort of non-technical, but at the same time specialized, use of the phrase.[46] But the reason for adopting the term in Daniel would be to suggest a contrast between the *beastly* pagan kingdoms and the righteous kingdom which has upon it God's imprimatur, a contrast found in the Psalms (e.g., 80:13, 17).[47]

H. H. Rowley has recently raised the question whether the "Son

---

very well come from Isa. 11:2 and kindred passages. Note the striking parallel which he quotes:

> And in him dwells the spirit of wisdom,
> And the spirit which gives insight,
> And the spirit of understanding and might.
> (I Enoch 49:3.)

> And the spirit of the Lord shall rest upon him,
> The Spirit of wisdom and understanding,
> The Spirit of counsel and might.
> (Isa. 11:2.)

[44] Similarly, in I Enoch the "Son of Man" is referred to as "the Anointed One" (48:10), an idea which may well be derived from Ps. 2:2: "The kings of the earth set themselves, and the rulers take counsel together, against the Lord and against his anointed."

[45] *Ibid.*, pp. 14 ff.

[46] I have assumed in the above discussion that the usual view is correct, to the effect that the figure in the Similitudes is intended to represent an individual supramundane person. This has been disputed by T. W. Manson in his *Teaching*, pp. 228-29. If he is right, then the origin of the conception in Dan. 7:13 receives added force.

[47] See Glasson, *op. cit.*, p. 38.

of Man" of the Similitudes is messianic at all in the strict sense of the word. He argues that "there is no evidence that the Son of Man was identified with the Messiah until the time of Jesus," and lays stress on the fact that in I Enoch, chapters 37–71, this figure is not one who brings deliverance or salvation, but rather dominion and judgment.[48] This, as far as it goes, was the view also of Rudolf Otto,[49] and represents the tendency of Goguel's thinking when he writes, for example, "Thus at the time of Jesus the term 'Son of Man' was a rather rare designation of the Messiah envisaged in his rôle as Judge" and "The fact that Enoch always uses the term 'this Son of Man' shows that this term is not a Messianic title which was in current use, but a somewhat mysterious designation, an allusion to a passage in which it was thought there was a reference to the Messiah." [50]

The question is by no means easy to decide. A solution depends in part upon a decision as to whether the term "Anointed One" in the Similitudes is used in the technical sense of Messiah, or more generally—as of the high priest (Exod. 28:41), of the king of Israel (I Sam. 9:16), or even of Cyrus (Isa. 45:1). It is perhaps in favor of Rowley's thesis that, if used in the strict sense, this is the first time that the phrase "Anointed One" is found in Jewish literature.[51] The Son of Man is also denominated the "Elect One" in I Enoch (cf. 40:5; 46:3), a phrase taken from Isa. 42:1, where it is definitive of the "Servant of Yahweh," as is also its usage in Luke 9:35; 23:35. But it will hardly be argued that the intention of the author of the Similitudes is to identify the Son of Man with the Suffering Servant! If the late date of the work adopted by Bousset, Dalman, and Nathaniel Schmidt was to prove acceptable, then the threefold equation, Messiah=Son of Man=Suffering Servant of Yahweh, would be intelligible under the influence of the church's New

---

[48] Op. cit., pp. 29-30, 56-57.
[49] Op. cit., pp. 190, 214 ff., pp. 219 ff.
[50] The Life of Jesus, p. 576.
[51] As Charles himself admits; see op. cit., II, 217, on I Enoch 48:10.

Testament.[52] Otherwise, Rowley's thesis affords interesting possibilities. If true, it would eliminate the only distinctively apocalyptic contribution to the growth of the doctrine of the Messiah outside the New Testament. For as we have observed, the nonprophetic apocalyptic otherwise has no messianic teaching whatever.

The Transcendent Order

The prophets were little concerned with the problem of a future life for the reason that their absorption in God's government of affairs in this world gave them no time to think about the next. The *vaticinium in situ* resulted from the word always "finding" the prophet *in situ*—i.e., it was always relevant to his needs and those of his people. And since that word found him and, so to speak, "put him on the spot" with divine relentlessness, it succeeded in keeping him at his God-appointed task of dealing realistically and fearlessly with the problems of his day. The apocalyptist who chronologically followed the prophet came on the scene in a day of tribulation and despair. The solution he afforded his contemporaries therefore varied according to the degree in which he shared the prophetic spirit and even the prophetic word. Speaking generally, because he perceived that the vindication of the righteous—or alternately with the prophets, of the righteous Yahweh—was not to be accomplished in this life, he looked forward to a resurrection life in which it would be.

And many of them that sleep in the dust of the earth shall awake, some to everlasting life, and some to shame and everlasting contempt. And they that are wise shall shine as the brightness of the firmament; and they that turn many to righteousness as the stars for ever and ever.
(Dan. 12:2-3.)[53]

---

[52] See above, pp. 77-83, and Glasson, op. cit., p. 61.

[53] The above-outlined logic of the origin of the apocalyptic doctrine of the resurrection is essentially that accepted also by H. H. Rowley, op. cit., pp. 50-51. This seems to me more likely than that it should have been taken over from various foreign sources which have been suggested.

As this doctrine of the resurrection developed under the apocalyptists it took on several different forms according to the belief advanced regarding the final judgment and the kingdom of God. Those who shared the prophetic outlook sufficiently to hold to any messianic rule on this earth at all looked for the resurrection to occur either after that rule (I Enoch 101–104; Ps. Sol. 3:16; 14:7; 15:15, and so forth), or before it (I Enoch 1–36; Test. Jud. 25:4; Test Benj. 10:7-8), while the nonprophetic apocalyptists who denied the doctrine of a messianic kingdom held that the resurrection would come after the judgment (II Bar. 51:6). It is significant for the doctrine of Scripture held by both Jewish and Christian Churches that Daniel and the Revelation of John at this point, as at so many others, prove to be prophetic in character. For both these apocalyptic works in true prophetic fashion find room for a kingdom of the Messiah realized on the historical plane.[54]

On the character of those who would share in the resurrection three views were advanced. Charles has analyzed these as follows: first, some held that "all Israelites are to rise" (Dan. 12:2; I Enoch 1–36; II Bar. 5–51:6), the usual Pharisaic attitude as illustrated in M. Sanhedrin 10:1;[55] again, there were those who claimed that "all righteous Israelities" would rise (Isa. 25:8; 26:19; Ps. Sol. 3:16; 13:9; 14:7; 15:15; II Bar. 30; I Enoch 101–104); third, still others taught that "all mankind are to rise" (IV Esdras 7:32, 37; Test. Benj. 10:6-8).[56] In this connection it is to be noted that there was some discussion in the apocalypses relative to the nature of the resurrection body. Some denied it entirely, holding to the resurrection (or resuscitation) of the spirit only (I Enoch 91–104); others held it would be a spiritual body (I Enoch 37–71); still others suggested that the body would be changed in the resurrection, in the case of the damned to "become worse than it is," and

---

[54] Cf. Dan. 7:14, 18, 22, 27-28; Rev. 20:4-6. The important prophetic element here is the fact of the earthly messianic kingdom; its relation to the final judgment is an incident of no special importance.

[55] It reads, "All Israelites have a share in the world to come" (Danby).

[56] See Charles, op. cit., II, 218, on I Enoch 51:1.

in that of the saved to gain a new "splendour" and "beauty" (II Bar. 50–51).[57]

Much is made in the apocalypses of the final judgment. This is only what one would expect of the religion of the throne. It is to be held before God (IV Esdras 7:33; Rev. 20:11-15), or before his "Elect One" (the Son of Man, I Enoch 45:3). The "day" of final judgment is variously described as the "day of tribulation" (I Enoch 1–5), the "Great Day of Judgment" (II Enoch 22:11; 84:4), the "Day of Judgment" (I Enoch 81:4), "the day of tribulation and pain" (II Enoch 55:3), the "day of the Elect One" (II Enoch 61:5), the "day of destruction . . . , of tribulation . . . , and of the great judgment" (II Enoch 98:10), the "day of repentance . . . and visitation" (Assump. Mosei 1:18), and the "day of the Mighty One" (II Bar. 55:5-6). Whether held before, after, or entirely apart from any thought of a messianic kingdom, it will at all events be in the "consummation of the times" (Test. Reub. 6:8; II Bar. 13:3; 30:3), or in the "consummation of the end of the days" (Assump. Mosei 1:18). There is also the rather general teaching in the apocalypses that judgment will be according to one's deeds in this present life. To this end there will be opened before the Lord or his Messiah "the book of life" (I Enoch 108:3; cf. Exod. 32:32; Ps. 69:28; Isa. 4:3; Ezek. 13:9; Dan. 12:1; Phil. 4:3; Heb. 12:23; Rev. 3:5, and so forth).[58]

In some cases the Gentiles share in both the judgment and its results, good and bad.[59] These are, on the one hand, "eternal life" or some equivalent (Test. Asher 5:2; I Enoch 65:10); on the other, "eternal punishment" (Test. Gad 7:5; I Enoch 53:2 ff.). Other expressions used to describe the result of the judgment are: the

---

[57] See I Cor. 15:35-50. On the rabbinic teaching regarding the resurrection body, see Moore, Judaism, II, 379 ff.

[58] This "book" is called in the apocalypses the "books of the Living" (Jub. 34:19-20; II Enoch 47:3), the "book of the deeds of mankind" (II Enoch 81:2), the "book of the memorial of life" (Test. Levi frag. vs. 59), and the "heavenly tablets" (II Enoch 103:2; Jub. 33:10).

[59] Cf. I Enoch 48:4; 68:6; II Enoch 90:30-31; Test. Sim. 4:4; Test. Jud. 24:6, et al.

"abyss of fire" (II Enoch 10:13; 90:24 ff.), the "new earth . . . tilled in righteousness" (II Enoch 10:18 ff.), "the accursed valley" (II Enoch 27:2-3), the "Garden of Righteousness" (II Enoch 32:3), the "New Jerusalem" (II Enoch 90:28-29), the "mansions of the elect" (I Enoch 41:2; cf. 61:2), the "New Heaven and New Earth" (I Enoch 45:2, 4 ff.), the "Valley of Gehenna" (I Enoch 54:1 ff.; 85:13), "the furnace of fire" (I Enoch 98:3), "Hell" (I Enoch 108:5-6), "Heaven" (II Enoch 1:8 ff.), and the "eternal inheritance" (I Enoch 55:2). The similarity of many of these phrases to biblical terminology is so patent as not to require particular reference.

Where belief in the coming of the Messiah existed, this was to be preceded by wars (Test. Jud. 22:1 ff.; II Bar. 48:37-39); by *internecine strife in families* (I Enoch 100:1 ff.); by *famines, earthquakes, pestilence,* and the like, called the "woes of the Messiah" (II Bar. 27–29, 70:1 ff.); and by *the antichrist* (II Bar. 40:1 ff.).[60] The latter is stated in one passage as about to arise out of the tribe of Dan (Test. Dan 5:6). The description of the messianic age is given at times in terms of Isa. 11:6-9 (II Bar. 73–74; cf. II Enoch 58:6); and in the same book (II Bar. 29) the prosperity of that age is stated in terms of the earth's extraordinary fruitfulness and the size of the sea life, behemoth and leviathan to be the measure of the fish produced therein (cf. also IV Esdras 6:51-52). The rabbinical literature drew upon these same conceptions of unusual fruitfulness in describing the messianic banquet which was to inaugurate the age.[61]

The point of major importance to be gathered from this infinitely diverse medley of details regarding the eternal order is that already stated (p. 211). These details constitute so many stage props required by the apocalyptist to further his ends. They have no function to perform other than this. He can accordingly deal

[60] The "woes" are referred to as "the footprints of the Messiah" in M. Sotah 9:15, where reference to the strife in families is referred to in the words of Mic. 7:6; cf. Matt. 10:36.

[61] See Moore, *op. cit.*, II, 298, 363-64, 378.

with them with considerable freedom, placing them in a variety of orders and adding to or subtracting from them at will. All that we have any right to do by way of evaluating the apocalyptist's materials, therefore, is to note the general direction which his employment of them gives to his belief in the divine government of the universe. From this we may hope to gather how far he approximates the prophetic spirit and shares the prophetic moral and spiritual insight. And it is by reference to this norm that the religion of the throne must be judged.

The Transcendent Ethic

The strong ethical interest which we have observed in Pharisaism is found in the apocalyptic literature as well. A particularly strong ethical emphasis occurs, for example, in the Testaments, in the Psalms of Solomon, in II Baruch, and in IV Esdras. The Testaments are especially striking for the way in which their author has undertaken to warn his readers against the deplorable consequences of certain sins. He takes representative ones which he finds exemplified in the lives of the patriarchs—such as fornication (Reuben), envy (Simeon), debauchery (Judah), deceit (Issachar), lying (Dan), guile (?-Naphtali), hatred (Gad)—and warns Israel against repetition of them, indicating that these examples were intended as warnings to Israel throughout her history. The same work contains the highest doctrine of forgiveness found outside the pages of the New Testament (Test. Gad 6:3-7)[62] and is the first Jewish book to combine the two commandments of loving God and loving one's neighbor after the manner of Mark 12:30-31. (Test. Iss. 5:2; Test. Dan 5:3; cf. Test. Iss. 7:6).[63]

The pessimistic attitude of nonprophetic apocalyptic which exalted the throne farther and farther above sinful man and his world brought forth fruit in two directions, so far as the subject of

[62] See Charles, op. cit., II, 293.
[63] This is not too striking, however, in view of Mic. 6:8; cf. Amos 5:15 and Wright, Challenge, pp. 42 ff.

practical ethics is concerned. In the first place, it had the effect of leaving the function of judgment in this present world in the hands of men. For this they had the Torah to guide them so far as the immediate present was concerned; and as we have seen (pp. 223 ff.), at "the end of the age" they would have the "Son of Man" to come for final judgment. Accordingly the Torah and the Messiah (or alternately, the "Son of Man") became the two focal points of interest for much apocalyptic writing; and as Canon Charles has observed, "the more one is emphasized, the more the other falls into the background." [64] This is particularly evident in II Baruch, where the "Messiah Apocalypses" (27–30 and 53–74) alternate with praise of the Law (31–48, 49–52, and 75–87).[65] Indeed, the typical Pharisaic allegiance to the Law emerges in all the apocalypses almost, if not quite, without exception (cf. IV Esdras 7:89, 94). In consequence apocalyptic rather generally makes the Law and its obedience the means of man's justification,[66] though in one passage at least it seems to fall back on the prophetic doctrine of God's unmerited grace in dealing with his people (Assump. Mosei 12:8); and several writers combine both ideas, making justification the product of both faith and works.[67]

The second fruitage of the nonprophetic apocalyptic in the realm of ethics was the denial of the possibility of man's attaining to anything more than the "relative righteousness" already known to Pharisaism. Even God, according to such apocalyptic, could not vindicate his rule on the plane of history and in the world as we now know of it (cf. above, pp. 198-200). But if this is so, then what is to be thought of man in his predicament? He is trapped, so to speak, in an imperfect world in which it is impossible for him to perform the high demands of God upon him; and the only possible solution for the moment is, therefore, for God to lower those

[64] Charles, op. cit., II, 478.
[65] Ibid.
[66] Cf. II Bar. 51:3-7; 67:6; 75:7.
[67] Cf. IV Esdras 9:7-8; 13:23; Sir. 16:14. However, IV Esdras 7:102-115 specifically denies the doctrine of "imputed righteousness."

demands. This is essentially, of course, to deny that goodness is feasible in a sinful situation and to affirm that moral character is, to some degree at least, a function of environment. Accordingly apocalyptic, together with Pharisaism, failed to afford any radical solution for the problem of specific evils and their elimination from man's world. The only ethical contribution it had to make was a "transcendent ethic" for a supramundane heavenly order which man might look forward to beyond the pale of history (I Enoch 12:4; 15:3)[68]

I should like to suggest that fundamentally there were two reasons for apocalyptic's failure at this point: (1) a transcendent God who is the "wholly Other" cannot come in contact with his world with a view either to giving his people an Example of how they may properly live righteously in an evil world or to aiding them to do so and thus saving them in the situation. Note in this connection the significance of the fact that apocalyptic made no contribution to the development of the messianic doctrine of the prophets other than that provided in the figure of a "son of Man" who comes to judge and not to save. (2) The ethic of apocalyptic is a crossless ethic. As we shall see in chapter 14 below, the only ethic that will function in a sinful world is one with a cross at its center; and this is one after the pattern of those prophetic characters who are prepared to "suffer for righteousness' sake." Modern "consistent eschatology" with its *Interimsethik* for a limited period and perfect conditions only runs true to type at this point, be it noted, as does every example presented by the apocalyptic messianisms of the current political world. For these latter, like the nonprophetic apocalyptic within Judaism, claim that for their godless ethic to

[68] In consequence of what is said above, within Christian circles apocalpticism represents a virtual denial of both the Incarnation and the work of the Holy Spirit in the church. A Docetic Christ and a humanistic church are the logical bedfellows of consistent apocalyptic. For obviously, if the Christian ethic will not work on the historical plane, then our Lord cannot have been genuinely human, nor can the Holy Spirit contribute his "fruitage" of life and character to his church.

work they must first be allowed to make over the world according to the pattern of their messianic faith.[69]

[69] In speaking of apocalypticism's ethic as a "crossless ethic" I do not wish to be understood as denying that many apocalyptists have been prepared to suffer "for right-eousness' sake." This would be entirely unfair and untrue to the historic facts. The point I am making is that in so doing, however, they have considered the "cross" merely a necessary evil attendant upon the essential inability of the Christian to live the "good life" in an imperfect world and, therefore, to be born until a time of retribution (cf. Rev. 6:9-11). The prophetic view, on the contrary, is that to take up the "cross" is an integral and necessary part of the plan of salvation, on the part of Christ's people, equally with Christ himself (cf. below, pp. 292-95).

12

Jesus and the Apocalyptists

To determine our Lord's attitude toward the subject of apocalyptic is one of the really urgent tasks at the present time confronting New Testament scholars, and, indeed, all who are concerned about what he taught. It is also one of the most difficult. The reasons for these two statements are closely related. We have already seen that the apocalyptic literature on the whole originated within the bounds of Jewish orthodoxy but that its acceptability there proved short-lived, so much so that it gave birth to no sect or party. Commenting on this fact Oesterley suggests that, rather than regard the apocalyptists as "a party in the strict sense," we should think of them as representing "an attitude of mind." [1]

If then, Jesus actually dealt with their views on any occasion, he had no means of labeling them, for purposes of either commendation or adverse criticism, with a party name such as he used in speaking of the teachings of scribes and Sadducees. In any given case, accordingly, we can determine whether he is dealing with such teachings only by careful comparison of his own with the extant writings of the apocalyptists.

But again, by reason of its very orthodoxy and therefore apparent harmlessness, apocalyptic was enabled to capture the church almost

[1] *A History of Israel*, II, 319.

from her inception. This was no doubt partly because the majority of those in the Jewish Christian community came out of the ranks of the orthodox Hasidim—the good, religious group among the Jews who belonged to no party and constituted in reality the "prophetic element" in contemporary Judaism—whence also much of the apocalyptic literature emanated.[2] But there was additionally a parallelogram of forces which converged on the thinking of the early church from the beginning and which suggested apocalyptic as the normal direction for her teaching to take. Among these may be mentioned: the false assumption that the "this-worldly" is necessarily materialistic and the "other-worldly," spiritual; a misinterpretation of our Lord's teachings about the nature of the kingdom and its "coming" and in like manner about the coming of the "Son of Man"; a misunderstanding relative to those who should not "taste death" until they should "see the kingdom of God come with power" (Mark 9:1); a confusion regarding the temporal relation between the destruction of Jerusalem (or the appearance of the Abomination of Desolation, Mark 13:14) and the "end of the age"; and other items of like character.[3]

Since the church wrote the Gospels, there is always the antecedent possibility to be reckoned with that she colored her account of our Lord's teachings with her own apocalyptic outlook. We need not be as pessimistic at this point, I think, as some wish us to. A formula which appears generally to prove out is that the church was a good witness to what Jesus taught even when she herself misunderstood his teachings. Nonetheless it is to be borne in mind at all times that our Lord's views on the subject of apocalyptic must not be confused with those of the church, nor is the latter's belief on the topic a criterion to that of Jesus.

Jesus' Use of the Apocalyptic Literature

As in the case of the scribes, so here there is a great volume of materials illustrative of the similarity between the teachings of our

[2] *Ibid.*; see also above, p. 210.
[3] See Glasson, *op. cit.*, pp. 151-213, especially p. 197.

Lord and those of the apocalyptists. Strack and Billerbeck in their massive work, *Kommentar zum Neuen Testament aus Talmud und Midrasch*, and Canon R. H. Charles in his two volumes, *The Apocrypha and Pseudepigrapha of the Old Testament in English*, have done yeoman service in pointing out and discussing the relations between these and the possible dependence of one upon the other. It is impossible here to attempt anything like an exhaustive statement on the subject or to bring together a complete list of references to all the materials involved. With a view, therefore, merely of indicating how extensive it is, I have collected in Appendix B some of the more suggestive passages and their New Testament parallels.

The sheer volume of these is impressive. Moreover, the similarity to apocalyptic teachings in our Lord's is vouched for by all of our gospel sources, though there appears to be a preponderance in Mark and M, a large number of the references in Mark being found in chapters 13 and 14. The excessive apocalyptic material in M or Special Matthew accords with Canon Streeter's observation that this Gospel favors apocalyptic.[4] But that our Lord used the apocalyptic terminology and that his teachings were colored by apocalyptic ideas seem certain.

Several considerations, however, serve to rob this datum of its apparent significance. In the first place, as we have already seen in chapter 9, the same may be said for Jesus' use of the rabbinic terminology and doctrines; to a lesser degree it is true also relative to the priestly literature, particularly in the case of the Zadokite Fragment (chapter 6). There would probably be rather general agreement that the approximation between our Lord's teachings and those of the scribes far exceeds that of the former to apocalyptic. No doubt the reason for such concurrence in both instances is the same, or at any rate, similar. Herford, it will be recalled, attributes this in the case of Jesus and the Pharisees, not to Jesus' wish to agree or disagree with the latter sect, but rather to the

[4] *The Four Gospels*, pp. 520 ff.

common source of their knowledge of religious truth, namely, the synagogue.[5] Similarly, here our Lord will have acquired his custom of teaching and speaking after the apocalyptic fashion through mingling with the Hasidim and Pharisees, among whom the apocalyptic literature was known and accepted to a degree. As a skillful teacher and one who knew men, he spoke their language— whether that be of rabbi, priest, or apocalyptist—and in that language taught them the gospel of the kingdom.

A second consideration serves to carry forward the above observation a step farther: in spite of the observed similarity in their teachings there is no reason to think that Jesus knew the literature of the apocalyptists. He never refers to any of it or to its authors, nor does he ever appear to quote it.[6] This, it would seem, is an excellent example of the church's faithfulness in transmitting his teachings in the form in which he gave them. For had he known this literature—or alternatively, had the church wished to make it appear that he did—there was no reason why he should not have quoted or cited it directly. Its use within Jewish circles was not banned until the day of Rabbi Akiba (A.D. 135), and even then the assumption that it was forbidden rests upon a particular interpretation of "external books" referred to in M. Sanhedrin 10:1. The church itself could cite or even quote an extracanonical book when it wished to, as may be the case in I Pet. 3:19-22 (I Enoch) and appears to be certain at Jude 9 (Assump. Mosei), though admittedly this was not frequently done.[7] In our Lord's case, his use—if such it was—of both rabbinic and apocalyptic literature was of the same nature—a chance similar phrase or clause, a technical or semitechnical use of a term, a nearly quoted sentence, never more than this. Probably the nearest approximation to a direct quotation is: for the rabbinic literature, Jesus'

[5] See above, p. 168.

[6] Except, of course, the canonical apocalypses (Dan.; Ezek.; Isa. 24–27; Zech. 9–14).

[7] Canon Charles has collected a number of likely quotations in the Revelation of John from extracanonical literature; see his commentary (I.C.C. series), I, lxxxii-lxxxiii.

utterance of the Golden Rule which occurs in various forms (most nearly to his own in the letter of Aristeas, para. 207); and for the apocalyptic, his uniting of the two commandments which appears in several forms in Test. Iss. 5:2; 7:6; Test. Dan 5:3, and so forth. Whatever may be said of the former of these two instances, it seems that Jesus need not have gone to the Testaments to find the commandments united after this fashion, as they had been united in essence in Mic. 6:8 long before. However it is probable that the particular form given the union of these two duties in the Testaments—that which brought together Deut. 6:4-5 and Lev. 19:18 —had become popular by our Lord's day and that this prompted his employment of it (Matt. 22:34-40 and parallels). In this case Jesus obviously need not have even known of the origin of the popular combination of the two commandments.

This leads to the final observation that in numerous cases the similarity between our Lord's teachings and those of the apocalyptic literature is due, as in the case of the scribal writings as well, to their having a common source in the Old Testament prophetic teaching. Reference to Appendix B will make this evident. This was because, as we have seen, all Jewish religious culture stemmed from this great source. Accordingly it would have been exceedingly strange had there not been much agreement between every branch of this culture. That this is so, however, proves nothing in regard to the fundamental nature of the teaching of these groups; their interpretations and usage of this prophetic literature varied greatly.

It is less popular today than in a former generation to speak of our Lord's "accommodating" his teachings to current usage and thought frames. But in point of fact every true teacher "accommodates" his materials to the intellectual level of his students. There can be no teaching otherwise. A sane critical method ought certainly to recognize that the prophets and our Lord were compelled to do just that by reason of the spiritual and moral immaturity with which they were forced to deal. Jesus, like Paul, might well have said to his hearers, "I, brethren, could not address you as spiritual men, but as men of the flesh. . . . I fed you with milk, not solid food; for you were not ready for it . . ." (I Cor. 3:1-2 R.S.V.). This was the reason—or one major reason, at any rate, as he said himself (Mark 4:10 ff.)—for our Lord's employing the parable, allegory, and the *argumentum ad hominem*. And it will also be the reason, we may well believe, that he cast much of what he had to teach in the apocalyptic, priestly, or rabbinic molds with which his hearers were familiar. But in the end these molds must not be confused with the gospel which Jesus had to preach and teach and live; that, as we shall see in chapter 14, was something else, and it was about this that he was greatly concerned. In the meantime the intellectual "bait" employed by this Master Fisherman was carefully chosen for its appropriateness to the "fish" with whom he had to deal.

Jesus and the "Vision" Motif

Jesus may have employed the apocalyptic "vision" technique as a framework for his teachings, but he did not claim to be able to solve riddles or mysteries. The Talmud, indeed, states that our Lord was condemned to be stoned and hanged as a magician.[8] This was the common fate of the "soothsayer" and "sorcerer" (M. Sanh. 6:4; 7:4). But there is no further evidence of this on Jesus' part. The Talmudic charge may be, indeed, as Klausner has observed, an independent account of the scribal claim that he was in league with Baalzebub.[9] But there is rather strong evidence in proof of our Lord's disclaimer to expert knowledge of the future (cf. Mark 13:32; Acts 1:7); he had neither "familiar spirit" of the type condemned by the prophetic scriptures (Deut. 18:11; Isa. 8:19; cf. M. Sanh. 7:4) nor "angel" interpreter of the common sort which usually accompanied and interpreted for the apocalyptic writer (Rev. 1:1).

[8] Cf. Baby. Sanhedrin 43a; Strack and Billerbeck, op. cit., I, 1023, 1037; Joseph Klausner, *Jesus of Nazareth*, pp. 27-28; Maurice Goguel, *The Life of Jesus*, pp. 72-73.
[9] *Op. cit.*, p. 272; Mark 3:22-30.

Our Lord's one certain experience in this field was his "call-vision" of the prophetic type (Mark 1:9-11). This, as we have seen, is in quite a different category from that of the apocalyptic literary vision device, and it is in no sense comparable with it. There are, however, four passages which have been claimed as typically apocalyptic.

The first of these is the temptation narrative found in both Q (Luke 4:1-12=Matt. 4:1-11) and Mark (1:12-13). This is classified by the form critics as a piece of church "polemic"—almost a theological debate in fact, says Dibelius, who holds that probably it had associated with it originally a "legend" which has become lost.[10] Another suggestion is that of William Manson, to the effect that "the temptation narrative" may be "an epitome of the *whole* spiritual history of Jesus," that is to say, of various narratives which "have become conflated with the wilderness experience" following the baptism.[11] The result of both these views is to separate the temptations from the baptism of Jesus. A saner critical approach, however, and one preferred by Manson himself, would suggest that these two events are closely related in their significance and that "already at the threshold of his ministry" Jesus "had a vision of the future in which the subsequent issues of his work were fully precognized." [12]

In my judgment this last is the correct approach to an understanding of the temptations. In all three Synoptics the point is made to stand out clearly that there was an inner connection between baptism and temptation which had to do with the type of messiahship Jesus was to accomplish in the world. The baptism and its associated phenomena indicated that this would be one which would combine the Suffering Servant motif with that of the Messiah one; Jesus was to be a vicariously atoning Messiah.[13] The temptations which followed, then, represented so many endeavors

[10] *Message*, p. 185.
[11] See *Luke* (Moffatt series), p. 39.
[12] *Ibid.*
[13] See my *Intention*, ch. i; Wm. Manson, *Jesus the Messiah*, p. 155.

to escape the logical implications of that association of concepts; and it seems clear that they are not intelligible on any other view of messiahship than this paradoxical one. They involved the decision to be *loyal* to this conception of the messiahship (third temptation, to be Satan's Messiah and not God's); to *obey* the Father in his wish that the Messiah, like man in his humiliation and weakness, should live by that Father's will alone (first temptation, to make bread of stones); and to *trust* the Father, even as man must trust him, to measure up in every crisis of one's life (second temptation, to jump from the pinnacle of the temple).[14]

Was this "vision," then, of the apocalyptic type? The answer seems on the whole to be that it was not. It will hardly be claimed that it was a mere literary fiction like the usual apocalyptic vision, although it may very well be that our Lord cast his experience into this form for his purpose in teaching those who could best understand matter when so presented. The doctrine of the "two kingdoms" is indeed involved in the words of Satan in the third temptation on Matthew's reckoning (cf. Luke 4:6), an undoubted apocalyptic touch. But as Major observes, instead of citing the apocalyptic Daniel, Jesus here goes back to Deuteronomy for his inspiration—to "the great practical summary of the prophetic teaching of Israel's Golden Age," [15] and one, therefore, which may advisedly serve as an example of an equally prophetic future messianic kingdom. But the really determinative factor here which shows us the "mind of Christ" in the matter is the fact that the conception of the Messiah involved in this vision, if such it be, is by no means that of the apocalyptic supramundane and so glorious "Son of Man," but rather that of the wholly prophetic lowly Messiah who can be tempted as other men, who in his weakness must find strength as they in his Father, and who must trust and obey him as they also are required to do. The temptation vision, then, does not stand for a glimpse into a dark future, as

---

[14] See T. W. Manson, *Teaching*, pp. 196-97.
[15] *The Mission and Message of Jesus*, p. 30.

the words of Satan about "the kingdoms of the world" present and future might lead us to imagine. It stands rather for a time of challenge and intense struggle on the part of the Messiah when he must finally make a choice between two courses of action which lie before him. The experience was a unique one, the like of which is not to be found in the apocalyptic literature or anywhere else. That it should be related of one whom the church believed to be the Messiah is the best proof of its authenticity. It must go back to Jesus, for a church believing in a supramundane apocalyptic Messiah would never have portrayed one of this type. And since this is so, it becomes clear that this "vision" was simply a modification of the usual "call-vision" of the prophets, an elaboration of that which began on the banks of the Jordan, and exclusively for the prophetic Suffering Servant-Messiah.

A second "vision" which is treated, for example by Schweitzer, as apocalyptic in nature—that is, as revealing a "mystery" regarding the future—is the Transfiguration.[16] This view depends for its cogency upon a reversal of the chronological order of the confession of Peter at Mark 8:27-30 with this event at Mark 9:2-8. To this end he adopts the common critical theory of a double recension of the incidents included in the section Mark 6:1–8:26.

To this theory of Schweitzer it is sufficient to reply: First, unfortunately for his view the double recension hypothesis does not involve the passage with which he is concerned. His argument that 8:34 ff. "points to the circumstances of the time just after the return of the disciples, when Jesus was sometimes alone with the disciples, and sometimes calls the eager multitude about Him"[17] lacks force. On the contrary this passage fits best where it stands— an example of how Jesus after the confession of Peter urges not only his disciples but also the multitudes to share the experience of the cross with the Messiah. Before that event and our Lord's consequent willingness to speak of the nature of his messiahship

[16] *The Quest of the Historical Jesus*, pp. 384 ff.
[17] *Ibid.*, p. 383.

(as at 8:31 ff.) any reference to either his own cross or the one his disciples must take up would have been an anacronism.[18] Again, it is significant that Luke, who as is well known omits everything in Mark 6:46–8:27b, yet retains the Marcan order—confession followed by transfiguration—showing as above argued that any dislocation in Mark 6:1–8:26 did not concern these events and their ordering.[19] Third, as I have already shown (p. 31), it is peculiarly un-biblical and artificial to suggest that Matt. 16:17 ("For flesh and blood has not revealed this to you, but my Father who is in heaven.") is a reference to the "voice" at the Transfiguration. The divine voice under such circumstances does not communicate new truth, but rather confirms or at most calls those with the prophetic insight to have known already what it would say. Instead of this experience constituting the disclosure of a divine mystery, then, it was the "call-vision" of the church to "hear" (Mark 9:7) what the Incarnate Word of revelation had to say.

A third supposed apocalyptic vision experienced by our Lord is found in Luke 10:18-24. Johannes Weiss, for instance, thought it "one of the most useful aids to an understanding of Jesus"[20] as it enshrines his vision of the downfall of Satan after true apocalyptic fashion. It is true that some of the phraseology of the passage is apocalyptic in origin, or at least in usage: "Satan fall . . . from heaven" (cf. Rev. 12:9), "your names are written in heaven" (cf. Dan. 12:1; Rev. 3:5). But it can be duplicated either verbatim or in sense from the prophets as well, and this was no doubt its source (cf. Isa. 14:12; Ps. 69:28; Exod. 32:32), whence it was taken over by apocalyptic and became the common property of the average Jew. The apocalyptic interpretation of the passage therefore depends essentially upon the verb ἐθεώρουν

[18] Such, in fact, Matthew's placing of the reference to the cross at 10:34-39 actually is!

[19] See Streeter, op. cit., pp. 172 ff.; James Moffatt, Introduction to the Literature of the New Testament, pp. 627-28.

[20] See Klostermann, Das Lukas-Evangelium, p. 117.

(vs. 18), here translated "I saw." But as Klostermann among others has pointed out, the verb is in the imperfect tense and might perhaps best be translated "I was watching," the reference being, then, to the work of the "seventy" which Jesus means to say has begun to destroy the power of Satan in the world. While, therefore, it may be granted that the language of the passage owes something to the current apocalyptic teaching, the interpretation which makes of it a "vision" on Jesus' part is misleading; no vision motif is intended. This is simply our Lord's usual metaphorical way of referring to the coming of the kingdom, which, be it noted, is transpiring before his eyes, not in the eternal order as apocalyptic thought demanded, but on the historical plane.[21]

The fourth example of the apocalyptic vision motif which some would find in our Lord's teaching is in Mark, chapter 13, the so-called Little Apocalypse. It is strange how generally the dilemma involved in the interpretation of this section is overlooked by New Testament students. It may be stated thus: either (a) the passage is a Little Apocalypse (in the technical sense of an insertion by or into Mark's Gospel from extraneous apocalyptic sources), the rather general view among New Testament scholars today, including Schweitzer,[22] in which case it is not from the lips of Jesus and therefore cannot be cited as an example of his use of apocalyptic method; or (b) it is from Jesus and in this case needs to be re-examined entirely as to its character and message.

Accepting the latter alternative as probably correct, T. W. Manson explains the apparent confusion in the chapter as due to disarrangement of actual sayings of Jesus, which as now arranged commit him to temporally relating the destruction of

[21] Cf. for much the same interpretation as above, Wm. Manson, Luke (Moffatt series); Major, Manson, and Wright, Mission and Message of Jesus, p. 279; see also Moulton, A Grammar of New Testament Greek, p. 134.

[22] See Quest, p. 387, n. 1.

Jerusalem and the end of the age.[23] This is a real possibility. I have offered another suggestion to the effect that the chapter is in reality an "anti-apocalypse" in the sense that it contains throughout a number of hints that, whereas "signs" pertain to historical events and should be looked for by those of prophetic insight, no "sign" is to be expected of the end of the age.[24] In the nature of things no "sign" can possibly pertain to that last of all events for the same reason that fundamentally no "sign" ever relates to an "event" in the eternal order (Matt. 12:38-45). Such an "event" is, as Barth has remarked of the eternal word, "vertical" in relation to the historical plane, coming straight down from above; it cannot, therefore, give any precursory signals of its coming on the historical—i.e., horizontal—plane. "Of that day or that hour no one knows," says our Lord, "not even the angels in heaven, nor the Son, but only the Father." (Mark 13:32 R.S.V.)

But in any event, however Mark 13 is to be accounted for, it is not an apocalyptic "vision"; for there is no reference in it to the vision motif. So far as the destruction of Jerusalem is concerned, that is clearly *predictive prophecy*; and its explanation is not to be arrived at by reference to a supposed apocalyptic vision, but rather after the manner of Rudolf Otto when he writes:

The gift of prophetic divination known in ancient Israel emerged anew in Christ. . . . Like them [the prophets], he prophesied the fall of Jerusalem and the destruction of the temple. His prophecy, like theirs, rested on knowledge of and insight into the politically ominous situation of Jerusalem and a menacing and aggressive world power.[25]

Such a historical event Jesus, like the prophets, could foresee for the reason that he could "read the signs of the times," because he had rich insight into God's ways of governing his universe.

[23] *Teaching*, pp. 262-63.
[24] See my *Intention*, pp. 57 ff.
[25] *Kingdom*, p. 358; see also my *Intention*, pp. 59-60.

Jesus and the End of the Age

The supposed temporal reference to the end of the age and the coming of the Son of Man in Mark 13 is to be dealt with in the larger context of Jesus' teaching as a whole. It is almost universally held at the present day that our Lord believed these "events" to be near at hand and that they would come to pass certainly within the lifetime of some then living. It is accepted further on all hands that the church from the beginning followed our Lord in this expectation. While one hesitates to oppose an almost universally accepted teaching of modern New Testament scholarship, I must register my long-standing conviction that the former of these propositions is based on the flimsiest of evidence.[26]

Upon examination it appears to rest on three main supports. In the first place, it is suggested that our Lord must be conceded to have been capable of committing a historical blunder. This proposition is laid down in opposition to the contrary bias of orthodoxy which has endeavored to dodge this contingency by associating the "coming" of the Son of Man with a variety of historical events, such as Pentecost and the destruction of Jerusalem.[27] I share the feeling of repugnance on the part of New Testament scholars to such unethical "dodges," and readily concede the possibility that our Lord could have been mistaken regarding the date of a future event. But it has not been sufficiently recognized that to admit this possibility is one thing, whereas to suggest that our Lord could have mistakenly predicted the end of the age as about to occur within a certain temporal limit is quite something else. For the latter would mean not only committing a historical blunder but allying himself with an entire point of view—the apocalyptic. The latter I do not accept, for in my judgment the evidence is quite to the contrary.

The second main support of the view in question is the general one that, the teachings of Jesus being of an apocalyptic nature,

[26] One may now cite Glasson, *The Second Advent*, to the same intent.
[27] See T. W. Manson, *Teaching*, pp. 279 ff.

one would expect him, like all apocalyptists, to make the mistake of looking for the end of the age in his own generation. This is the first argument in reverse. The thesis to which this section of the present volume is dedicated is this: Jesus stood squarely in the stream of the prophetic revelation; and any items of identity between his views and those of the apocalyptists are the result of the fact that at these points apocalyptic is following for the moment in the path of its great precursor, the prophetic revelation, or else that our Lord found just here that he could without compromising his own convictions "accommodate" himself to the thought frames of his auditors.

As the above two supports for the theory that Jesus contemplated the sudden approach of the "end of the age" are both of an a priori nature, the only real grounds for it are yet to be examined. These are of an exegetical nature; and for our present purpose it will be sufficient to examine in detail the three passages upon which, in T. W. Manson's view, the theory rests. They are: first, Mark 14:62, "And Jesus said, 'I am; and you will see the Son of man sitting at the right hand of Power, and coming with the clouds of heaven'" (R.S.V.). This is, of course, our Lord's reply to the high priest's question at his trial, "Are you the Christ, the Son of the Blessed?" (vs. 61). The usual interpretation of this passage is well stated in the words of Otto, who happens to agree with it. "They themselves [the members of the Sanhedrin] will live to see and know Him as the exalted Son of man, and they *themselves* must then concede that Christ spoke the truth when He confessed, 'I am.'" [28]

But a detailed examination of the passage leaves one far from convinced. It has long been recognized that our Lord's reply here is made up of two Old Testament quotations, one from Ps. 110:1 (the Son of man sitting at the right hand of Power), the other from Dan. 7:13 (coming with the clouds of heaven). This in itself is sufficient to give us pause; when one quotes Scripture,

[28] *Kingdom*, p. 227.

he does not necessarily mean that he wishes to apply the whole
of it to the matter in hand, but rather that such quotation forms
a convenient vehicle in which to present his thought of the
moment. The question had been, Are you the Messiah? And the
answer is, Yes, and you will have good opportunity to vouch for it.

If, however, the language is to be pressed, then it appears to
yield most surprising results which cut directly against the theory
with which we are dealing. The former of the two passages was
previously quoted more fully by our Lord at Mark 12:36.

> The Lord said to my Lord,
> Sit at my right hand,
> till I put thy enemies under thy feet.
> (R.S.V.)

Regarding Jesus this passage yields an intelligible meaning and
one quite in accord with his teaching generally, if we suppose
him to mean that he is about to go to his Father, there to be
received in regal state and await the reduction of all his foes on
the historical plane to submission to himself. This prophetic
idea will refer, then, to the progressive accomplishment of Jesus'
rule among men within history; and as Glasson has very aptly
observed, "the meaning of Jesus' reply would therefore seem to
be that although He was about to be put to a shameful death He
was really entering upon His reign. The idea is brought out by
Philippians ii.8-11, where the supremacy of Jesus springs from
His humiliation." [29]

As regards the second passage, that of Dan. 7:13—"And, behold, there *was coming* [LXX] with the clouds of heaven one like
unto a son of man, and he came even to the ancient of days, and
they brought him near before him"—the church under the influence of apocalyptic has not unnaturally referred this to the
so-called parousia or second coming of our Lord. But as Glasson,
again, has pointed out, the "coming" referred to in the passage is

[29] *Op. cit.*, p. 64.

rather to the Ancient of Days and not to earth. In other words, it corresponds in essence exactly to the former part of the verse as now interpreted—i.e., the portion taken from Ps. 110:1—for like the former it refers to the Son of Man's acquiring "dominion, and glory, and a kingdom" from the Father himself. And further, as Glasson has taken pains to discover, this has always been the Jewish interpretation of the passage. They knew of no advent of the Messiah on the clouds; these stand, to their way of thinking, merely in a figurative manner for the Messiah's majesty and glory.[30]

To Jesus' auditors, accordingly, the passage as a whole meant, "I am the Messiah; and you will live to see me reigning, for though my death may seem to you now the end of my ambitions, really it is the beginning of my triumph; and from now on my Father will progressively bring my servants into submission to me." Our Lord's reference, as so often in his teachings, is to a spiritual fact that he conveys to his hearers through the medium of the imagery with which they are acquainted.

Manson's second passage is Mark 9:1, "And he said to them, 'Truly, I say to you, there are some standing here who will not taste death before they see the kingdom of God come with power'" (R.S.V.). Manson curiously renders the perfect participle ($\epsilon\lambda\eta\lambda\upsilon\theta\upsilon\hat{\iota}\alpha\nu$) as though it were a present progressive, "coming." [31] It is true that the perfect may at times stand for the present tense, but I know of no justification for rendering it as a present progressive. In any case, it would appear to be begging the question to insist on its being so rendered here. As it stands, the Greek rather clearly seems to mean, as C. H. Dodd has rendered it, "There are some of those standing here who will not taste death until they have seen that the Kingdom of God has

---

[30] Op. cit., pp. 186, 230 ff. He has pointed out too that the Jewish interpretation of Dan. 7:13 was also accepted by Cyprian (p. 187).

[31] Teaching, p. 278. Manson's own theory appears to demand that Mark 9:1 shall refer to the "coming" of the kingdom on the historical plane through Peter's confession (cf. pp. 119, 130).

come with power,"[32] Dodd further comments, "The bystanders are not promised that they shall see the Kingdom of God *coming*, but that they shall come to see that the Kingdom of God *has already come*, at some point before they became aware of it."[33] That is to say, standing on the plane of history and in their lifetime, some of Jesus' auditors are to be able to look back and see that the kingdom of God has come in their midst "with power." This does not sound like the so-called parousia or the end of the age. It is hard to imagine men looking back with a certain satisfaction on having experienced the Eternal coming into time like a stroke of lightning.

The interpretation of this passage which sees in it a reference to the parousia is based on its connection with the immediately preceding verse (8:38), in which there occurs an undoubted mention of it. But that verse was added, almost as an aside or at most as a warning parallel to and interpretative of the similar one—both in form and meaning—found in verse 35. And both warnings refer back to the original theme of the passage found in verse 34, "If any man would come after me, let him deny himself, and take up his cross, and follow me." The kingdom comes, as Manson himself has shown with great force,[34] as men acknowledge his messiahship and, taking up the cross, follow him. It is, then, to such a coming of the kingdom that 9:1 refers. This verse is introduced by the formula, "And he said . . . ," which appears to have been Mark's characteristic way of introducing the conclusion to an incident or teaching of Jesus (cf. 2:27, 4:9; 7:9); and its intent is to assure his hearers that in their lifetime the kingdom will come through men following him as demanded above. By the same token the phrase "with power" means that great numbers in that generation will accept Jesus' lordship, for the power of the kingdom is a power to convict and to inspire to noble endeavor and action in line with verses

[32] *The Parables of the Kingdom*, p. 53. Italics mine.
[33] *Ibid.*, n. 1.
[34] See his *Teaching*, pp. 201-11.

34 ff. (cf. the use of the word in I Cor. 2:4-5). On this reading of the passage, then, the thought of the parousia as something to be expected in that generation simply disappears. It is instructive to note that Luke omits the words "come with power" (Luke 9:27), thus, as Streeter has pointed out,[35] "interpreting the 'Kingdom of God' as the Church," a quite proper interpretation of Mark's words in my judgment. Matthew, however, substitutes the words "the Son of man coming in his kingdom" for "the Kingdom of God come with power" (Matt. 16:28). I shall leave this Matthaean change for discussion in a somewhat larger context after looking at Manson's third passage.

This is Mark 13:26, "And then they will see the Son of man coming in clouds with great power and glory" (R.S.V.). Manson again appears to beg the question at issue by placing "after the troubles in Judea" in brackets after "And then." As the text of Mark reads, "And then" refers, not to the Jewish War, but rather to the catastrophic events connected with the end of the age and narrated in verses 24-25. That is to say, the end of the age and the events associated with it are definitely related to the parousia. But whether both are conceived as coming soon after the Jewish War is by no means clear. We have only the words of verse 24—"But in those days, after that tribulation"—to guide us, and they are of little assistance as the time span indicated is indefinite. Manson himself, however, seems to me to have given us a clue to a solution of this difficult problem.[36] For he has demonstrated, along with others, that Jesus' general teaching is to the effect that no "sign" will be given of the end of the age. This is true of all the sources, including Mark himself outside chapter 13. Instead, according to these sources, the end will come suddenly and without warning. Thus for Mark see 13:33-37; for Q, Luke 17:26-27, 34-35=Matt. 24:37-39, 40-41; Luke 12:39-40=Matt. 24:43-44; for M," Matt. 25:1-13; for

---

[35] *The Four Gospels*, pp. 520-21.   [36] *Op. cit.*, pp. 260 ff.

L, Luke 12:35-38. This was the teaching of Paul from the beginning of his writing career, as I Thess. 5:1-11 testifies. It seems certain, therefore, that Jesus taught after this manner.

But if this is so, and one accepts the suggestion that Mark 13 came from Jesus, then obviously the "signs" referred to in that chapter cannot refer to the parousia and the end of the age, nor can the Jewish War be temporally related to these eschatological events as itself a "sign" of the end. The intention of our Lord in the words, "But in those days, after that tribulation," accordingly must be, not to unite the war with the end of the age, but contrariwise to separate them. It would help somewhat if verses 24-27 were to be transposed with verses 28-31; the simple possibility that these two sets of verses have somehow gotten reversed in the manuscripts would account for the present apparent confusion. In the meantime, on Manson's own hypothesis of what Jesus taught, it seems impossible to base on Mark 13:26 the view that he expected his advent to occur in that generation.[37]

Canon Streeter's reference to Matthew's predilection for apocalyptic has already been mentioned (p. 237). While agreeing that this is so, I am not certain of Streeter's explanation of it.[38] He thinks it to be "subservient to a moral purpose"—with which generally one of course would agree—"in view of the immediacy of the Great Assize, between which and the date of writing perhaps not more than four short years remained"; and he holds that Matthew expected "the visible Return of Christ . . . within the lifetime of those who saw and heard Him." In addition to the passages above cited from Manson, Streeter uses in support of this thesis Matt. 10:23, the Matthaean alteration of Mark 9:1 (Matt. 16:28), and the additions in Matt. 24:29 and 26:64 of phrases suggestive of the immediacy of the Son of Man's parousia.[39] The key to an understanding of these passages is

[37] See further on Mark 13 my *Intention*, pp. 56-61.
[38] *Op. cit.*, pp. 520 ff.
[39] *Ibid.*; for Manson's thesis about the Son of Man in the corporate sense, see his *Teaching*, pp. 227 ff., also C. J. Cadoux, *The Historic Mission of Jesus*, p. 100.

furnished, I am inclined to believe, by the suggestion of T. W. Manson—and of others—that the phrase "Son of Man" was used at times by our Lord in the corporate sense of Dan. 7:13. Assuming that Matthew was aware of this fact, it was possible for him to substitute the phrase at 16:28 for "kingdom of God" of Mark 9:1, meaning thereby exactly what Luke did (Luke 9:27), who achieved it by dropping the phrase "come with power" as we have already seen (p. 252). That is to say, Matthew here, like Luke, means that the establishment of the church is the equivalent of the kingdom of God coming with power; and both in turn may be expressed by the words, "the Son of man coming in his kingdom."

The same solution, strangely enough, appears to work also at Matt. 10:23, "I say to you, you will not have gone through all the towns of Israel, before the Son of man comes" (R.S.V.). A close analysis of Matthew's chapter 10 discloses, as is well known, that he has conflated his sources (Mark and Q) alternately throughout this passage, assembling them after his own fancy to a degree. In general Matthew had been following Q (Luke 10:3-12) throughout verses 7-15; then follows a section in which he inserts material from Mark 13:9-13 (vss. 16-23). Toward the end of the former passage (at vs. 15) he had strangely omitted Luke 10:11b, which reads, "Nevertheless know this, that the kingdom of God has come near." But after the second passage we find the words "You will not have gone through all the towns of Israel, before the Son of man comes." The suggestion is very tempting that this again is Matthew's version of the Q passage and is to be explained by the equation, Son of Man=kingdom of God. H. H. Rowley suggests the same equation and solution for Mark 8:38, and remarks that in view of the fact that "Mark has perceived that the Son of Man here meant the kingdom of God," Mark and Matthew are essentially in accord.[40] It is possible also that the same solution will explain Matthew's "immediately" and

40 Op. cit., pp. 115-16.

"hereafter" at 24:29 and 26:64, though I am inclined to agree with Rowley that the symbolism involved in the equation can be carried too far. That our Lord believed he would come again for the consummation of his kingdom appears too deeply imbedded in his teachings to suppose that his references to it are always to be interpreted in terms of metaphor.

On the whole, the best proof of our Lord's prophetic—i.e., non-temporal—standpoint relative to the end of the age and his own advent as Son of Man is to be derived from his clear intention to found the Christian fellowship which we call the church. It is inconceivable that he should have spent his major efforts toward this end if he anticipated that his advent would occur in that generation. His creative purpose relative to the church, therefore, is the rock upon which founders the view that our Lord was so misled as to adopt at this point the apocalyptic philosophy of history.[41] The deep significance of this fact for the Christian faith we shall examine in chapter 14 below.

Jesus and the Transcendent Messiah

A variety of messianic and related conceptions presented themselves for our Lord's approval or rejection. There were the "righteous branch," king and leader of the "remnant" (Jer. 23:3, 5), a genuine spiritual figure of great stature; the Suffering Servant of Deutero-Isaiah; the nationalistic figure of the Pharisees and Zealots; the priestly Messiah of the Testaments; the otherworldly "Son of Man" of I Enoch, a judge and ruler but no saviour.

There are weighty reasons against the view that Jesus adopted the last of these as descriptive of himself. It is perhaps significant that John the Baptist, who seems to have been influenced by the current apocalypticism, never spoke of the figure for whom he came as forerunner as the Messiah, but rather as the "Coming

[41] See my *Intention*, ch. vi.

One" (Mark 1:7; Matt. 11:3=Luke 7:19 [Q]), and that he thought of him as a Judge (Matt. 3:11-12 [Q]) as well as Redeemer (Mark 1:7-8).[42] Most if not all of the elements of this conception the Baptist may have derived from Malachi (cf. 3:1 ff.). The element of judgment could have been taken from the picture of the Son of Man in I Enoch, but that figure is never referred to as the "Coming One" in this work. In any case, our Lord hastened to disillusion John regarding his own mission as he conceived it, for the picture he portrayed of himself was not that of Judge but of Saviour (Matt. 11:2-6=Luke 7:18-23).

Moreover, though our Lord often referred to himself as the Son of Man—a fact testified by all of our sources,[43]—yet the picture he drew of himself in this character was far other than that of the figure of the same name in I Enoch. Referring to Dan. 7:13-14, Professor William Manson observes, "Nothing in this passage suggests that the transcendent figure here introduced makes his entrance on his glory through humiliation and suffering, not to say through abandonment by God and death."[44] This observation will apply as well to I Enoch and its picture of the Son of Man. In that book he is and remains a transcendent figure. Not so the Son of Man of the Gospels. Here the motif of *humiliation* is attached to the figure in most of our sources: thus in Mark (8:31; 9:12, 31; 10:33, 45; 14:21, 41), in Q (Luke 9:58; 17:22), in L (Luke 22:48), in John (6:53; 8:28; 12:34), being absent only in M. The *exaltation* motif is there also, to be sure, but this comes after the "abandonment" of Manson's thesis.

The impression one gleams from a study of all these passages —and it can be only an impression at the present stage of our study—is that generally speaking the humiliation passages are those in which the *individual* reference to Jesus is intended most

[42] Cf. Walter Lowrie, *The Short Story of Jesus*, p. 11; also Goguel, *op. cit.*, pp. 267-68; W. Manson, *op. cit.*, pp. 247-48.

[43] The proof of this statement is summarized in my *Intention*, ch. iv; cf. p. 236 also.

[44] *Jesus the Messiah*, pp. 23-24.

clearly, whereas the exaltation passages are those in which the corporate Son of Man is in mind. Rowley asserts as much also: "The passages which speak of this future coming of the Son of Man . . . are, however, the passages where the collective understanding of the phrase is attended with the least difficulty." [45] This assertion is made in conscious opposition to T. W. Manson's view that Jesus expected his disciples as constitutive of the Son of Man to go with him to his cross.[46] The answer to this view, as to that of apocalypticism generally regarding the near approach of the parousia in Jesus' conception, is that it makes nonsense out of our Lord's endeavor to gather together the "remnant" as the new "people of God," his church. But if the impressions just referred to are correct, then it would seem likely that the ultimate origin of the phrase "Son of Man" on our Lord's lips would be: for the *individual, humiliation* aspect, the Psalms (e.g., 8:4), together with Isa. 42:1; 53, and so on, whence came the Suffering Servant motif attaching to this lowly aspect; for the *corporate, exaltation* aspect, Dan. 7:13.

Our Lord's prophetic definition of the term "kingdom of God" also militates against his adoption of the Son of Man motif from I Enoch. For in his view this was not something to be realized in the distant future and on a heavenly plane with the *apocalyptists*, but rather on the plane of history. It was already present in Jesus himself (Luke 11:20) and had "come," with the confession of Peter to his messiahship, in human experience (Mark 9:47; 10: 15). This theme remains to be developed in the light of the gospel as a whole in chapter 14 below.

It seems highly probable, therefore, that Jesus did not conceive of himself in terms of the Son of Man of I Enoch—the extraworldly figure come to judge. The words of John 12:47b, "For I did not come to judge the world but to save the world," seem

[45] *Op. cit.*, p. 115. Exaltation passages include: Mark 8:28; 9:9; 13:26; 14:62; from Q, Luke 12:8; 12:40; from M, Matt. 19:28; 24:30; 25:31; from L, Luke 21:36; from John 6:27, 62; 12:23; 13:31.
[46] *Op. cit.*, pp. 231-32.

almost like a direct denial of such a claim; and one cannot but feel that in combating the current apocalypticism at this point John had the "mind of Christ."

Addendum

No attempt has been made in this chapter to deal at length with our Lord's attitude toward the subjects of demonology and angelology. This is because of the vastness of the series of problems involved in such a discussion. To do them justice would require a book in itself. I should like, however, herewith to register my conviction that demons and angels are for Jesus' gospel mere surds or irrational elements without obvious functions in his teachings as a whole. They may be eliminated, and the gospel will sustain no visible loss. It is therefore providential and, one would fain believe, under the Spirit's guidance that the Christian Church has never given them a place in her creeds.

Jesus' attitude toward the transcendental ethic will be covered in positive fashion in chapter 14.

PART

V

New wine into fresh wine-skins.
—Mark 2:22

Thou hast kept the good wine until
now.—John 2:10

THE RELIGION of MATURITY

Synopsis

Chapter 13:—In spite of the earnestness of the religious leadership in the Judaism of our Lord's day, it was on the whole unworthy and inadequate. The frustration of Saul of Tarsus is evidence of what it did to a man who was better than his religion. The religions of altar, book, and throne cater respectively to a man's EMOTIONAL, INTELLECTUAL, and VOLITIONAL needs. Separately, therefore, they are fragmentary in their several religious and ethical expressions. The net product of each of them is an egocentricity which is detrimental alike to the cause of true religion and to the production of godlike personality.

Chapter 14:—In the New Testament there is given a REVEALED RELIGION answering to the revelation of the word in the Old Testament and constituting its God-intended human response. Its AUTHORITY is the Incarnate Word who was what God expects man to become. Its sole TECHNIQUE is the Spirit of Christ who guides his people in the Christian "way" of life. Its PRODUCT is the *Imago Dei*, which fulfills God's purpose in creation. Its INSTITUTION is the Body of Christ, an "eternal" fellowship enjoyed within history.

Chapter 15:—Our Lord gave little thought to the FORMS of the religious response for which he gave his life. In the matter of sacrament and organization, however, the church has had the "mind of Christ." In the light of the foregoing, the church's watchword may well be, "Let the Christian be the Church" in every phase of his life in the world of time.

CHAPTER

13

The Old Wine

WE HAVE been looking at three attempts of postexilic Judaism to implement the prophetic word of revelation and so to bring about its realization in human experience. There should be no doubt regarding the general sincerity of purpose on the part of those concerned in these endeavors. The disciples respectively of altar, book, and throne were earnestly desirous of putting men in touch with the living God of the prophetic word; and the techniques devised by them were intended at any rate to serve that end. The fact that for each of the three religions resulting from these efforts there is documentary evidence of a spirit of self-criticism is sufficient proof of the earnestness of purpose underlying them.[1]

Again, it is notable that however far the leaders of the religions of altar, book, and throne seemingly departed from the revelation

[1] This spirit is, of course, to be credited to what these religionists had imbibed of the prophetic ethic; for it was not native to the religions as such, as can readily be seen in its total absence where such religions have not come in contact with an ethical movement like that of the Hebrew prophetic word. Examples of its existence are to be seen: in the religion of the altar in the special provision for a sin-offering for the high priest and the other priests on the Day of Atonement (Lev. 16:6 ff. 11 ff.), an ordinance associated with "repentance" in M. Yoma 8:8; in the religion of the book in the six kinds of false Pharisees listed in the Jerusalem Talmud (see Moore, op. cit., II, 193); and in the religion of the throne in the sense of creaturehood and of consequent ethical unworthiness that is never absent from the motif inspiring the apocalyptic literature.

of the word in evolving the techniques which they adopted for their several faiths, they nowhere give evidence of consciously or willfully repudiating the prophetic spirit or the revelation which provided its motivation—rather the reverse. For they were concerned to exhibit the continuity between the religions they severally represented and the word of prophecy which they were claiming to implement. Perhaps the best point in their favor is the fact that they acknowledged that "when the last prophets, Haggai, Zechariah, and Malachi, died, the holy spirit ceased out of Israel," that is to say, that they themselves were by no means men of prophetic stature, however much they might admire and seek to emulate the attainments of such men.[2] At the same time numerous flashes of moral and spiritual insight in their writings afford evidence of the presence still of the spirit of the prophets in their midst.

Nonetheless the history of religion is replete with examples of earnest and sincere leaders who, while they thought themselves in the right, were by and large tragically wrong. When the fruitage of such misguided leadership issues in *physical violence*, its inadequacy becomes apparent for all the world to see. One need but mention a few names like the following to win instant assent to this thesis: Ignatius Loyola and Francisco de Xavier, with the latter's use of the Inquisition for securing conversions by force; Cotton Mather and belief in witchcraft; Mohammed and the slogan, "The Koran or the sword"; the Genevan *Consistoire* and Servetus; the Council of Constance and the burning of John Huss; Adolph Hitler and modern European Jewry.

The tragedies in the realm of the *spirit* which result from sincere but enlightened leadership are not so readily discerned, but they are not the less real. One might mention: a sense of frustration over or despair of ever finding God by the techniques employed, or contrariwise an unbalanced assurance that God has become wholly known and consequent self-righteousness, religious exhibitionism,

---

[2] *Ibid.*, I, 421; the rabbis, however, claimed still to hear the *bat qōl*, or echo of the divine voice.

and genuine spiritual stagnation and loss of a sense of reality. Indifference to moral issues and downright antinomianism or immorality have frequently been the product of wrong religious guidance, even as agnosticism and atheism are the natural fruitage of that which is unintelligent or uninformed.

That the leadership in the religious milieu of the Judaism of Jesus' day was on the whole inadequate and unworthy there can be no doubt. There were exceptions, of course, like the fairminded Rabban Gamaliel I and his earnest grandson, Gamaliel II; the inquiring Nicodemus; the saintly priest Zacharias, father of John the Baptist; above all the thoroughly frustrated Saul of Tarsus, who was "so extremely zealous . . . for the traditions" of the fathers. But these exceptions—or partial exceptions, for they are hardly more—only serve to "prove the rule" that the leaders of the religions of altar, book, and throne in the Judaism contemporary with Jesus were insensitive to the moral and spiritual degeneracy of the causes they represented.

It has sometimes been argued that the internal struggle pictured in Rom. 7:7-25 could not have been experienced by Saul in his Pharisaic days, as this would have involved his already sensing the inadequacy of the religion of the book and his having become, therefore, its ethical superior. The suggestion of this contingency, however, offers no barrier to the adoption of the view that it is intended to refute. The history of religion affords numerous examples of men who were better than their religions. Were it otherwise, there would be far fewer cases of conversion from one religion to another. A sense of the inadequacy of one's own faith is indeed a *sine qua non* of conversion to a higher one. From a psychological view, therefore, the persecuting zeal of Saul of Tarsus is the best proof one could wish that he had such a feeling with reference to his religion of Pharisaism.

When, accordingly, modern writers—Jewish and Christian—indulge in acrimonious attacks on Saul for his persecuting zeal, claiming that his feeling of frustration was by no means representative of the contemporary Pharisaism, they are unwittingly lowering the score of the ethical and spiritual insight of the leadership of that faith.[3] It was Paul's "finely drawn sensitiveness" [4] that led him to defend a faith which he had come to see was morally inadequate to the demands placed upon it by the needs of man. Enlightened modern Judaism makes no attempt to defend the unwholesome legalistic spirit that compiled the Mishnah, for example. That Saul of Tarsus should have sensed its inadequacy and experienced the feeling of frustration which that sense was bound to engender in one earnestly desiring to know God is much to his credit, not the reverse. The Torah which was intended to be "unto life" had become for him, as the result of his Pharisaic training and understanding of it, "unto death" (Rom. 7:10). The best explanation that can be offered for Paul's persecuting zeal, therefore, is that is was a sort of "defense mechanism", born of his sense of frustration and endeavor to cover up the inadequacy of his Pharisaic faith. And that he had no peers in that experience by no means redounds to the praise of the Pharisaism of the day. The same may be said for the leadership of the other two religions of altar and throne. Saul of Tarsus was no psychopath, as some would have us believe; he was merely gifted with an ethicospiritual insight beyond his fellowmen.[5] Let anyone who doubts this study the Mishnah with care.

It was but natural, one imagines, that the three religions of altar, book, and throne should have grown up about the prophetic word as so many wild shoots to sap away its life if possible and to divert its energy to unproductive channels. For curiously these three religions represent the three sides of the human personality—feelings, intellect, and will. It would seem inevitable, therefore—human

[3] See Joseph Klausner, From Jesus to Paul, pp. 313, 424.
[4] The phrase is that of Donald W. Riddle (Paul, Man of Conflict, p. 53).
[5] For a like exegesis of Rom. 7:7-25 see A. C. McGiffert, A History of Christianity in the Apostolic Age, p. 126, n. 1; A. H. McNeile, St. Paul, His Life, Letters, and Christian Doctrine, p. 12; Sanday and Headlam, Romans (ICC series), in loc.; C. H. Dodd, Romans (Moffatt series), in loc.

nature being what it is—that not only in the postexilic Judaism but throughout the course of Christian history as well, they should be found endeavoring to implement the word of revelation and, so to speak, to bring it "down to earth."

The Old Wine of the Altar

The religion of the altar is the religion of the emotions or senses. It appeals to those of artistic temperament, who love the pomp and ceremony of its rituals, the beauty of its temples, the symbolism of its altars and sacrifices. Polytheistic religions have a great advantage here—as is seen in the great temples of Babylonia, Egypt, and South India—with their ornate representations of the gods and goddesses and of all the hosts of heaven and hell. But theism is able after a fashion to make up its deficiency at this point through employing certain geometrical and other conventional patterns and even the exquisite use of writing as in Islam, through the development of an elaborate ritual of sacrifice accompanied by many changes of garments as in the case of the high priest in Judaism, or through the composition of the grandiose music of the Mass as an accompaniment of the mystery of the Divine Tragedy portrayed amidst the most colorful surroundings of altar and vestments as in Catholicism.

The altar with its time-honored ceremonies appealing to the senses rather than to the reason is the natural center of orthodoxy in any religion. Its priests by virtue of their office are the bulwarks of traditionalism and the status quo, opposed to change and innovation of every sort, lacking in moral fervor and spiritual insight. They owe their livelihood to their ability to cater to the aesthetic instinct in man and to make his approach to the Deity as agreeable an experience as the phenomenon of sacrifice will permit. In consequence the priest instinctively endeavors to cover the crudities of his art—as every true artist should do—with a rich display of furnishings, garments, music, pomp, and rubric to divert the worshiper's attention and to give him the satisfaction he craves.

Protestant orthodoxy since the reformation has been at a peculiar disadvantage here, as it cannot adequately represent its altar. For the historic struggle within the Roman Church, out of which it had its origin, made the adoption of the symbols of the old faith impossible for it. It finds itself, therefore, in the paradoxical position of being a religion of the altar destined by its genius to appeal to the aesthetic in man but without the visible means of fulfilling its proper function. Historically it has tended as a consequence to break down and to gravitate in the direction of either the book or the throne or toward both together. Its true genius of religion of the altar is perpetuated today in its purest form among the smaller tangential sects, where it appeals to man's emotional nature chiefly through the imagination, portraying the invisible altar and the sacrifice on Calvary. It cannot display the bloody sacrifice, so it speaks with deep emotion of the "blood atonement" with no more attempt to analyze the meaning of that phrase or to state the same in intelligible terms than the priest who performs the bloody ritual at the altar of other faiths.

The religion of the altar characteristically appeals to the neurotic type of person who is looking for balm for his conscience and salvation for his soul. If he has an inferiority complex, that is cared for by the inflation of his ego, which the thought that God has planned his individual salvation brings him. In its extreme forms, therefore, this religion tends to be egocentric and as a result is without ethical interest, being in practice amoral or even antinomian. It is this altar religion in every community, including the Christian Church, which produces the so-called "piety" or "religiosity" that is so unwelcome to the Christian of the prophetic tradition.

The Old Wine of the Book

The religion of the book is the religion of the intellect, as its name suggests. The theological movement known as "Liberalism" has been within Christian circles the modern exemplar of the worship of gnosis (knowledge), even as Gnosticism was in ancient times. This appears, for example, from its development of the sciences of textual and literary criticism, and of the grammatico-historical method of exegesis. Its entire interest, indeed, centered in the book first and last. That it denied holding to any—or at most held very tenuously to any—doctrine of inspiration is of no significance. It is quite possible to stake one's life on an object without having a well-formulated reason for doing so.[6] This is in fact exactly what the priest does at the altar as he performs the sacrifice whose significance he cannot explain but which he would on no account desist from offering. The somewhat curious position of the old guard "liberals" today is a rather clear indication that they have done just about the same. For having drunk to the dregs the old wine of their marvelous techniques for the study of Scripture, they are at a loss to know what to do with what they have found. Still it is much to their credit that they have traveled this road, and they have laid every other student of Scripture under their debt to an incalculable degree.

This religion of the book, wherever it is found, tends to be legalistic. This was so of Pharisaism in ancient times, as it is of Islam and Sikhism today. Roman Catholicism also, though essentially a religion of the altar, has always manifested such legalism. This is partly because the altar religions have their own interest in enforcing the ritual parts of religious or canon law, as we have seen to have been true of the high priests or Sadducees within Judaism, partly also in view of the peculiar brand of Catholicity nourished by the Roman Church. This allows for the existence within its bounds of an extremely legalistic system like that exhibited in any one of the great monastic orders, such as the Franciscans or Dominicans, alongside the altar mysticism of the Spanish Mystics, St. Catherine of Siena, St. Francis of Assisi, and others.

This legalism of the religion of the book is generally due to its

---

[6] Liberalism's allegiance to the Scriptures was due, in my judgment, to an unreasoned and essentially irrational carryover from the like interest on the part of traditional theology, in which the "Word of God" has always been so largely identified with the words of Scripture.

wholesome, if unbalanced, emphasis on ethics. For if the religion of the altar tends to be amoral, pious, even antinomian, that of the book looks in the direction of being downright irreligious and anti-theological. In the last generation it was represented within the fold of evangelical Christianity by the "Social Gospel," a movement which had the meritorious effect of restoring the social emphasis where it should always have been in the thinking of Christian people.

The danger inherent in the religion of the book stems from its virtues: intellectual superiority and worthy ethical interest. The conscious possession of these two dominant traits tends to produce a superiority complex which exhibits itself in self-righteous attitudes and develops in the end into a species of self-worship. This religion usually appeals to the paranoic or self-assured person. It produces in each generation on its left a crop of cynical, "hard-headed," irreligious individualists who neither fear God nor regard man. Their worship becomes—for exactly opposite reasons but none the less truly— like that of the people of the altar, a species of ego-culture. If the altar religionist is insipid by reason of his piety, the book moralist is obnoxious for his intolerable arrogance.

The Old Wine of the Throne

The religion of the throne is the religion of the will. Albert Schweitzer is the outstanding modern exemplar of that fact. A "consistent eschatologist" on his own avowal, he announced that Jesus' teaching was irrelevant to the intellectual demands of our day. Jesus was for him the Leader who showed the way to utter obedience of the Father's will at whatever cost and who called his disciples to undertake a like consecration of life. Accepting that challenge himself, Schweitzer gave up a brilliant professorship in New Testament at Strasburg, studied medicine, and went out to "darkest Africa" as a medical missionary. That was consistent and sincere at all events, whatever one may think of Schweitzer's views generally.

The religion of the throne, however, tends to be extremely pessimistic regarding the possibility of saving the world and becomes in consequence progressively "other-worldly" as the implications of its viewpoint are understood and accepted.[7] Men generally, it discovers, are unprepared even to consider the merits of God's will, far less to resign their own to it. Lacking then both the divine perspective and the divine patience, the disciples of this faith can see no hope for the present evil age or world.

This throne-religion, moreover, can find no place for ethics—save as *Interimsethik* for a select group living under ideal conditions—for the reason that this world is too bad to tolerate anyone attempting to fulfill God's demands for human living. The disciples of this religion are unconsciously frustrated by the absolute character of these demands on the one hand, and the extreme difficulty and even danger of attempting to carry them through in a morally imperfect world on the other. They rightly see that such an attempt will call for great sacrifice and even eventual crucifixion but not that it is an integral part of the plan of salvation. The religion of the throne accordingly is transformed into a religion of despair; it flees from the contemplation of this present evil age to focus its interest wholly upon a perfect state of bliss that the denizens of this world know not of. There is much truth in the charge, therefore, that the religion of the throne offers its devotees a "fire-insurance policy" for the hereafter.

The superiority complex is again manifest among these religionists, but for a reason contrary to that operating in the people of the book. There an overweening optimism prevails as the legalist feels assured that in the end he will succeed in saving the world by means of his ethical culture. "Knowledge is power," and the religion of the book has it. Paul was thinking of just such intellectuals when he

---

[7] The use of the word "pessimistic" is sometimes denied as applicable to the apocalyptists. H. H. Rowley, for example, in *The Relevance of Apocalyptic* claims that these religionists were merely "realists" (p. 153). But realism in the sense of the acknowledgment that the present world or age is evil is compatible with the Christian hope and belief that one day the kingdom of God will be established here in full measure, and it is just this of which the apocalyptists in the end despair. It is such despair that is labeled above "pessimism."

wrote that "knowledge puffs up" (I Cor. 8:1). But the people of the throne also nourish a superiority complex—and that because by some trick of imagination the function of judgment pertaining to the throne is transferred from its Divine Occupant to themselves. This is due, I am inclined to believe, to an imperfect doctrine of the Spirit shared by a majority who think themselves individually so far in possession of the Spirit as to be able to speak ex *cathedra* for God himself. Sitting, therefore, presently with the Lord in his throne they are able to look down virtuously upon a world that is fit only to be burned. A sound doctrine of the church and of the Spirit as given, not to the individual, but to the church and therefore to the individual only as he partakes of the community life and its benefits would go far toward correcting this sort of religious egotism.

For the net product of such teaching is again an egocentric religion. It produces in each generation a crop of "holier-than-thou" folk whose self-esteemed holiness and consequent intolerance of their brethren in the Christian community is the antithesis of that true humility of spirit without which men cannot recognize, far less receive, and certainly will never enter into, the kingdom of God. For this reason also the throne religion is inconducive to unity and peace within the Church of Christ. Intolerant criticism of others leads to division and yet more division, as is bound to occur in a group which sadly fails to understand that "Judge not, that you be not judged" is aimed at just such a schismatic spirit.

It is relevant to cite here an example from outside the bounds of the biblical revelation and its religious milieu in support of the contention with which this chapter opened—that the three religions of altar, book, and throne correspond to the nature of man's psychology.[8] This is taken from the oldest ethnic religion extant, Hinduism. Here the three are represented respectively by *Bhakti-marg*, the way of devotion or love (the religion of the altar); *Gyanmarg*, the way of knowledge (the religion of the book); and

Karmmarg, the way of action (the religion of the throne). It is of the utmost importance to note that all three of these religions or "ways" have equally good standing within Hinduism, as that system has no absolute, transcending category or standard by reference to which they may be evaluated. This, Hinduism considers, is evidence of outstanding merit in herself as a system of tolerance; actually from the Christian standpoint it is the sure sign of her inadequacy and inability to rise above the *hubris* of man's spirit.

And indeed it may now be said with a degree of finality that, judged from the Christian standpoint, these religions are together but reflections of the self-assertive nature of man. Their value in each case is relative to his needs, on the one hand, and to their ability severally to enable him to hear the prophetic word, on the other. They represent characteristic responses on man's part to the divine word and are in no sense to be confused with that word itself. They are, in the strictest sense, religions and not revelation. To confuse them with revelation, or to equate any one of them with it, or to suggest that any one of them is the logical and necessary outcome thereof, is in reality the result of failure to take the concept of revelation seriously. The transcendent factor, then, which unlike Hinduism is found in Christianity and by reference to which these three religions may be evaluated, resides not in them but in the prophetic word which is heard in the biblical revelation.[9]

---

[8] See above, p. 264.

[9] It is strange, to say the least, how seldom this fundamental difference between the work of the prophet, on the one hand, and that of the priest, scribe, and apocalyptist, on the other, has been discerned by even Christian scholars. Pfeiffer, however, contends for what has been my thesis in the first twelve chapters in this book, though I had not observed this until arriving at this point. It is worth while, I think, to append to this chapter, therefore, a quotation from his work. "On what evidence O. Eissfeldt (*Einleitung in das Alte Testament*, p. 615, Tübingen, 1934) asserts that 'in Israel there are four different types of utterance that are regarded as Word of God' (namely, the instruction [Torah] of the priest, the oracle of the prophet, the song of the singer, and the proverb of the wise man) is not clear. The case of the Decalogue . . . is unique. Laws, songs, and proverbs were eventually deemed divinely inspired by regarding their authors as prophets: as a result, these compositions came to be considered prophetic oracles and were included in the collection of sacred scriptures" (*Introduction to the Old Testament*, p. 51, n. 1).

271

CHAPTER

14

The New Wine of the Gospel

THE ULTIMATE reach of the Old Testament prophetic revelation had been the challenge it offered to that people calling itself "the people of God" to achieve the status of a "redemptive community." [1] The religions of altar, book, and throne made earnest efforts to meet that challenge by the "ways," respectively, of *sacrifice*, of *instruction*, and of *judgment*. These were all man-conceived ways, and they failed because of the essential incompleteness of the revelation itself. To be complete, revelation, as we have seen, must present to man's view the two sides of divine word and divine act.[2] And the prophetic revelation of a "redemptive community" had consisted of word only. In reality, therefore, the failure of the three religions mentioned was the failure on man's part to complete a revelation which in the nature of things could only be completed by God himself. These biblical religions, while historically the highest of all religions for the reason that they were "responses" to a genuine revelation of the prophetic word, were still only responses and not revelation itself, as their disciples were the first to acknowledge.

The New Testament religion of maturity continues the pro-

[1] See above, pp. 36-39.
[2] The Johannine formula for this is "the Word became flesh" (John 1:14)—that is, the divine word was fulfilled in the divine act.

phetic revelation of the Old Testament, being the divine act required to complete the divine word at the point of achievement of the "redemptive community." This is its sole intention. The function of this New Testament religion is epitomized in the words, "I have come not to abolish . . . but to fulfill" (Matt. 5:17 R.S.V.). It is the divinely ordained response to the revelation of the word and is therefore an integral part of revelation itself. To adopt the terminology of an older generation, it is the "final religion," in the sense that it is the only religion that forms an integral and therefore necessary part of divine revelation. As such, however, its potentialities are only gradually discovered by its own adherents. Its finality for the most part remains a mystery to the very people who profess to believe in it.

The religion of maturity is, in a word, the "way" of incorporation of the divine word in the "redemptive community" so that the latter becomes the divine act fulfilling the former. The community captures the word, so to speak—or rather, is captured by it—and by its life and effort achieves that word's purpose to redeem humanity. The community's watchword becomes, "Let your light so shine before men; that they may see your good works, and glorify your Father who is in heaven" (Matt. 5:16). The community does not glorify itself in living its life and in performing its "good works" for the reason that by virtue of its being the divine act its works are not its own but those of its divine creator. It is conscious at all times of the truth that "we are his workmanship, created in Christ Jesus for good works, which God prepared beforehand, that we should walk in them" (Eph. 2:10 R.S.V.).

This "way" of the religion of maturity is, by contrast with the techniques of the three religions studied, utterly unique with the uniqueness of God's thoughts as contrasted with man's. Only God could cause his word of revelation to be completed by an act which should incorporate that word in a community of morally mature personalities. Hence it never occurred to men as a possibility or even as a necessity. The religion of the altar had a suggestion

273

of this in its "whole-burnt offering" with the idea of utter consecration which it involved, as did the religion of the book in the
meticulous care with which it endeavored to erect a protective
"hedge" about the Torah with its numerous ordinances, and the
religion of the throne, with its declaration of the divine judgment
upon the unworthiness of man's life in God's sight. But each
of these failed, either at the point of sensing the necessity which
the word of God laid upon man of fulfilling all the "righteousness"
of God's moral person and of God's moral demand, or else in regard to the possibility of man's doing so on the plane of history.

The unique divine thought that the divine word and purpose
could be achieved within time was always stultified at the start
under the aegis of these several religions through the hypnotic attraction of the *symbolical factor* in each. Because of this factor
none of the three has ever been able to come to grips with the
intentioned realism of the divine word. For the religion of the
altar, attention to the ritual of the sacrifice; for that of the book,
concentration upon minutiae of interpretation; for that of the
throne, contemplation of the divine judgment—these interests have
severally absorbed the entire thought and effort of their disciples.
The religion of the altar *dramatized* God's demand that man show
forth His righteousness; the religion of the book *indoctrinated* it;
and the religion of the throne *condemned* man for falling short
of it. These were all religious "ways" conceived by man. But none
within these groups ever was able to find the divinely-intended
"way," *which is that of leading the community out into the
fullest expression of the meaning of the word of revelation for the
life of man within time.* It remained for the religion of maturity
to give a demonstration of this, and this she has done, first in the
person and work of Jesus, and then in the church which is his
"body."

The new wine of the gospel, then, is the assurance, through the
medium of a living demonstration, that the divine word can be
realized in the contemporary historical situation, though only

and always by a divine act. New wine is always a new creation; the "new wine of the gospel" no less. We turn, therefore, to an analysis of this creative act as found in the New Testament's religion of maturity.

The Gospel's Authority—Jesus Christ the Lord

The demonstration of the above claims for the religion of maturity resides in the person and work of Jesus. Jesus therefore is its authority. *Jesus is Lord.*[3] He is the Lord of the church's conscience, of the church's mind, of the church's passion, of the church's will, of the church's morality, of the church's religion, of the church's life in the world of human affairs. This is a conviction on the part of the Christian Church which grows with the years; and it is the testimony of experience that the greater the Christian spirit, the more earnest that spirit is to confess itself the "slave of Christ." "For although there may be so-called gods in heaven or on earth . . . yet for us there is one God, . . . and one Lord, Jesus Christ." (I Cor. 8:5-6 R.S.V.)

Here, then, is the place to start for an understanding both of the person and work of Christ, and of the religion of maturity—at the point, that is to say, of *the church's common witness.* The Christian gospel is the record of an experience. And when, ignoring that fact, theology has endeavored to begin at any point other than that provided by that "which we have heard, which we have seen with our eyes, which we have looked upon and touched with our hands, concerning the word of life," it has only succeeded in running out into the sterile sands of dogma unrelated to life and without moral and spiritual value.[4] Hence the disrepute into which theology periodically falls, and rightly! *You shall be my witnesses,* says the risen Christ; and men can only witness to what

[3] I Cor. 12:3.
[4] I John 1:1 (R.S.V.). John's way of saying that the divine word of revelation is fulfilled by the divine act in Jesus is, of course, "the Word became flesh" (John 1:14).

they have experienced. The church's witness, accordingly, is the record of the church's experience of Jesus. And that experience has taught her that Jesus is her Lord.

In endeavoring to define in what sense and why she knows Jesus to be her Lord, the church has employed with reference to him such terms as: Word of God, Messiah crucified, Wisdom of God, Power of God, Image of the Invisible God, First-born of all Creation, Only-begotten Son, the Glory of the Father, Saviour, Author of Eternal Salvation, Our Righteousness and Consecration and Redemption. These terms are intended separately and collectively to say that the church has found the man Christ Jesus to be the God-given means of mediating God to man. On her testimony he has been the divine act answering to and fulfilling the divine word on the historical plane. In her witness, therefore, he is the final revelation of God and the divine demonstration that the prophetic revelation was entirely realistic in its claim that the "good life" can be lived in an imperfect world. According to her gospel he is the God-proposed response of man to the word of revelation and is the manifestation in personality of what religion ought to be. Jesus is the church's religion.[5]

It is to faith, of course, that these things are so—to faith arising out of the experience which the church enjoys with her Lord. One does not say "only to faith," as though faith were a weak or inadequate epistemology. Faith is the highest and noblest method of apprehending truth that man possesses, for it is the only means at his command for coming into possession of the highest truth.

[5] Professor F. C. Grant has some fine words to say on this subject in his *Gospel of the Kingdom*, p. 129. The school of comparative religions (*Religionsgeschichte*) has long led us up a blind alley in insisting on the importance of the sources of the terminology used by the church to describe her Lord. These have been sought in every conceivable philosophy and religion. But the only value that attaches to such studies is the more perfect elucidation of the meaning of the words in themselves. As for the underlying religious concepts to which they are intended to give expression, however, there can be no doubt. The church was conscious of the fact that Jesus stood in the line of the Hebrew prophetic revelation and that he was the divine act answering to the divine word. The attempt to make him out something else, therefore, by reference to other religious notions or verbiage is simply an example of what the late William Sanday termed "not only wrong, but wrong-headed."

The five senses and the ability to transmute the information which they provide into intelligible "idea" give man knowledge of the natural world about him; reason makes him the possessor of concepts, which, incidentally, may or may not be true; faith puts him in touch with the spiritual and ethical realms, provided it is attached to the proper subject. This is not, of course, to deny that the lower media for the communication of knowledge—the senses and the reason—come into play at the higher level; rather it is to affirm it. But it is to deny that these will serve the function of the higher instrument, faith, or that the function of that higher instrument is in any way invalidated by the inadequacy of the lower for discovering the higher type of truth.[6]

Moreover, to say that the revelation of the divine act in Jesus is conditioned by its acceptance on the part of the church through faith, is only to say what must be said of the prophetic revelation of the divine word at every stage. The same sort of "assurance" attaches to the faith in the one case as in the other. No prophetic word ever became the divine word of revelation, either to the prophet himself or to his auditors, except as it was received by faith. By faith, therefore, Jesus has become for the church as surely the divine act as ever the prophetic word became for the Hebrew people the divine word.

But faith has its "signs," for it is not blind superstition. It was to communicate a knowledge of these "signs" that the Gospels were written.[7] On first thought one would imagine that nothing pertaining to Jesus and his historical life could prove irrelevant for the revelation of the divinely intended response of man to the word of revelation. For the prophets made it abundantly plain that God is interested in every phase of man's life. But one does not read far into the Gospels before discovering that these are by no means simply collections of "facts" about Jesus—indeed, that they are not "lives" at all in the usual sense of that word. Some selective

[6] See the thesis of Paul S. Minear, "Eyes of Faith," before quoted.

[7] One of the contributions of form criticism to our thinking has been the discovery of much of the motivation for what has gone into the canonical Gospels.

principle has obviously been at work here. It is instructive to note the results of that selective activity, for thereby one may hope to discover the divine intention underlying it.

To begin with, nearly everything from infancy to the beginning of the ministry was eliminated from the church's witness to Jesus. The several stories of the miraculous birth, one brief incident of two or three days duration in boyhood—this is all that remains of this period of our Lord's life. At first it seems surprising that nothing of even the adult career of Jesus is mentioned before at the age of "about thirty" (Luke 3:23) he was ready to enter upon his life's work. Children mature more rapidly in the East than in the West, and the Mishnah places the age of maturity for boys at thirteen years (M. Aboth 5:21), when they are ready "for the commandments." The conclusion is patent: the church was not interested in perpetuating a life pattern to serve as a guide for Jesus' disciples.[8] The importance of Jesus for the church's faith does not lie in the direction of imitation. The question which she asks herself is not "What would Jesus do?" The church did not perpetuate enough of his activities to make possible an answer to such a question in detail. It is important to remember this, as entire theologies and codes of ethics have been written about a misunderstanding at this point.

It is only from the time that our Lord was "ready for authority," to use the Mishnaic term—that is, at "about thirty" (M. Aboth, 5:21)—that his career becomes of interest for the church's gospel. This is what one would have expected, if we have been right in speaking of Jesus as the church's religion—remembering that this is the religion of maturity—inasmuch as maturity implies the power of bearing fruit;[9] and that power in the moral and spiritual fields, being the highest in man's development, usually comes later in life than in the physical and intellectual realms. The creative period of our Lord's life, then, lay between his baptism and resur-

[8] Even the much-publicized idea that Jesus was a carpenter depends for its verification upon a single verse in one gospel source (Mark 6:3).
[9] See above, p. 15.

rection; and judging from the space given to them the church thought of his death and resurrection as the most important and creative events even here.

It was the creative power implicit in everything that Jesus said and did during this period which impressed the church and in the end proved determinative for her faith. There was little unique about his teachings, as we have already seen. But there was about them an unmistakable "authority" (Mark 1:22) which was impressive, and the same "authority" was sensed in his acts (vs. 27). And the church has perpetuated the tradition in her Gospels that Jesus himself attributed that unique "authority" to the fact that the kingdom of God had come among men through himself and through the "something" that functioned in and through him (Luke 11:20 [Q]; 11:29-32 [Q]). That "something" was no doubt the moral kinship which existed between the Son and the Father and which made possible our Lord's saying, "All things have been delivered to me by my Father; . . . and no one knows the Father except the Son and any one to whom the Son chooses to reveal him" (Matt. 11:27=Luke 10:22 [Q]), where to "know" the Father is to experience "a new personal relation between God and man"[10] after the fashion of that taught by the prophets in their time. It is to be morally and spiritually en rapport with God (Hos. 6:1-3; Jer. 31:34). Jesus, then, was so attuned to the will of his Father that when he spoke it was the word of his Father, and when he acted it was the act of his Father. Hence, to speak a word against that "authority" which functioned in him was to blaspheme the Spirit of God, whose authority it was (Mark 1:10, 12; 3:28-30).

The will of the Father for our Lord is summed up in the word which Judaism had taken over from the Hebrew prophets as definitive of the moral person of God and indicative of his dealings with mankind, and particularly with his own people—namely, righteousness. Though only Matthew's special source, M, reports

[10] Manson, Mission, p. 371.

our Lord's use of this term, there can be little doubt that he would have acknowledged that it summed up what he would have wished to say on the subject of his Father's will for him (Matt. 3:15; 6:33). In any case, there can be no doubt that the church understood our Lord's "authority" to be related to, or even the product of, the righteousness of God which he manifested to his disciples while he resided with them and that she attributed the latter to that "Spirit of holiness" which was his (Rom. 1:4). As that righteousness was, on the one hand, God's moral person functioning on the plane of history (see p. 46), it was, on the other hand, that *Imago Dei* which God expects to see in man. And in the latter capacity it stood for the perfection of moral character which made such an impression, as the Gospels record, upon Jesus' contemporaries (Mark 7:37)—in a word, for morally mature personality.

The greatest of all our Lord's teachings were those spoken intimately to his disciples after the confession at Caesarea Philippi; and here the form critical principle that the intimate words of Jesus to the disciples were teachings, not of Jesus himself, but of the later church, completely fails. For otherwise the whole tenor of Jesus' ministry and teaching fails to reach its logical climax. Those teachings concerned his death and resurrection.[11] They reached their peak in the "upper room" when he said, "This is my blood of the covenant, which is poured out for many" (Mark 14:24). These words are the explanation of a life of service which was to issue at the last in the pouring out of that life in death (Heb. 9:12-13), in the obedience unto the cross (Phil. 2:5-11), in the love of God giving his Son (Rom. 5:6-11). For the ultimate demand which the church understood the Father's will to have made upon Jesus was his obedience unto death, even the death of the cross (Phil. 2:8). There was nothing distinctive or disjunctive about the cross as such, however. Jesus' whole life of obedience was one continuous cross; and all along the way he went—to alter the figure

[11] Cf. Mark 8:31-33; 9:30-32; 10:32-34.

slightly—there was a series of crosses of which that on Calvary was simply the climactic one. The term which perhaps best describes our Lord's work in this respect is that of "Suffering Servant of Yahweh," a term which he apparently never used himself as he used that of Son of Man to describe his person, but one nonetheless which he recognized to be descriptive of his activity, as both his words and actions testify.[12]

It is a term which brings to the fore the idea of vicarious suffering and consequent atonement as the final intent of Jesus' life. The sublime Sufferer of Deutero-Isaiah had been one who, whether as an individual or as a group, had suffered and died for the sins of mankind with a view to their salvation.[13] This figure served admirably, therefore, as interpretative of the way that Jesus was leading his disciples through suffering—on the part of both himself and them—into the status of the redemptive society. Because of its implicitly vicarious nature it became permissible to say with Paul that Jesus is our righteousness (I Cor. 1:30) and that "in him" we become the righteousness of God (II Cor. 5:21)— two obviously vicarious phrases—even as by him "the righteousness of God" had been manifested on the temporal plane (Rom. 3:21 ff.)

Inasmuch as all that our Lord did, reflected at once the will of the Father for his life, and at the same time the moral person of the Father himself, his acts, therefore, as the church saw from the beginning, were, taken together, God's act, even as the prophets' words collectively and in their final intent were God's word; and both the one and the other were with a view to man's redemption (II Cor. 5:21). The gospel formula at this point, accordingly, is: God gave his Son and his Son gave himself (Rom. 5:8-11; II Cor. 5:19).

God's act, however, is always last, even as it was also first. In the raising of Jesus from the dead, man had no part to play, not even

---

[12] See my *Intention*, ch. iv.   [13] See Isa. 53.

Jesus himself. This was God's act of re-creation. Hence, Jesus is for the church at once "the first fruits of these who have fallen asleep" (I Cor. 15:20), and at the same time "the first-born of all creation" (Col. 1:15), inasmuch as having gone beyond death, through resurrection, to "newness of life" he has achieved that which every man "in him" is to achieve. Having lived the "good life" in time and by his resurrection wiped out the bounds that separate the life of time from that of eternity, he returned from the grave as God's act, to demonstrate to the church the validity of the life which he had lived. He, therefore is the "resurrection" and "the life," and they who believe in him "shall never die" (John 11:25-26), or rather, they are raised to "newness of life" (Rom. 6:4)—in this present age and on the plane of history (Rom 6:4, 11; 7:4-6; Eph. 2:6).

Jesus' authority for his people, then, rests first on his *vindication of God's righteousness within time*, as the prophets had declared God would contrive. As God's act he accomplished God's righteous will for man's salvation and so manifested the Father to his people. At the same time he also vindicated man in God's sight by achieving on man's behalf the *Imago Dei*, which it had been God's purpose that man should become—an equally prophetic teaching (cf. Jer. 31:31-34; Ezek. 36:23-31; and Gen. 1:26 [P], which is based on such prophetic passages as the two former). In the former capacity Jesus was God's act of revelation; in the latter he was equally man's response to that revelation.

The Gospel's Method—The Gift of the Spirit

But if Jesus, while constituting the church's authority for her religion, did not furnish her with a conduct pattern by which she might lead her life, it is difficult to see how the Christian "way" in the life situation is to be discovered. I recall a conversation with a Moslem mullah in the course of which he remarked, "Sahib, I have read the Gospels, and I do not see where you can discover how to act in particular life situations. Now, as a Moslem I experience no difficulty at this point, for the Koran and Hadith cover every case and every conceivable situation, and I simply follow their directions." The same, of course, can be said for Pharisaism and for every legalistic system which provides a system of casuistry capable of resolving general laws into their concrete expression for particular occasions.

The answer lies again in the church's witness to the divine revelation which the Spirit of Christ is, in this instance, in her midst. For as by faith the church came to see in Jesus the divine act of revelation, so by faith she has become aware that he lives and guides her by his Spirit. It was the church's experience before it became her doctrine, that the Spirit was given to her as a community in the first instance, rather than to the isolated individual (Eph. 2:19-22),[14] so that to have the Spirit became "the distinctive mark of the Christian life and of the new Messianic age." [15] Christ lives again and is present by his Spirit in his church— such has been the content of the church's resurrection faith dating from that event. It is thus that she has from the first explained the resurrection "appearances" (I Cor. 15:1 ff.; cf. II Cor. 3:17-18), the experience of Pentecost (Acts 2:17 ff.), and the charismatic "gifts" of God to his church (I Cor. 12:4 ff.).

Once again, this Spirit is to the church both God's act ("the power of God", I Cor. 2:4-5) and God's word (I Cor. 2:16), or as Paul would say, the medium of communication to the church of the "mind of Christ." Moreover, the Spirit as a medium of revelation reverses the order which we have just seen to pertain between the prophets, representing the divine word, and Jesus, the divine act, relative to the establishment of the "redemptive society." The challenge of the word to establish that society having been met in the act of Jesus, the old prophetic order of divine act followed by divine word interpretative of the same is re-estab-

[14] Cf. C. A. Anderson Scott, *Christianity According to St. Paul*, p. 160; I Cor. 12:4.
[15] So Millar Burrows, *op. cit.*, p. 78.

lished. This order—the opposite to that found in the scheme of creation, where the normal order is, of course, word followed by act ("God spake and it was so")—is proper within a "redemptive society." For in dealing with his people God as sovereign naturally acts first and thereafter interprets his acts to his people.

Such at all events has been the experience of the church from the beginning. The church at Pentecost first experienced the power of the Spirit and thereafter that illumination which converted her into a flaming evangelist of the word (Acts 1:8; 2:2-4). And as it was with the church as a whole, so the individual first experienced the Spirit as the "power of God" and then as the "mind of Christ;" and Paul is constrained to pray that his Christian readers may have the spiritual insight to discern the work of God which has already transpired in their lives (Eph. 1:15-23). This is, indeed, the rationale of the church's doctrine of "regeneration" (John 3:3, 5 ff. Rom. 8:2, 9 ff.) or "adoption " (Rom. 8:14 ff.) as a first creative act on God's part relative to the individual. The church's formula is, "If any man's will is to do his will [and this can come only through the divine afflatus], he shall know whether the teaching is from God" (John 7:17 R.S.V.). First the act of God by the Spirit; thereafter the word of God by the same Spirit.

It is, then, by the medium of the Spirit of Christ that the latter becomes to the individual Christian "righteousness and consecration and redemption" (I Cor. 1:30). By "righteousness" here Paul means, of course, what from the Reformation forward the church has enshrined in her doctrine of "justification." The Spirit as God's act, having given one the new "life in Christ Jesus" (Rom. 8:2) above referred to, has thereby put that one in the way of vindication in the sight of God. Viewed in this light—i.e., from the angle of actual experience—this doctrine becomes wholly rational and is in no way unethical, as the enemies of the Reformation have always held it to be. It would be unethical only on the assumption implicit always in apocalypticism that what happens on the historical plane lacks that quality of "actuality" which the prophetic revelation showed God to have imparted to his acts within history. If to be "in the church"=to be "in the Spirit"=to be "in Christ" is a series of equations which represents a mere mouthing of words and nothing more, then, of course, the doctrine of justification is an unethical farce. But only on this assumption can it be considered so. If, contrariwise, the prophets are right and one may say with the great Augustine *"Extra ecclesiam nulla salus"* for the reason that the church in time is God's real church—made actual with the actuality imparted to all his acts by God himself— then it follows that to have the Spirit of Christ is to be justified in time along with that church, because in true prophetic fashion as we have seen Jesus accomplished in time the justification at once of God and man by the life of perfect righteousness which he led. And the same will be true, as we shall see in the next section, of sanctification and redemption.

In the meantime it is to be noted that following the divine act there comes the divine word in the experience of the individual Christian, again by the same Spirit. The Christian Church by her faith in the living Spirit of Jesus has been converted into a community of witnesses (Acts 1:8; 2:16 ff.), witnesses, that is to say, to Jesus and to his meaning for human life. All the Lord's people receive the illumination by the Spirit (II Cor. 4:4 ff.; Eph. 1:18; Heb. 6:4) which enables them to apprehend divine truth and to know the "way" in which they should walk. The question which that Spirit raises in their consciences and answers for them, as we have seen, is not "What would Jesus do?" Rather it is this: "Having committed my personality to the Father's will, as Jesus did, what must I do in my day and generation?" There can be no doubt that such a high spiritual principle of guidance will seem eminently unsatisfactory and illusory for those who are legalistically minded, but that it is exactly in line with the prophetic method of the revelation of the word is patent; and it serves to link the average Christian, therefore, with that great line of God-inspired men of old in the Hebrew tradition. Moreover, it is because of this universal distribution of the Spirit's guidance among all members of the Christian community that the New Testament writers forebear from giving more than the most general statement of principles in the matter of Christian ethical living, leaving it to the individual Christian under the Spirit's leading to work out his own salvation with fear and trembling (Phil. 2:12). It would have been highly presumptuous for Paul, for example, to have written to the Spirit-guided church other than he did write in words like these;

I . . . beg you to lead a life worthy of the calling to which you have been called. (Eph. 4:1 R.S.V.)
I appeal to you therefore, brethren, by the mercies of God, to present your bodies as a living sacrifice, holy acceptable to God, which is your spiritual worship. (Rom. 12:1 R.S.V.)
But I say, walk by the Spirit, and do not gratify the desires of the flesh. (Gal. 5:16 R.S.V.)
If then you have been raised with Christ, seek the things that are above, where Christ is, seated at the right hand of God. Set your minds on things that are above, not on things that are on earth. (Col. 3:1-2 R.S.V.)
Therefore be imitators of God, as beloved children. And walk in love. (Eph. 5:1-2 R.S.V.)

It would be a great mistake, however, to infer from the general nature of such apostolic admonitions that no answer can be given by the Spirit-led Christian to specific problems in the realm of ethical living. This is, indeed, the mistake which is made by all who have adopted the apocalyptic view of history and who, together, with their denial of God's ability to vindicate himself within the sordidness of time, are forced also to affirm the Christian's equal inability to know what God wants of him in specific situations and to do it, granted it were possible for him to acquire such knowledge. At this point much of the continental theology with its swing of the pendulum between God's "yea" and "nay"—a sort of dialectic *thesis* opposed to its *antithesis* for which on the avowel of this theology there can be found no final syn-

thesis within time—has succeeded in stymying the church's endeavor to give a clear word for the ethical problems of our day.
Thus to deny the church's ability to formulate solutions to specific
ethical problems is essentially to deny the doctrine and reality of
the Holy Spirit, even as it is equally to deny the validity of that
righteousness of God which Jesus manifested in his life on the
plane of history. It ought to be obvious—to all who hold to the
prophetic view of history at all events, as against the apocalyptic
view with its ever-present pessimism—that as the word of God
came to the prophet in the situation and not *in vacuo,* so the
Spirit is given to the church to solve the problems that face the
church in its day. Accordingly the reason the apostolic writings
are not full of specific solutions is, not because such cannot be
given by the Spirit-filled church, but because the apostle believed
in the prophetic interpretation of history, in the reality of the
Spirit's guidance of his church, and in the consequent ability of
the Christian under that Spirit's leading to discover the solutions
to his ethical problems. Herein is seen the consummate faith of
that apostolic band to which the Spirit first was given. I am re-
minded of the remark of a modern "apostle" to India: "I am content, having seen the Church in India under the Spirit's guidance,
to leave it there. It is in Safe Hands!"

What has just been said regarding the Spirit's guidance of every
member of the church fellowship is not intended to preclude,
however, the complementary truth that God still raises up in his
church the few of prophetic stature. All are not prophets even in
a prophetic church (I Cor. 12:29). As the Spirit is given to the
church, it is the church that by and large through the centuries is
guided by the Spirit in the ecumenical decisions she must make.
But it often happens that the first impulse to make such moves
and the guidance as to the direction which they are to take is as
of old manifest to the church through the medium of Spirit-filled
men of prophetic stature. In this, too, the Spirit functions in

accordance with the *modus operandi* of the word of God which came to the Hebrew prophet.

The Gospel's Product—The Imago Dei

The aim of the religion of maturity, as its name implies, is the production of a community of morally mature personalities who shall reflect God's moral person on the plane of history. According to the priestly writer of Gen. 1:26-28 this was the purpose of God in creation—a conception undoubtedly derived from such prophets as Jeremiah (31:31-34) and Ezekiel (36:23-31), and in any case interpreted by the prophets along ethical lines. The *Imago Dei* must of necessity be sketched after this manner for the reason that the pattern of God's own person was conceived along such lines by the prophets, as we have seen. God's holiness— his person, that is, in its transcendent awesomeness—did not greatly concern this Hebrew realist; but his righteousness—his ethical stature as he dealt with man in judgment and salvation— was for the prophet the pattern of right living and right acting on the part of man.[16] Moreover Jesus accepted that pattern of righteousness for his own life and by fulfilling it became the divine act answering to the prophetic word which demanded that man thus become the *Imago Dei*.

But the Spirit interpreting to his church "the mind of Christ" has made it clear that it was not enough that Jesus become the *Imago Dei* on the historical plane. To attain this same pattern of God's moral person is, not only the duty, but also the privilege of Jesus' church. No standard lower than this will suffice. The Spirit has said it both negatively and positively to the church in words like these:

"For I tell you, unless your righteousness exceeds that of the scribes and Pharisees, you will never enter the kingdom of heaven." (Matt. 5:20

[16] See p. 50.

[M].) Human ethical standards will not be acceptable to God, who demands perfect righteousness on man's part.

"You, therefore must be perfect, as your heavenly Father is perfect" (Matt. 5:48 [Q or M?]), or perhaps better, "Be merciful, even as your Father is merciful" (Luke 6:36). Whichever way the saying is read, the eventual teaching is the same, namely, that the standard or pattern for man's ethical living is the moral person of the Father.

"And we all, with unveiled face, beholding the glory of the Lord, are being changed into his likeness from one degree of glory to another; for this comes from the Lord who is the Spirit" (II Cor. 3:18)—a verse which takes that Jesus who has proved himself the *Imago Dei* as the equivalent of the righteous standard to be found in God himself, even as Paul does in his prayer for the church at Eph. 4:13, "Until we all attain . ... to mature manhood, to the measure of the stature of the fullness of Christ."

The achievement of the *Imago Dei* on man's part, which we saw in the last section to involve the application of the divine act and the divine word by God's Spirit to his needs, from the standpoint of man's effort involves a routine which is wholly prophetic in its atmosphere and development. It begins with the assumption that God's sovereign power is present in the world of human affairs and is available for the needs of men. We have three gospel sources upon which some effort has been expended with a view to giving them chronological arrangement—Mark, L, and John. Although these differ in numerous details, yet they are alike in suggesting that Jesus' ministry began in an atmosphere heavily charged with eschatological imagery of the prophetic, not apocalyptic, type. Thus Mark writes that Jesus began his work with the proclamation, "The time is fulfilled, and the kingdom of God is at hand; repent, and believe in the gospel" (1:15). Likewise L, which, I would agree with Streeter, was a little volume circulated as a sort of pre-gospel,[17] began with our Lord's proclaiming "the acceptable year of the Lord" as "today" having been "fulfilled" (Luke 4:19 ff.) John too placed at the forefront of his Gospel immediately

---

[17] *Four Gospels*, pp. 232 ff.; T. W. Manson, *Teaching*, pp. 39 ff.

following the prologue the testimony of certain individuals and a series of events—the changing of water into wine and the cleansing of the temple—both of which were intended to show in startling vividness how in Jesus God's sovereign rule over human life, over nature, and over religious worship had come to unique expression (John 1:29–2:22). Even the form critics, who generally find so little chronological material with which to reconstruct a "life" of our Lord, are agreed that he began his ministry, as the Baptist had done before him, in such an eschatological atmosphere.[18] In Jesus, or with him, the *eschaton* of the prophets was being realized among men; the kingdom of God was come near.

All this amounts to saying that with Jesus the power of God becomes available for men, for Jesus is God's act of salvation. As Bultmann remarks, "The Kingdom of God is deliverance for men"; "It is not *they*, with their fellowship and their activity, who constitute the Kingdom, but God's power alone";[19] and, as he would agree, that power is released to men through Jesus (Luke 11:20 [L or Q]). It is apropos at this point also to remark that the Spirit of Jesus continues throughout the history of the church to afford to men this same power of the kingdom that first appeared in history through Jesus (p. 283).

How, then, may man appropriate this power of God for himself? How may he proceed to work out his own salvation with fear and trembling (Phil. 2:12), confident the while that it is God who is at work within him? It is at this point that apocalyptic and prophetic teaching is at the greatest variance, the former being wholly unable to interpret the Sermon on the Mount realistically and to find any real place for a Christian ethic on the plane of history, being in consequence essentially antinomian. Contrariwise, the prophetic view with its usual realism sees in the sermon the part which man is legitimately asked to play in achieving the *Imago Dei* on the

---

[18] See, for example, Bultmann, *Jesus and the Word*, pp. 27 ff. Bultmann says among other things, "Jesus thus *rejects the whole content of apocalyptic speculation, as he rejects also the calculation of the time and the watching for signs*" (italics his).

[19] *Ibid.*, p. 38.

historical plane—a challenge, as it were, after the manner of the challenges which the prophetic word time and again threw out to the "people of God" of old. And when seen in this light, the sermon is discovered to follow the "pattern" of prophetic teaching to a remarkable degree. What can be done with it from the standpoint of modern psychological analysis is well illustrated in the two books by Professor Ernest M. Ligon, *The Psychology of Christian Personality* and *Their Future Is Now*. In what follows I shall endeavor to state the prophetic interpretation more nearly in the terminology of the prophets (and Jesus) themselves.

As is well known, there were originally two sermons—a Q sermon to be found in large part in Luke 6 and an M sermon embedded in Matthew's present version of the Sermon on the Mount in chapters 5–7. Each sermon began with a series of four beatitudes which were in the form of Aramaic poetry, and each set of beatitudes set forth a portrait of the "son of the kingdom." The Q portrait in true prophetic imagery delineated the progressive stages through which the true disciple must go in order to arrive at that perfection which is like to the Father. These are:

Beatitude 1: *Realization* on man's part of his poverty of spirit in the sight of a righteous God (Luke 6:20=Matt. 5:3; cf. Isa. 57:15)

Beatitude 2: *Repentance* in the Hebrew sense (shūb) of a "turning away" from the husks of the old life to God and his demands upon man's obedience (Luke 6:21=Matt. 5:4; cf. Isa. 57:18; Joel 2:12 ff.) [20]

Beatitude 3: *Consecration* of oneself to the "good life" as expressed in the earnest desire to be satiated at the banquet table in God's kingdom (Luke 6:21=Matt. 5:6; cf. Isa. 41:17; 44:3; 55:1)

Beatitude 4: *Endurance* to the end or the courage to risk all for the kingdom which is being realized in experience (Luke 6:22-23=Matt. 5:11-12; cf. Isa. 51–53) [21]

[20] For a statement of the meaning of repentance in the Hebrew sense, see my *Intention*, pp. 29 ff.

[21] The third beatitude in Matthew's present order (5:5) was evidently inserted by Matthew when he combined the Q and M series. See my article "An Exposition of the Beatitudes" in *Journal of Bible and Religion*, July, 1947.

Attention should be called to the fact that all of the materials which went into this little poem were derived from Deutero-Isaiah, a fact of great importance from the standpoint of its interpretation, as we shall see below.

The M series of beatitudes was derived from Ps. 85:10, and here we have the portrait of a personality in which various elements are compounded with a view to indicating the varicolored nature of that character which fulfills God's demands of perfect righteousness —in other words, the portrait of the *Imago Dei*. These elements are:

Beatitude 1: *Mercy*, the quality demanded in social ethics (Matt. 5:7)

Beatitude 2: *Sincerity* or *Truth*—that without which true religion cannot be achieved (Matt. 5:8)[22]

Beatitude 3: *Peace*, which with the prophets stood for right relations between God and man and between man and his fellowman (cf. Isa. 52:7 ff.; 57:19 ff. and Eph. 2:14 ff.), the proper content of an evangel (Matt. 5:9)

Beatitude 4: *Righteousness*—that is, the *Imago Dei*—to achieve which the true disciple is prepared to undergo persecution, to take up the "cross" (Matt. 5:10)

Each series of beatitudes comes, then, to the same end; each expresses the thought that the realization of the kingdom of God in human life effects an inward transformation of the personality and character. There is little novel about such teaching, it is true. It was all derived from the prophetic scriptures, and the rabbis had adopted the *Shema'* (Deut. 6:4 ff., etc.) as the symbol of the individual's commitment to such transformation.

And yet it is clear that there is a novel element in our Lord's use of these old materials. In the Q version of the Beatitudes—taken in substance from Deutero-Isaiah, where it was understood that the redemption of God's people and the achievement of their righteousness in God's sight would be through a labor of love on the part of the Suffering Servant, at once a corporate and an individual figure—the surrender that is made to God's sovereignty and the

[22] See the above article on this beatitude.

consequent persecution that is suffered are "for the sake of the Son of Man" (Luke 6:22 [Q]) or "for my sake" (Matt. 5:11—Matthew's modification of Q). That is to say, commitment to God's kingdom has a vicarious intent in view, and its aim is the blessing of the Son of Man—again both an individual and a corporate figure standing both for the Redeemer himself and for the people of God whom he redeems. Accordingly, in painting the portrait of the true disciple in the Q Beatitudes our Lord has all the while been sketching the "saving remnant" or the "redemptive society," and his intent is to suggest that salvation for the individual is the result of his taking his legitimate place in and assuming his proper responsibilities with reference to the community.

The M version of the Beatitudes also gives us a picture of redemption. The first seven verses of Ps. 85, from which this version was taken (vs. 10), are a prayer for the "salvation" which God will give his people; the remainder of the psalm, beginning with verse 8, is a prophecy of the direction which the promised salvation will take. Verse 10 is a summary of this in terms of God's righteousness in every aspect of life.

> Mercy and truth are met together;
> Righteousness and peace have kissed each other.

In this M version, as in the other, utter commitment to God's kingdom involves eventual persecution (the taking up of the "cross"), though the idea is introduced into the Beatitudes from the Deutero-Isaiah context, as it is not found in the psalm. The group who suffer it are those denoted by the phrase "sons of God" (Matt. 5:9)—i.e., God's own peculiar people who are his "sons" in that like him, for this is what the Hebrew idiom "son" means, they serve man's highest good regardless of every personal cost.[23]

---

[23] The introduction of the motif of suffering and persecution here is very significant, and one doubts if New Testament scholars have given it due consideration. It can only have been done by our Lord—and not by the author of the Gospel or of M—as its elimination would destroy the poetic form of the stanza. Moreover the church held to an apocalyptic eschatology, and this passage teaches a prophetic one

293

It seems clear that in the Beatitudes the two sources, Q and M, are at one in giving us Jesus' own analysis of the meaning of his Marcan saying, "The kingdom of God is at hand; repent ye, and believe in the gospel" (Mark 1:15). He meant thereby to call men to wholehearted allegiance to God's rule over their lives, and this would eventuate in an inward transforming experience resulting in the willingness to undergo vicarious suffering on behalf of the people of God, the "redemptive community." In other words, to achieve mature personality in Jesus' teaching is, like him, to acquire that toughness with reference to the world and that ability to stand alone against the world's inducements which we call "character." And had our Lord given us a definition of that term, it is safe to say that he would have defined it as the *Imago Dei* acquired by the true disciple through commitment to the will of God and the suffering which that commitment must entail in an imperfect and sinful world.

The Q sermon continued with a series of woes corresponding to the Beatitudes and directed against the failure to commit onself to the kingdom (Luke 6:24-26). These in turn were followed by a section on loving and doing good to one's fellow men (6:27-45), whose theme is found in verse 36 (cf. Matt. 5:48), "Be merciful, even as your Father is merciful" (R.S.V.). By means of various parables it was suggested that social righteousness would be achieved in the world when men were made right at the core of personality —when, in other words, they had acquired character (vss. 39-45)— for "the good man out of the good treasure of his heart produces good, and the evil man out of his evil treasure produces evil; for out of the abundance of the heart his mouth speaks" (vs. 45, R.S.V.). Here "heart" is used after the manner of the Hebrew psychology to stand for the entire inner or higher side of a man's nature. Finally the Q sermon closed with the parable of the house on the rock and that on the earth (sand) (6:46-49), in which the picture of two

---

for a realistic world in which persecution is possible. There is here no *Interimsethik* for an ideal situation.

individuals is seen. One has failed through lack of commitment, and the other has achieved through wholehearted allegiance and consecration to the sovereignty of God.

In M the beatitude call to commitment was followed by an analysis of human personality and the teaching that it is sacred at every point and must be reverenced and cultivated. The teaching is divided into five headings: (a) *reverence for personality* as such and consequent desisting from anger against another's person (Matt. 5:21-26); (b) *equality of the female personality* and the necessity of reverencing it even in thought (vss. 27-32); (c) *reverence for the intellect* (or truth, its standard) and the requirement that a man's word be as good as his bond (vss. 33-37); (d) *reverence for the will* and the willingness to merge one's interests in those of the group (vss. 38-42); and (e) *reverence for the emotional life* and the loving of men for their own good quite apart from anything lovable which may appear to be in them, even as God loves men without distinction (vss. 43-48). M also contained a section on true religion whose theme was a call to sincerity in man's relations with God (6:1-8, 16-18).

Each sermon, then, had as its theme the achievement of character or moral personality through reverencing it in others and through merging one's interests in those of the community. In both the thesis is that they who lose their lives will save them, a theme on which our Lord dwelt on more than one occasion, as both Mark (8:35) and Q (Luke 9:24) bear witness.[24] The Christian, then, individually and as a member of the Church of Christ, is to partake of his Lord's Spirit, to accept his evaluation of human personality in terms of moral character or the *Imago Dei* as this is achieved through the incorporation of the divine word, and to follow him in total surrender to the will of God and so in apparent loss of what paradoxically can only be won by abandoning.

This theme of the development of Christian personality through

[24] The parables labeled by C. H. Dodd "Parables of Crisis" are all concerned with confronting men with the challenge to achieve life through death and surrender (*The Parables of the Kingdom*, ch. v).

various stages until it arrives at "maturity" (Heb. 6:1) is, to be sure, a very common one in the New Testament. I have selected the Sermon on the Mount as representative because of the clarity of the development here. In theological terminology it is called "sanctification" (Rom. 8:1 ff.; I Cor. 1:30; 6:11; Gal. 5:22 ff.). It finds a legitimate place in the Christian's career only against a background of the prophetic view of history and of God's ability to vindicate his righteous rule on the plane of history. Against this background it becomes the capstone of the religion of maturity, which is essentially the religion of a divine optimism. Sanctification is far more closely and organically related to "justification" in Paul's writings than in most post-Reformation theologies. Professor Millar Burrows has rightly remarked:

Traditional Protestant theology uses the term "sanctification" to distinguish it from justification, but Paul's own terminology is not so clear-cut or systematic. From his unfettered and varying use of several expressions it is evident that for him the experience of salvation meant both the cancellation of past sins and the power to overcome sin from then on.[25]

It ought to be obvious, one imagines, that it is only on the basis of a realistic prophetic view of history and of God's giving the character of "actuality" to all his acts on the historical plane that these things can be so. First and last they assume man's spiritual and moral "educability," that is to say, his capacity for moral growth even under the adverse conditions which confront him within time. At this point the modern Christian psychologists are fast coming to the prophet's assistance, and much that they are writing sounds like a page out of Jeremiah or Paul. I cannot do better, therefore, than close this section with a quotation from one of them, my own colleague, Professor Donald G. Stewart.

Educability defines the Deity's method of dealing with man. By man's very creation he has been constructed to grow, to improve, and

[25] *Op. cit.*, p. 185.

in God's "saving grace" there is found the pattern for the measurement of the Creator's intention. From the standpoint of educability . . . God's "favor" does not begin to operate at the moment man decides to accept the Deity's gift of salvation, but long before and after this, for God has created in man the power to respond to His challenge. The individual who "press(es) on to the high calling of God in Christ" does so with God-given power.[26]

It is this unique combination of "challenge," "response," and "God-given power" which underlies and serves to explain the development which characterizes the religion of maturity.

The Gospel's Institution—The Church of Christ

It is a mistake to contrast the prophetic standpoint in the Old Testament with the apostolic view in the New in terms of "community" versus the "individual." Religious experience under the aegis of the prophetic word of revelation was always an individual one, and before the close of the canon under the Old Covenant it was explicitly said to be so (Jer. 31:27-34; Ezek. 18:1-4; 36:23 ff.). At the same time, however, the prophets retained in the doctrine of the "remnant" the communal conception of God's dealings with men. Experience taught the Christian Church that this twofold view was the correct one, and no essential alteration was ever made in it. The church became the "remnant," and to it the Spirit was given, but the individual felt His regenerating power.

The individual's experience of salvation, therefore, is always in the church fellowship. This is because the equation "in Christ"= "in the Spirit"="in the Church" is a true one corresponding to reality.[27] It is true of religious experience as of every other kind that man does not live his life alone like a sort of Robinson Crusoe cast ashore on some deserted isle in the cosmic sea. Christian mysticism is at this point quite unlike every sort of pagan mysticism, which may always be represented by an ellipse with two focuses, one

---

[26] First Principles of Christian Education (inaugural address, 1947).
[27] C. A. Anderson Scott, Christianity According to St. Paul, p. 158.

297

divine and the other human. This relationship is a wholly amoral one, as it leaves one's fellow man entirely out of the picture. The figure that serves to exemplify Christian mysticism is rather the humble cobweb with the strands uniting every member to the Lord of life at the center, but with also connecting filaments uniting all the members in a unique fellowship with one another.[28]

Both *benefits* and *responsibilities* accrue to the individual from his sharing in this genuine fellowship. It is not possible to discuss these separately as they tend to merge into one another. In the first place, the individual as a member of the Christian community through the work of the Spirit finds himself a partner to and sharing in God's final act of redemption of mankind. He is on consecrated ground, and the advantage of that fact becomes gradually clear to him. These others with whom he associates, like himself, "are being sanctified in Christ Jesus" and have been "called to be saints" (I Cor. 1:2). The church fellowship is, so to speak, the "advance guard" of God's outreach in the world; it is through this rich spiritual experience that he is working out his saving purpose. It is his tilled ground (I Cor. 3:9) in an otherwise pagan jungle. It is his house rising above the crude abodes of heathen idols (I Cor. 3:9).

While, therefore, it is true that the individual by reason of the act of the Spirit in his own life is progressively sanctified and receives that degree of illumination which he requires for his personal needs, he shares additionally a wider "sanctification" of the entire fellowship. Individually he experiences that "newness of life" which is the result of being genuinely in fellowship with Christ by his Spirit (Rom. 6:1 ff.; 8:2 ff.). Negatively this means that sin is progressively put out of his life.[29] Positively it means that his motivation is set right and that he purposes under the power of the

---

[28] It is intended throughout this discussion that the terms "church," "fellowship," "community," and the like shall stand for the real Church of Christ which exists within time and about which the prophetic scriptures of the New Testament show concern. This is the Communion of Christ, the people who really know the Lord. Such a community has always existed from the first century forward; it is found in every organized church and in none.

[29] Burrows, *op. cit.*, pp. 185-86.

Spirit to do all of God's will in every situation which confronts him. As this purpose is the product of God's act by his Spirit, it partakes of the "actuality" of all of God's acts within time, and in consequence merits the adjective "perfect" in the sense of Matt. 5:48 (M).[30] This is perfection in the prophetic and realistic sense of motivation, and the possibility of its achievement by the Christian can only be denied on the assumption of apocalyptic that nothing within time partakes of the nature of "actuality" and hence can serve to vindicate either God's righteous rule or man's religious response. It is such perfection that our Lord has in mind in Matt. 6:33 and again in 7:13-14. Essentially it consists of the acquisition of direction for one's life—a genuinely prophetic conception (cf. Luke 13:24 [Q]; also Ps. 1). As such *perfection of motivation* is an act of God, the Christian has no ground for glorying thereby (Eph. 2:7-9); but its reality cannot be denied by anyone who adopts the prophetic view of history and who believes, accordingly, that we are "created in Christ Jesus for good works, which God afore prepared that we should walk in them" (vs. 10).

But there is a higher type of perfection still. This is the *perfection of achievement* in company with the others who are in fellowship with Christ.[31] The Christian in the fellowship finds himself strangely captured and enthralled by that acme of God's righteousness, love. On analysis this is seen to be, in the first instance, the "love of Christ" for himself; then, the love of the brethren for him; and finally a constraining and redemptive love within himself for Christ and for all those for whom Christ died.[32] This interacting love produces a *perfection of achievement* which the individual could never have experienced alone. No single individual could ever achieve the totality of the righteousness of God or of the *Imago Dei* which the Incarnate Son was and is either in the world or out of it. Nor could anyone alone attain to the "measure of the stature of the fullness of Christ" (Eph. 4:13).

[30] *Ibid.*, pp. 163-64 for a fine exegesis of the passage.
[31] Cf. John Mackay, *Heritage and Destiny*, pp. 45 ff.
[32] Cf. Rom. 14:15; I Cor. 8:11 ff.; II Cor. 5:14.

But in the community of Christ's people the individual is privileged to share in a perfection of achievement which takes in all of the other members of the fellowship in any given age and also all those who in successive ages to the end of time shall partake of Christ. To speak of this experience also is to be wholly realistic. This is true for two reasons: in the first place, Paul's term for the church, the "Body of Christ," is more than metaphor. It stands for a spiritual reality which again is as "actual" as anything God ever does within time. Indeed, the Body of Christ is the supreme reality of all and the one which represents the goal of history as conceived and achieved by God himself (Eph. 3:10). The church is the God-appointed medium for the accomplishment of all of God's will in the world. It is the "redemptive society" at last brought into being by God's own act by his Spirit. It performs, therefore, not its own will, but the will of its creator. In the end, accordingly, when the scroll of history is finally unrolled, it will be seen that the church has perfectly accomplished God's will for man. Because he is a member of this fellowship the individual Christian shares in this perfection of achievement.

But again, to speak so is wholly realistic because genuine sharing is the product of genuine concern. Every member of the fellowship makes the contribution which he is empowered to make (I Cor. 12; Eph. 4:16) through the "talents" God has given him as these are used by the Spirit in whose "power" he shares. Under the Spirit's guidance he discovers his God-appointed task which accords with the "talents" he has received. Paul is stating in I Cor. 12 what was experienced by the church before it became her doctrine, when he suggests that the Christian who has found his "niche" in the Christian fellowship harbors neither a superiority (vs. 21) nor an inferiority complex (vss. 15-16). The church's supreme task as the "redemptive society" is "the building up of itself in love" through bringing all peoples into its fellowship (Eph. 4:16) and seeing that everyone makes that contribution to the common good which he is individually empowered by the Spirit to make.

This ofttimes means sacrifice and the bearing of the "cross" by those who make their contribution to this great end (Col. 1:24 ff.); for the church is not only the Son of Man in his glorious estate but also the Suffering Servant in humility and suffering. The church, however, with her prophetic outlook knows what the apocalyptist never grasped: in the divine economy it is through suffering that the world's redemption is achieved. Hence she "rejoices" in her "tribulations" while the redemptive agony is upon her.

CHAPTER

15

The New Wineskins

CHILDREN dancing in the sun-
light stretch out their hands to grasp the sunbeams and are disappointed that there is nothing tangible there to be added to their
little store of treasures. So men have always demanded something
tangible in religion. This doubtless is the origin of "sacrament," the
material symbol of "things not seen." Wine requires a container,
even the "wine" of religion; and "new wine" must have "fresh
skins."

What, then, of the "fresh skins" of our Lord's parable? (Mark
2:22 R.S.V. mg.)[1] He obviously intended that there should be such
to contain the "new wine" of the gospel, for he spoke of the old
skins as worn out (παλαιούς), and by implication at least this
meant that the old ones were to be displaced with new ones. And
yet characteristically he did not condemn the old forms and rituals
adopted by the religions of altar, book, and throne; he merely
prophesied their disuse and passing away from the religious scene.[2]
But equally he did not give as clear a lead as we could wish in regard
to the nature of the new ones. This, we may well believe, was
symptomatic of his generally prophetic attitude and of his stress
on spirit rather than on the formal side of religion. The implication

[1] See above, p. 130.   [2] See above, pp. 129-31.

302

of these facts would appear to be that in Jesus' view "fresh skins" can be found as they are needed and that it may well enough be left to men to discover them in the situation as it arises.

We need not be overmuch disturbed, I think, that our Lord has left us in a condition of uncertainty at this point. But let us first see just how extensive this is. It is no secret that it is difficult to demonstrate that the external forms by which the religion of maturity endeavors to express itself owe their origin to Jesus, though it is probable that the difficulty here has often been exaggerated. Thus only with some hesitancy can the observance of the Christian sacraments be traced in each case to a specific command on his part. It was not Jesus' own practice to baptize. John 4:2, which says as much, certainly represents the true state of affairs in spite of 3:22, 26; and as Strachan remarks, "the real meaning seems to be that while Jesus sanctioned Christian Baptism, in His lifetime He baptized only through His disciples."[3] This conclusion is fundamentally in agreement with the Synoptic tradition which indicates that our Lord baptized, not with water, but with "the Holy Spirit" (Mark 1:8) or with "fire" (Luke 3:16 [Q]), or with both together.[4] Moreover, that our Lord commanded his church to baptize rests finally on the witness of a single verse in the special source lying behind one Gospel only (Matt. 28:19 [M]). The co-ordinate passages in the other Gospels (Luke 24:48-49; John 20:21; cf. Acts 1:7-8) do not contain the reference to baptism, Mark 16:16 being, of course, unauthentic.

Burrows may be right, therefore, in suggesting that the practice of Christian baptism "may have been introduced into the church through the influence of John's followers."[5] At all events there was good precedent here. And if this is the case, there would be every reason for Jesus' disciples to have begun the custom even

[3] The above statement stands, I think, in spite of the uncertainty of the text in John 4:2 to which Strachan alludes (*The Fourth Gospel*, p. 147).

[4] John also speaks of Jesus baptizing only with "the Holy Spirit," as does Mark (John 1:33).

[5] *An Outline of Biblical Theology*, p. 270.

while he was with them. This would have served to indicate, as was done in other ways also, that the movement of the Baptist and that of Jesus were essentially one in spirit and in intent.[6] There was no hint, it is true, at the first sending forth of the disciples at Mark 6:7-11 (cf. Matt. 10:7 ff.; Luke 9:2-5) that they were to baptize, nor does the New Testament generally suggest that this was a characteristic mark of an "apostle." Paul, indeed, specifically denies that this was his function as an apostle (I Cor. 1:17).

And yet it is clear from Acts 2:38—and thereafter throughout the book—that baptism was from the first an accepted rite in the Christian Church.[7] Paul also assumes its prevalence throughout the church (Rom. 6:4; Eph. 4:5; Col. 2:12). This can hardly have been the case unless Jesus had in some way sanctioned the rite while he was with his disciples. There is just a hint in the curious saying to the sons of Zebedee regarding the drinking of his "cup" and the being baptized with his "baptism" that he had done so (Mark 10:35-45). There can be no question, of course, that the "baptism" and "cup" here both refer to the same experience in our Lord's case, namely, to his crucifixion; the phrases employed in his saying constitute a nice example of Hebrew—or at any rate, of Semitic— parallelism. But the use of such metaphorical language regarding his cross requires itself to be explained. And the natural explanation which occurs to one is that Jesus is here drawing upon the deeper symbolism of the Christian sacraments, just as Paul did after him to the same intent (Rom. 6:1-14; I Cor. 10:16-17).[8] The same may be said for the Q saying, "But I have a baptism to be baptized with; and how I am constrained until it is accomplished!" (Luke 12:50).[9] But if this is so, it would seem to be imperative that these Christian sacraments should have already been in existence in some form previous to our Lord's metaphorical references to them. It will

[6] *Ibid.*, p. 235; cf. Mark 1:4, 15; Matt. 4:17.
[7] *Ibid.*, p. 270.
[8] I am inclined, however, rather strongly to agree with Professor Burrows that in Rom. 6:3-4 "Paul refers to the inner experience of 'baptism into death' and not at all to the ceremony" (*ibid.*, p. 240).
[9] See my *Intention*, p. 148-49.

serve to fulfill the demands of this thesis, I believe, if it can be
determined that baptism was already being practiced by his disciples
and that the common meal with bread and cup had taken on the
chabūrāh aspect of Oesterley's suggestion, which it may well have
done long before the evening of the Last Supper.[10]

Again, that our Lord desired the perpetuation of the Communion feast as the center of the Christian communal life probably
rests on the testimony of one apostle, Paul—and he was not himself
present at the Last Supper, nor can we be certain of the literal
intent of his words (I Cor. 11:24-25). But if the Last Supper was
simply the last of a series of chabūrāh feasts held by Jesus with his
disciples—the "fellowship meal" par excellence at which he sealed
the new covenant by pointing out the significance of bread and
cup—then it seems certain that he

did have in mind the perpetuation of the feast! A "fellowship meal" is
given for exactly that purpose. Every time it is repeated the old fellowship ties are strengthened, the bonds of love are tied the tighter, and
the comradery is renewed. In coming together for "fellowship, in the
breaking of bread and the prayers," therefore, the primitive community was undoubtedly fulfilling our Lord's desire, if not his express command.[11]

As with the sacraments, so in the case of the Christian Church
and its structure there is some room for doubt about our Lord's
attitude and desires. H. J. Holtzmann and Adolf Harnack in modern
times have been leading exponents of the view that Jesus neither
used the term "church" nor envisaged the existence of a redemptive
community corresponding to that name. The argument in chapter
6 of my book, The Intention of Jesus, leads me, at any rate, to conclude that

By direct saying, by parable, through challenging men to an expression of faith in himself, by means of the strange acted parable of the

[10] W. O. E. Oesterley, The Jewish Background of the Christian Liturgy, pp. 172 ff.
[11] Intention, p. 223. As is well known, the injunction in Luke 22:19b is a
Western "noninterpolation."

305

"twelve," and through the establishment of the "fellowship meal," Jesus made it evident to his intimate disciples that he desired to form a group who should live the Kingdom life in the closest fellowship with himself as its Mediator,[12]

which group is what I understand the New Testament to mean by the word "church." Whether, therefore, Jesus ever used the Aramaic term for "church" in this sense of his congregation, as over against the Old Testament usage of it to refer to the "people of Israel," is in my judgment immaterial. He conceived at any rate of such a new people of God; his intention embraced the establishing of such a people; and to that end he directed all his energies. It is such "intention" on his part that is of the utmost importance for us, for because of it we may surely conclude that in the most real sense Jesus was the Founder of the church.[13]

"The Mind of Christ"

The relative indifference which, as we have just seen, our Lord showed toward outward forms and rites is not to be explained by the assumption of the modern apocalyptists that he looked for a speedy end of the "age." Such a theory is entirely irreconcilable with his prophetic world view and his purpose of establishing the "remnant"—the Church of God transformed into his image and likeness. Jesus was not concerned about the "fresh skins" because he knew that form is a matter of relative indifference. It was important for him and should be equally so for us that the church as the living fellowship in union with him as its Lord should incarnate the prophetic word in its communal life and live out its implications for the day in which it is placed.

The form which the church's embodiment of the word assumes from age to age necessarily varies with the conditions and therefore may very well await the event itself. It is for this reason no doubt

[12] *Ibid.*, p. 224.
[13] Millar Burrows has a good short résumé of the whole subject of "The People of God" as that term is intended in both Testaments (*op. cit.*, pp. 146 ff.).

that Jesus gave little thought to ecclesiastical structure and organization, leaving it to each local or temporal community to work out its own salvation in this matter. And we cannot doubt that it has been under the guidance of the Spirit of Christ that the church has from age to age succeeded in adapting its form and structure to the changing needs of men. Thus it is a striking fact that, when at the close of the Middle Ages the system known as "feudalism" was falling to pieces by reason of its own rottenness and men were searching for a new principle upon which to erect their social structure, the church rediscovered that "liberty of the children of God" (Rom. 8:21) which not only contributed to its own rebirth but also gave the system of democracy with its large place for individual freedom and initiative to the western world at large. Similarly in our own day, when again our social and economic life seems to have searched to the limit its own resources and found them wanting, the church—surely under the guidance of the Spirit of Christ and partaking of his mind—is in the process of perceiving anew the bearing of the principle of corporate living upon the needs of its own life and that of the world beyond its borders. It scarcely requires prophetic insight to foresee a new day when both the church's internal organization and the socioeconomic structure of society without will exemplify the functioning of both gospel principles of *individual freedom* and *communal fellowship* in nicer adjustment than has hitherto been attained by either.[14]

Equally, one believes, in perpetuating the sacraments the church has accorded with the "mind of Christ." Christian baptism gives expression to the principle of *individualism* which is indigenous to the church's prophetic faith. It is the symbol of the fact that true religion is not a matter of race or people, of blood or class, but of personal allegiance to God. Its prophetic authority is found in the principle set forth by Jeremiah and Ezekiel in passages like these:

[14] Bishop Charles Gore as long ago as 1928 was a pioneer in discerning with prophetic insight the coming of this new day; see his *Christ and Society*, particularly lectures ii and v.

In those days they shall no more say, The fathers have eaten sour grapes, and the children's teeth are set on edge. But everyone shall die for his own iniquity: every man that eateth the sour grapes, his teeth shall be set on edge. (Jer. 31:29-30.)

But if the wicked turn from all his sins that he hath committed, and keep all my statutes, and do that which is lawful and right, he shall surely live, he shall not die. (Ezek. 18:21; cf. vss. 1 ff.)

The church's baptism conserves the permanent elements in the rite as practiced by the Baptist—namely, its symbolical suggestion of the individual's repentance of his sins and his pledge of allegiance to God's sovereign will. But it goes far beyond John's baptism in that it no less signifies induction of the individual into the fellowship of the community of Christ, the Redeemer and Lord of life, in which community alone the Christian can live and move and have his being. Baptism into Christ, to the mind of the Church— and one must believe, therefore, also to the mind of Christ—is the "sign and seal" of our resurrection unto newness of life through fellowship at once with him and with his people, and apart from such resurrection we are all dead men (Rom. 6:1-11).

The Communion of the Lord's Supper likewise was perpetuated by the church, not because of a specific command of her Lord to do so—or at any rate, not for that reason alone—but because she acquired the "mind of Christ" sufficiently to "discern his body" in this sacrament. In celebrating this rite the Church of Christ perceived that she was giving expression to the corporate side of her faith and life. This is the phase of that life indicated in the idea of the "new covenant" of Jeremiah. "But this is the covenant that I will make with the house of Israel after those days, saith Jehovah: I will put my law in their inward parts, and in their heart will I write it; and I will be their God, and they shall be my people." (Jer. 31:33.) This new covenant includes, and therefore the Lord's Supper is intended to give expression to, a two-sided moral fellowship which is the ultimate reality in the church's existence. This is in the first instance with the Lord of life himself who died and yet continues to live and reign as Host at the head of his table and as Head of his church. "The cup of blessing which we bless, is it not a participation in the blood of Christ?"—that is, with our Host in his sacrificial death for his church (I Cor. 10:16a R.S.V.). At the same time and equally our fellowship is with those dedicated to allegiance to our Host's lordship. "The bread which we break, is it not a participation in the body of Christ? Because there is one loaf, we who are many are one body, for we all partake of the same loaf" —that is, of the bread which represents the "body of Christ," which with Paul is always his church. The Lord's Supper, then, in a unique way is qualified, as the Church has clearly seen, to give expression at once to the fact of this dual fellowship. That, therefore, she has the "mind of Christ" in perpetuating the sacrament cannot be seriously called in question.

The Church's Self-Dedication Versus Man's Arrogance

In the light of what has now been said, it should be clear that those movements in the Church of Christ which from time to time would have us return to the religions of altar, book, or throne as such have lost contact with the living Spirit of the Incarnate Word which is the be-all and end-all of the Christian faith, even as the presence of that same Spirit is the church's assurance that God is still "Emmanuel" and so in her midst. The church need never return to the religion of the altar for the reason that her one altar is the cross which she carries at the center of her life of unending self-dedication to her Lord's service. With Paul she may repeat each day of her ongoing life, "I rejoice in my sufferings . . ., and in my flesh I complete what remains of Christ's afflictions for the sake of his body, that is, the church" (Col. 1:24 R.S.V.). If the church is true to her Lord, she carries her altar already too deeply within her heart to learn anything from those who would have her carry it on her sleeve. For religious exhibitionism is not after the mind of him who went reluctantly up the hill Golgotha only because he was made to do so at the point of Roman spears.

Nor need the Church return to the religion of the book, for she requires no system of casuistry to decide between conflicting duties which do not exist. Her single duty, as she knows right well, is to love God by loving her fellow men; in a deeper sense perhaps than the evangelist knew, hereby is fulfilled all the Law and the Prophets. The church, therefore, is conscious of requiring, not a knowledge of commandments either old or new to teach her how she should "walk" in the world, but rather the power to perform what the Spirit makes clear to her to be her task from day to day. She has come at last to see that to love "the neighbor" is to love "God"; for the image of God is in that neighbor, and in the end it is that image that she loves, as prompted by her love of men she makes a sacrament of every kindly deed on their behalf.

Again, the church needs no more of the religion of the throne. For her function is, not to judge the world, but with her Lord and under his leadership to effect its salvation. The church need not judge the world any more than her Master, because both the one and the other were and are the world's Judge by virtue of their life lived among men (John 12:44-50; II Cor. 2:15-16). The world judged itself by its response—favorable or unfavorable, as the case may have been and was—to the word and life of the church's Lord as he walked among men; even so the world today pronounces its own sentence as it accepts or rejects the witness of that same word and life exemplified in the moral fellowship of Christ's people. But such judgment can never be the ultimate goal of either Christ or church, for that is best expressed in the words, "For the Son of man [both individually and corporately] came to seek and to save that which was lost" (Luke 19:10 R.S.V.).

It is an overstress on the element of judgment ($\kappa\rho\iota\sigma\iota\varsigma$) which is the major liability of the so-called "crisis theology" and of the "Neo-orthodoxy" which in America stems from it. These theological movements are essentially apocalyptic in origin and affiliation; that is to say, they are modern representatives of the religion of the throne. Their apocalyptic pessimism (cf. p. 269, n. 7) results from

310

the discovery on the part of their leadership of the bankruptcy of the "Old Liberalism" in which these leaders were trained in the period before World War I. That Liberalism, largely due to its embracing of the doctrine of evolution, could find no place for a doctrine of sin. The experiences of the past generation, however, convinced the adherents of this theology—in large measure, at any rate—that a view of mankind which left out the factor of sin was totally unrealistic. In consequence a group of younger theologians on the Continent and in this country have written the new theology of crisis about the idea of Brunner's expressive phrase, *Der Mensch im Widerspruch*, that is, *Man in Opposition* against God and his will.[15] This theology has made two valuable contributions to our thinking: it has restored belief in a genuine revelation, a word of God to man; and it has interpreted man as essentially in "revolt" against God. But it shares with apocalyptic generally a characteristic inability to transcend the pessimism which its origin in a period of gloom and tribulation appears to stamp upon it. One cannot but wonder when these theologians, who have at last discovered that sin is a reality in man's experience, will also learn that the gospel's central message is, not judgment upon this sin, but the "glad news" that there is under God such a thing as salvation from it.

Fundamentally the lack in the religions of altar, book, and throne is one. It is that each absorbs but a portion of the talents and attention of the disciple of Jesus; and its claim upon him, therefore, can in the nature of things be but a partial one. It demands *either* his emotional, or his intellectual, or his volitional powers, but *not all* three of these at once. The result on personality is in each case the same. This is the production of a self-assertive or arrogant attitude, because the disciple fails to see the totality of the demand of Christ on human life and in consequence becomes proud of his "Lilliputian" accomplishments. The religion of maturity never makes this mistake. It demands every ounce of simon-pure energy the individual possesses—*all* of his emotional or love life, *all* of his intel-

---

[15] See Brunner's book of the same name.

lectual powers, *all* of his will—and dedicates *all* of these to the cause of Christ and his gospel.

The normal product of such demand is that humility of which our Lord spoke in the parable of the unprofitable servants (Luke 17:7-10), who when they have done all that their Lord has demanded of them say, "We are unworthy servants; we have only done what was our duty." This is not a humility which sits down and folds its hands imagining that it can accomplish little for the cause of the kingdom, but rather one that drives a man out into the melee of the human situation and forces him by brain and brawn to work out the form which the obedience of the "law of Christ" shall require of him in his day and generation. And since our Lord has raised up such disciples from the inception of the Christian movement and continues to make them in every age, obviously he was wise above the wisdom of men in spending his time and energy when he walked here below with the problem of the nature of the gospel's "wine," leaving the fashioning of the "fresh skins" to faithful followers in each succeeding age.[16]

Let the Christian Be the Church

Those who complain that the Christian movement has no "cut and dried" program that will serve all men in every situation and for the church in every age have missed the *pièce de résistance* which constitutes the church what she is. The Church of Christ has no program because by reason of her genius she cannot have. But equally she does not need one. If the church were to acquire a program, she would cease to be the church. Her glory lies in this very lack, for this means nothing else than that her members are dedicated one and all to the attainment of her Lord's objectives as he communicates them to her by the Spirit. The Spirit of the living Christ is the church's program; the life she lives and the fruit she

---

[16] The remainder of this chapter is substantially taken from my inaugural address as Robert Dollar Professor of New Testament Interpretation in the San Francisco Theological Seminary, 1945.

312

bears are proof of that statement. The church in every moment of her life is placed by the Spirit of her Lord in the "crisis" of decision, and to arrive at a right decision requires the functioning of every power of personality and character of her every member.

It was this perennially unfinished task of the church, on the one hand, and the fact of the Spirit's guidance, on the other, which the Oxford Conference on Church, Community, and State (1937) had in mind when it coined the aphorism, "Let the Church be the Church." The expression is a good one but not quite good enough. It is a bit too abstract and smacks too much of the "theology" classroom. "Let the Christian be the church in his situation"—this is perhaps better and certainly more concrete. Let the Christian, in whom is the dynamic life of the Spirit of his Lord, be the church wherever he finds himself—in his social and economic, in his educational and religious, in his political and international groups. Let him live that life and show the courage and declare the gospel solution which is the only true and inevitable and Christian way under the circumstances, even as the church of the New Testament did in its generation before him.

If the church generally were only to realize that it is in the direction of this individual responsibility of her members to be the church-in-the-situation that her collective duty lies, much of the self-criticism to which during the past forty-five years she has subjected herself, together with much of the pessimism which has arisen by reason of her supposed ineffectiveness, would be dissipated. For it appears to have been assumed—doubtless without a clear analysis of the implications involved—that the church should bodily go out into the world to reconstruct its social, economic, educational, political, and other institutions along the lines of a Christian pattern. It is difficult to see just how this would work out in practice. It would seem to result in our having a Christian labor union alongside the several now existing, a Christian service club together with the "secular" service club, a Christian Red Cross, a Christian political party, and what not. Indeed, this very attempt has been made on occasion from the time of Calvin's Christian theocracy in Geneva down to the Christian Socialist party of the modern European state. And there are no doubt times when the church feels called upon to set up an institution in the world to serve as an example for it. Thus the church took the first hospital and medical college to the Orient.

But generally speaking this is not the New Testament way. The gospel calls rather for a ministry which shall seek at all times to do two things: first, to listen, like the true prophet which collectively it is, to "what the Spirit says to the churches," and then to transmit that word of the gospel to Christ's church for which it is meant; second, to inspire the members of that church—again under the guidance of the Spirit of Christ—with the courage and to give them the motivation and to fill them with the spiritual dynamic that will send them out into the world to become the church in all their relationships.[17] These individual Christians, then, become the Church in the existent service club, in the Y.M.C.A. and Y.W.C.A., in the Girl Scouts and Boy Scouts, in the Red Cross, in the amusement world and in the realm of art, in economic life, in the scientific laboratory, in the body politic, in the labor organization, and in the manufacturers' organization. And in each of these spheres of human activity, being the Church-in-the-situation, they as individuals— though ever conscious of the powerful spiritual fellowship of which each is a microcosmic replica—bring the gospel solution to bear on all the multifarious problems presented by the complex world in which the church finds herself. Thus, the Church of Christ discharges her redemptive task in the historic scene in which she lives, not as priest by sacrifices that cost her little (a pittance of this

[17] I am, of course, not forgetting that the New Testament does not recognize a moral dichotomy between "clergy" and "laity." This is a distinction for which the Roman communion is to blame, as is illustrated in its development of "secular" and "religious" in the monastery. The minister is also a layman in the sense that he must preach the gospel to himself as well as to others, and equally the layman is also a minister in so far as it is his duty to listen to the voice of the Spirit for himself and to give it forth with no uncertain sound. The above distribution of duties is to be understood as suggestive of a "functional" and not an "essential" difference among Christians. This is the truly gospel-oriented differentiation.

world's goods), nor as *scribe* in slavish adherence to the orthodoxy of a dead past, nor yet as *apocalyptist* with his crossless ethic for an unrealistic world—rather as the *prophet* that she is and prepared with her Lord and Redeemer to give herself in self-sacrifice for the word of God which she knows to be worth dying for.

This New Testament way, be it observed, is the only realistic one. For one thing it rids the ministry of the church of the intolerable burden of attempting to become an expert in every field at once. The minister's task is not to compete with the layman in being a better sociologist, and a better economist, and a better statesman, and a better psychologist, and a better financier than he. Rather it is to be an expert in the prophetic word of the gospel and its principles for life, and to bear witness with his soul aflame to his conviction that this gospel can solve all of life's problems. Again, this New Testament way gives the Christian layman a task of his very own; this is—with his knowledge of the gospel thus acquired and with his inspiration renewed by the fires of the fellowship in Christ, not to speak of the institutional church's "program of adult education," and equally with his expert knowledge in a limited field of his own profession—to put the two (gospel and *Fach*) together, to be the church in the world, and so to mold its life that "the way of the Lord" may be prepared, "his paths" made straight, "every valley" filled, "every mountain and hill" brought low, "the crooked" made straight and "the rough ways" smooth, to the end that "all flesh shall see the salvation of God."

There is little spectacular about such a "program." It leaves scant room for exhibitionism by either clergy or laity. Nor is the world likely to give much credit to a type of Christianity which makes her light shine with so little flash and sputter. But who wants its credit for the contribution a prophetic and therefore self-sacrificial gospel has to make to its life? They who do may "have their reward." But the Christian Church's concern is for God, who rewards his servants, laity and clergy alike, with the quiet mind and the happy assurance of a task well done.

315

APPENDIX A

Jesus' Use of the Old Testament Scriptures

I. PROPHETIC WRITINGS

Mk	10:7	Mk	Ge	2:24	J			
Lk	17:27	Q	Ge	7:7	J			
Mk	10:27	Mk	Ge	18:14	J			
Lk	17:29	L?	Ge	19:15, 24-25	J			
Lk	17:31	L?	Ge	19:26	J			
Mk	12:26	Mk	Ex	3:6	E			
Mk	7:10	Mk	Ex	20:12	E			
Mk	10:19	Mk	Ex	20:12-16	E			
Mt	5:21	M	Ex	20:13	E			
Mt	5:27	M	Ex	20:14	E			
Mt	5:21	M	Ex	21:12	E			
Mk	7:10	Mk	Ex	21:17	E			
Mt	5:38	M	Ex	21:24-25	E			
Lk	7:27	Q	Ex	23:20	E			
Mk	14:24	Mk	Ex	24:8	E			
Mk	12:1	Mk	Is	5:1-2				
Mk	4:12	Mk	Is	6:9-10				
Mk	13:24	Mk	Is	13:10				
Lk	10:15	Q	Is	14:13-15				
Mk	13:8	Mk	Is	19:2				
Mt	11:29	M	Is	28:12				
Mk	7:6-7	Mk	Is	29:13				
Lk	7:22	Q	Is	29:18-19				
Lk	7:22	Q	Is	32:58				
Mk	13:25	Mk	Is	34:4				
Lk	19:10	L	Is	34:16				
Lk	7:22	Q	Is	35:5-6				
Mk	1:11	Mk	Is	42:1				
Lk	13:24	Q	Is	49:12				
Lk	22:37	L	Is	53:12				
Jn	6:45	Jn	Is	54:13				
Mk	11:17	Mk	Is	56:7				
Lk	6:20	Q	Is	57:15				
Lk	4:18	L	Is	58:6				
Lk	13:29	Q	Is	59:19				
Lk	6:20	Q	Is	61:1				
Lk	7:22	Q	Is	61:1				
Lk	4:18-19	L	Is	61:1-2				
Mt	5:4	M	Is	61:2-3				
Mt	21:5	M	Is	62:11				
Lk	21:24	L	Is	63:18				
Mt	5:34	M	Is	66:1				
Mk	9:48	Mk	Is	66:24				
Mk	8:18	Mk	Je	5:21				
Mt	11:29	M	Je	6:16				
Mk	11:17	Mk	Je	7:11				
Lk	13:35	Q	Je	12:7				
Mt	7:22	M	Je	14:14				
Lk	13:35	Q	Je	22:5				
Mt	7:22	M	Je	27:15				
Mk	14:24	Mk	Je	31:31				
Mt	5:35	M	La	5:1				
Mt	9:13	M	Ho	6:6				
Mt	12:7	M	Ho	6:6				
Lk	21:22	L	Ho	9:7				
Lk	23:30	L	Ho	10:8				
Mk	9:29	Mk	Jl	4:13				
Mt	12:40	M	Jo	2:1				
Mk	13:12	Mk	Mi	7:6				
Lk	12:35	Q	Mi	7:6				
Mt	13:41	M	Zp	1:3				
Mk	13:27	Mk	Zc	2:10				
Mk	10:27	Mk	Zc	8:6				
Lk	7:27	Q	Ma	3:1				
Mk	9:12	Mk	Ma	3:23				
Mt	11:14	M	Ma	3:22				

II. PRIESTLY WRITINGS

Mk	10:6	Mk	Ge	1:27	P
Mk	1:44	Mk	Le	13:49	P
Lk	17:14	L	Le	13:49	P
Lk	10:28	L?	Le	18:5	H
Mt	5:33	M	Le	19:12	H
Mk	12:31	Mk	Le	19:18	H
Mt	5:33	M	Le	19:18	H
Mt	19:19	M?	Le	19:18	H
Mk	2:26	Mk	Le	24:5-9	H
Mt	5:38	M	Le	24:19-20	H
Mk	6:34	Mk	Nu	27:17	P
Mt	5:33	M	Nu	30:3	P
Mk	7:10	Mk	De	5:16	D
Mk	10:19	Mk	De	5:16, 20	D
Mk	12:29-32	Mk	De	6:4-5	D
Mt	4:10	Q	De	6:13	D
Mt	4:7	Q	De	6:16	D
Mt	4:4	Q	De	8:3	D
Mk	13:22	Mk	De	13:2-4	D
Mt	5:48	M	De	18:13	D
Mt	18:16	M	De	19:15	D
Mt	5:33	M	De	23:22	D
Mt	5:31	M	De	24:1	D
Mk	13:27	Mk	De	30:4	D

Lk	21:22	L	De	32:35	D
Mk	2:25-26	Mk	1 S	21:2-7	R^d
Lk	7:50	L	1 K	1:17	R^d
Lk	4:26	L	1 K	17:9	R^d
Mk	9:3	Mk	1 K	19:2-10	R^d
Mk	9:36	Mk	1 K	22:17	R^d
Mt	6:6	M	2 K	4:33	R^d

III. APOCALYPTIC WRITINGS

Lk	21:35	L	Is	24:17
Mt	6:6	M	Is	26:20
Mt	24:31	M	Is	27:13
Mk	8:18	Mk	Ez	12:2
Mk	4:32	Mk	Ez	17:23
Mk	4:32	Mk	Ez	31:6
Mk	6:34	Mk	Ez	34:1
Lk	19:10	L	Ez	34:16
Mk	13:7	Mk	Da	2:28
Mk	4:32	Mk	Da	4:9, 18
Mk	13:26	Mk	Da	7:13-14
Mk	14:62	Mk	Da	7:13-14
Lk	21:24	L	Da	8:10
Mk	13:17	Mk	Da	9:27
Mt	24:15	M	Da	11:31
Mt	24:10	M	Da	11:41
Mk	13:19	Mk	Da	12:1
Mt	25:46	M	Da	12:2
Mt	13:43	M	Da	12:3
Mk	13:14	Mk	Da	12:11
Mt	21:4-5	M	Zc	9:9
Mk	14:24	Mk	Zc	9:11
Mt	26:15	M	Zc	11:12
Mt	27:9	M	Zc	11:12-13
Lk	21:24	L	Zc	12:3
Mt	24:30	M	Zc	12:10-14

| Mk | 14:27 | Mk | Zc | 13:7 |
| Mt | 25:31 | M | Zc | 14:5 |

IV. POETIC WRITINGS

Mk	1:11	Mk	Ps	2:7
Lk	13:27	Q	Ps	6:9
Mt	21:16	M	Ps	8:3
Mk	15:34	Mk	Ps	22:2
Mt	5:8	M	Ps	24:4
Lk	23:46	L	Ps	31:6
Jn	15:25	Jn	Ps	35:19
Mt	5:5	M	Ps	37:11
Mk	14:18	Mk	Ps	41:10
Mk	14:34	Mk	Ps	42:6, 12
Mk	14:34	Mk	Ps	43:5
Mt	5:35	M	Ps	48:3
Mt	5:33	M	Ps	50:14
Mt	5:8	M	Ps	51:12
Mt	16:27	M	Ps	62:12
Lk	21:25	L	Ps	65:8
Jn	15:25	Jn	Ps	69:5
Mt	5:8	M	Ps	73:1
Jn	10:34	Jn	Ps	81:6
Lk	10:19	L	Ps	91:13
Mt	5:35	M	Ps	99:5
Mk	4:32	Mk	Ps	104:12
Lk	13:29	Q	Ps	106:3
Mk	12:36	Mk	Ps	110:1
Mk	14:62	Mk	Ps	110:1
Mk	12:10	Mk	Ps	118:22-23
Lk	13:35	Q	Ps	118:26
Mt	5:4	M	Ps	126:5-6
Lk	19:44	L	Ps	137:9
Mk	10:27	Mk	Jb	42:2
Mt	16:27	M?	Pr	24:12

APPENDIX B
Jesus' Teachings in Relation to the Apocalyptic Literature

Gospel	Code	Teaching	Source
Lk 21:35	L?	Sudden end of age	Is 24:17
Mt 6:6	M	Prayer in secret	26:20
24:31	"Matt"	Last trumpet	27:13
21:5	M-Jn	Thy King cometh	Zc 9:9
Mk 14:24	Mk	Blood of covenant	9:11
Lk 21:24	L?	Jerusalem and Gentiles	12:3
Mt 24:30	M	All peoples mourn	12:10-14
Mk 14:27	Mk	Smite the shepherd	13:7
Mt 25:31	M	Angels coming with Son of Man	14:5
Mk 13:7	Mk	Wars and rumors	Da 2:28
4:32	Mk	Mustard seed; branches	4:9, 18
13:26; 14:62	Mk	Son of Man on clouds	7:13-14
13:14	Mk	Abomination of desolation	9:27
Mt 24:15	"Matt"	ditto (in sanctuary)	11:31
Mk 13:19	Mk	Tribulation	12:1
Mt 25:46	M	Eternal punishment and life	12:2
13:43	M	Righteous shine as sun	12:3
Mt 18:10	M	Guardian angels	Jub 35:17
25:41	M	Abyss of fire	1 En 10:6, 13
Jn 14:17	Jn	Spirit of truth	20:1, 5
Mk 13:8	Mk	Famine, pestilence	23:3
Lk 12:21	L?	Poor in spirit, rich	25:4
Mk 2:28	Mk	Son of Man	37–71
14:21	Mk	Good were it for that man	38:1-2
Jn 14:2	Jn	Mansions of elect	41:2
Lk 9:35; 23:35	L	Elect One=Son of Man	40:5
Mk 9:43	Mk	Gehenna	54:1 ff.
Jn 5:22	Jn	Judgment given to Son of Man	69:27
Mt 25:31	M	Throne of his glory	71:1
Jn 10:3-4	Jn	Sheep follow leader	89:22
Lk 15:10	L	Joy of angels in heaven	104:4
Mk 12:25	Mk	Spiritual resurrection	104:4-6
Lk 10:20	L	Names written in heaven	108:3
Lk 17:3	Q?	Forgiveness	Test Gad 6:3, 6
Mt 25:46	M	Eternal life and punishment	7:5
Mk 12:28-31	Mk	Loving God and man	Test Iss 5:2
Lk 11:34	Q	Singleness of eye	3:4
Mt 25:35-36	M	Hungry, naked, etc.	Test Jos 1:6-7
Lk 13:24	Q?	The two ways	Test Ash 1:3, 6
Lk 21:28	L?	Redemption draweth nigh	2 Bar 23:7
Mt 13:29	M	Sowing, reaping evil	4 Esd 4:28
Mk 13:32	Mk	No one knows the day	4:36

BIBLIOGRAPHY

Abrahams, Israel. *Studies in Pharisaism and the Gospels.* Vols. I and II, Cambridge: Cambridge University Press, 1917, 1919.

Albright, W. F. *Archaeology and the Religion of Israel.* Baltimore: Johns Hopkins University Press, 1942

———. *From the Stone Age to Christianity.* Baltimore: Johns Hopkins University Press, 1940.

Bewer, J. A. *The Literature of the Old Testament.* Rev. ed. New York: Columbia University Press, 1933.

Bowman, J. W. *The Intention of Jesus.* Philadelphia: Westminster Press, 1943.

———. *Introducing the Bible.* Philadelphia: Westminster Press. 1940.

Box, G. H. *A Short Introduction to the Literature of the Old Testament.* 4th ed. rev. London: Rivingtons, 1930.

Branscomb, B. H. *The Gospel of Mark.* New York: Harper and Brothers, 1937.

Brunner, Emil. *The Divine Imperative.* New York: The Macmillan Co., 1937.

Bultmann, R. *Jesus and the World.* New York. Charles Scribner's Sons, 1935.

Burney, C. F. *Outlines of Old Testament Theology.* 3rd ed. London: Rivingtons, 1930.

Burrows, Millar. *An Outline of Biblical Theology.* Philadephia: Westminster Press, 1946.

Charles, R. H. *The Apocrypha and Pseudepigrapha of the Old Testament.* Vols. I and II. Oxford: Clarendon Press, 1913.

———. *The Revelation of St. John.* Vols. I and II. New York: Charles Scribner's Sons, 1920.

Danby, Herbert. *The Mishnah.* London: Oxford University Press, 1933.

Davidson, A. B. *Old Testament Prophecy.* Edinburgh: T. & T. Clark, 1905.

Deissmann, Adolph. *The Religion of Jesus and the Faith of Paul.* London: Hodder & Stoughton, 1923.

Dibelius, Martin. *From Tradition to Gospel.* New York: Charles Scribner's Sons, 1935.

———. *The Message of Jesus Christ.* New York: Charles Scribner's Sons, 1939.

Dillistone, F. W. *Continuing Stedfastly.* Toronto: University of Toronto Press, 1942.

Dodd, C. H. *The Parables of the Kingdom,* 3rd ed. New York: Charles Scribner's Sons, 1936.

Driver, S. R. *An Introduction to the Literature of the Old Testament.* 6th ed. New York: Charles Scribner's Sons, 1897.

Easton, B. S. *Christ in the Gospels.* New York: Charles Scribner's Sons, 1930.

Finkelstein, Louis. *The Pharisees.* Vols. I and II. Rev. ed. New York: Jewish Publication Society of America, 1940.

Glasson, T. F. *The Second Advent.* London: Epworth Press, 1946.

Gray, G. B. *Sacrifice in the Old Testament.* Oxford: Oxford University Press, 1924.

Harper, W. R. *Amos and Hosea.* New York: Charles Scribner's Sons, 1905.

Hebert, A. G. *The Throne of David.* New York: Morehouse-Gorham, 1941.

Klausner, Joseph. *Jesus of Nazareth.* New York: The Macmillan Co., 1925.

Klostermann, Erich. *Das Lukasevangelium.* (Handbuch z. n. Test.) 2nd ed. Tübingen: J. C. B. Mohr Paul (Siebeck), 1929.

Knox, John. *Christ the Lord.* New York: Willett, Clark & Co., 1945.

———. *The Man Christ Jesus.* New York: Willett, Clark & Co., 1941.

Lightley, J. W. *Jewish Sects and Parties in the Time of Christ.* London: Epworth Press, 1925.

Mackay, J. A. *Heritage and Destiny.* New York: The Macmillan Co., 1943.

Major, H. D. A., Manson, T. W., and Wright, C. J. *The Mission and Message of Jesus.* New York: E. P. Dutton & Co., 1938.

Manson, T. W. *A Companion to the Bible.* New York: Charles Scribner's Sons, 1938.

————. *The Teaching of Jesus.* 2nd ed. Cambridge: The University Press, 1935.

Manson, William. *The Gospel of Luke.* New York: Harper & Brothers, n.d.

————. *Jesus the Messiah.* Philadelphia: Westminster Press, 1946.

McCown, C. C. *The Search for the Real Jesus.* New York: Charles Scribner's Sons, 1940.

Meyer, Eduard. *Ursprung und Anfänge des Christentums.* Vols. I-III. Berlin: J. G. Cotta'sche Buchhandlung Nachfolger, 1921-23.

Minear, P. S. *Eyes of Faith.* Philadelphia: Westminster Press, 1946.

Montefiore, C. G. *The Old Testament and After.* London: Macmillan & Co., 1923.

Moore, G. F. *Judaism.* Vols. I-III. Cambridge: Harvard University Press, 1927-30.

Moulton, R. G. *The Literary Study of the Bible.* Boston: D. C. Heath & Co., 1895.

Oesterley, W. O. E. *The Jewish Background of the Christian Liturgy.* Oxford: Oxford University Press, 1925.

Oesterley, W. O. E., and Robinson, T. H. *A History of Israel.* Vols. I and II. Oxford: Clarendon Press, 1932.

Olmstead, A. T. *Jesus in the Light of History.* New York: Charles Scribner's Sons, 1942.

Ottley, R. L. *The Hebrew Prophets,* 6th ed. London: Rivingtons, 1929.

Otto, R. *The Idea of the Holy.* Rev. ed. Oxford: Oxford University Press, 1936.

————. *The Kingdom of God and the Son of Man.* Grand Rapids: Zondervan Publishing House, n.d.

Peake, A. S. *The People and the Book.* Oxford: Clarendon Press, 1925.

Pfeiffer, R. H. *Introduction to the Old Testament.* 5th ed. New York: Harper & Brothers, 1941.

Richardson, Alan. *The Miracle Stories of the Gospels.* London: Student Christian Movement Press, 1941.

Riddle, D. W. *Paul—Man of Conflict.* Nashville: Cokesbury Press, 1940.

Robinson, H. W. *Record and Revelation.* Oxford: Clarendon Press, 1938.

————. *Redemption and Revelation.* New York: Harper & Brothers, 1942.

Rowley, H. H. *The Relevance of Apocalyptic.* London: Lutterworth Press, 1944.

Schweitzer, A. *The Quest of the Historical Jesus.* 2nd Eng. ed. London: A. & C. Black, 1911.

Scott, E. F. *The Validity of the Gospel Record.* New York: Charles Scribner's Sons, 1938.

Skinner, J. *Prophecy and Religion.* Cambridge: Cambridge University Press, 1922.

Smith, J. M. P., Ward, W. H., and Bewer, J. A. *Micah, Zephaniah, Nahum, Habakkuk, Obadiah, and Joel* (ICC series). New York: Charles Scribner's Sons, 1911.

Strachan, R. H. *The Fourth Gospel.* 3rd ed. London: Student Christian Movement Press, 1941.

Streeter, B. H. *The Four Gospels: A Study of Origins.* Rev. ed. New York: The Macmillan Co., 1930.

Taylor, Vincent. *The Formation of the Gospel Tradition.* London: Macmillan & Co., 1935.

Walker, T. *The Teaching of Jesus and the Jewish Teaching of His Age.* London: George Allen & Unwin, 1923.

Wright, G. E. *The Challenge of Israel's Faith.* Chicago: University of Chicago Press, 1945.

INDEX OF REFERENCES

Old Testament

323

New Testament

Apocrypha

Pseudepigrapha

Mishnah

Talmud

Other Early Literature

INDEX OF NAMES AND SUBJECTS

335